A Detroit Story

D1595965

A Detroit Story

URBAN DECLINE AND THE RISE OF
PROPERTY INFORMALITY

Claire W. Herbert

UNIVERSITY OF CALIFORNIA PRESS

University of California Press
Oakland, California

Cataloging-in-Publication Data is on file at the Library of Congress.

Library of Congress Cataloging-in-Publication Data

Names: Herbert, Claire W., 1984– author.
Title: A Detroit story : urban decline and the rise of property informality / Claire W. Herbert.
Description: Oakland, California : University of California Press, [2021] | Includes bibliographical references and index.
Identifiers: LCCN 2020034104 (print) | LCCN 2020034105 (ebook) | ISBN 9780520340077 (hardcover) | ISBN 9780520340084 (paperback) | ISBN 9780520974487 (ebook)
Subjects: LCSH: Housing—Abandonment—Michigan—Detroit. | Gentrification—Michigan—Detroit. | Detroit (Mich.)—Economic conditions, 21st century.
Classification: LCC HD7304.D6 H47 2021 (print) | LCC HD7304.D6 (ebook) | DDC 330.9774/34—dc23
LC record available at https://lccn.loc.gov/2020034104
LC ebook record available at https://lccn.loc.gov/2020034105

Manufactured in the United States of America

29 28 27 26 25 24 23 22 21
10 9 8 7 6 5 4 3 2 1

To my family, especially my MBs

Contents

Illustrations and Tables

TABLES

Preface

Don't Think They Know

Frederick Williams

Don't think they know about us
They don't know

That I'm a crack baby
A product of that product

Don't think they know that

I was hand crafted by drug dealers
That police kicked in our front door
And put me face down on the floor
That I was told at seven years old not to blink nor flinch
When I seen someone get murdered
I would be murdered
If I snitched
Going to school my clothes had a stench
My clothes had holes and needed stitching
Or stitches
Because my parents didn't give a shit
Or addiction alters ability to make decisions

Don't think they know about them

We know where these drugs come from
Where these guns come from
Where these prisons come from

Don't think they know about us
They don't know

He carry a gun
More than he carry his son
Because people get buried everyday where I'm from
We hold grudges because judges only want to
Evict us
Convict us
Restrict us

They don't know

How it feels
being treated like you're about to steal
Or kill
Or both
They don't know what it's like to be black
To be black is to be hard
But being black is so hard at times I wanted to turn my back on black
To be black is to be
Not free
Yet to be black is
To be me
I wear a hoodie because I'm cool
Because I'm cold
Because I'm hot
Doesn't mean I deserve to be shot

Don't think they know about us
They don't know

Racial oppression is the root cause of our aggression
Yes I'm defensive

Don't think they realize
They paralyze

Us with government assistance
We can't have black power without general electricity

They pass bills through the senate
That makes it impossible to pay bills in the house
Hold
Holding us to a standard they can't stand next to
Policies that shove us into poverty
Dispossessed of property
Atrocities like boarded up houses and abandoned school buildings
Harsh reality for our children
My community is a cemetery
And I'm supposed to celebrate February

Don't think they know about us
They don't know[1]

In 2013, while studying informal property use in Detroit, I interviewed Craig, a resident and firefighter who told me "we live in an interesting town. If you could weather the storm you'll be alright, watch in ten years . . ." Detroit has certainly changed a lot since I began spending time there in 2008, and many residents in my study were optimistic about the prospects of their city. The timing of my research, from 2011 to 2016, was fortuitous. During our tenure in Detroit, my partner and I witnessed a host of unanticipated but significant changes signaling what may be looked back on as the turning point of Detroit: bankruptcy, the appointment of an Emergency Manager, election of the first white mayor in forty years, massive private investment in Downtown and Midtown by three white billionaire entrepreneurial stakeholders, and the first increase in the white population in sixty-four years.[2] When we arrived, residents said the city was hitting rock bottom. When we left, media sources had begun to hail the "rebirth" of Detroit. My project was not intended to be about gentrification, but the broader context of changes in Detroit revealed their significance along the way. It also meant that, while we did not intend (as most do not)[3] on *being* gentrifiers, structurally we probably were. This preface is a reflection on my experiences living in and learning about Detroit. The poem at the beginning is by my dear friend and incarcerated artist Fred Williams, born and raised in Detroit until he was wrongly sentenced to life in prison as a juvenile. This poem reminds me of how much, as outsiders or newcomers, we don't know about life in certain parts of Detroit and how much others can teach us if we're willing to listen and learn.

As white PhD students originally hailing from the West Coast, my partner and I rented a small house in Hamtramck, Michigan, in December of
2011. Hamtramck is a small two-square mile municipality surrounded by
Detroit that sits about four miles from Downtown. We were surprised to
find that renting a home closer to Detroit's Midtown (where we had hoped
to be) was out of our price range. I despise driving and all things car-
centric, which was a difficult feature of Detroit for me. Hamtramck was
the only walkable neighborhood we could afford and still have space for
the baby we were expecting. Anticipating spending at least a few more
years in Detroit, we decided to purchase a house, eyeing ones that were
cheap enough that even if we had to give it away, we would still have saved
money not paying rent. Just under a year and a half later, then with a one-
year-old daughter in tow, we purchased a house on a relatively stable block
in an area of the city that used to be called Piety Hill (due to several iconic
old churches nearby). Our block was not included in any specific neighborhood on city maps, a planner told me.[4] Instead, it was called "just
south of Boston Edison" for those who wanted to associate it with the historic districts filled with decadent mansions famously home to Henry
Ford and baseball legend Ty Cobb's old houses; "The North End" by those
who wanted to disassociate privilege and align with the urban agri-culture
energy in the city; or "Near New Center" for those hoping to capitalize on
the glimmers of gentrification in this area.

Our requirement was that the house be immediately livable, not having
the time nor resources for significant rehab (and our bar for "livable" being
quite low). The house we ended up buying was previously squatted, and
then renovated and occupied by a white family for fifteen years. It then
went through mortgage foreclosure and was resold to us for just over
43 percent of the delinquent mortgage value. The previous owners loved
the area so much they moved a block away, and we came to know them
well, giving us insight into the house we wouldn't likely have had access to
otherwise. The house was enormous and run-down after housing a family
of eight for so long, but the bones of the former owner's remodel were still
in good shape—new windows and roof, working furnace and air condi-
tioners. But the paint was chipping badly, and there were holes in the plas-
ter walls. Of three bathrooms, no single one was fully functional: we had
to shower in the basement. But it gave us space to accommodate various

friends, family, lodgers, and the occasional stray dog over the years ... We joked that when you have the space you take in guests of all kinds.

In the three years we owned it, the exchange-value of our property increased 258 percent. As young, highly educated white newcomers, we were frequently associated with and viewed as symbols of the changes taking place in Detroit. Some residents viewed newcomers like us with trepidation, as indicators of changes that weren't for them and wouldn't benefit them. But many others I spoke with viewed white residents wanting to live in Detroit as an affirmation of the goodness and potential of the city they loved so much. In one interview, a resident explained that having white folks move onto his block would bring resources to the neighborhood—the police would respond if a white person called, I was told.[5]

When we were purchasing our house, the home inspector—an elderly, Black, lifelong Detroiter—told us with a smile how happy he was to see young white people moving back into the city. *You all are modern day pioneers, here to help reinvigorate my city,* he said. My partner and I shared an uncomfortable smile, recognizing the problematic dynamic unfolding in the city indicated by his statement. Pioneers took over land made available to them because the government had stolen it from others there long before them, whose relationship to that land did not fit the framework of legal private property rights that was imposed by outsiders. Those pioneers were intent on extracting value and settling that land. We would come to understand that a similar process was unfolding with property in Detroit.[6]

The houses on our block were mostly occupied, with about one-third vacant and securely boarded up. When the three of us moved in, we brought the count of white folks on the block up to six. I found that being a mother was often a useful point of entry for me with my research. My child's verbose chatter and outgoing nature helped me make friends with other parents on the block, whose deep roots in Detroit provided connections to interview participants and their intimate perspectives. While trying to make contacts at community meetings and the like, residents often expressed feeling sick of being studied by white outsider researchers; I knew of several who had recently preceded me. We couldn't afford childcare while our daughter was young, so she tagged along for much of my field research. I believe that having a baby (and then toddler) strapped to my back and being a homeowner—which signifies investment, rooted-ness, and care—in the city enabled some residents to disassociate me from the other white outsider researchers they had been in contact with.

People often ask how I stayed safe during my research, commonly out-siders who weren't familiar with Detroit. I think this question often arises from prejudiced views of the city and persistent stereotypes of violence in impoverished Black communities. At the same time, living in Detroit brought a host of new experiences and required a steep learning curve to navigate a sociospatial environment that is very different from every other place I had lived. I was not equipped with any sort of "street wisdom"[7] to guide my navigating situations and scenarios that were initially unfamil-iar. I discuss this here to be transparent about my own experiences with this particular facet of field research in sociology.

In his book on the transformation of a DC neighborhood from a "ghetto" to a "gilded ghetto," Derek Hyra defines his concept "living the wire": white residents who move into an inner-city neighborhood for the hipness or cool-factor of living in an "iconic Black ghetto, where Blackness, poverty, and crime are associated with one another."[8] For urban scholars, "ghetto" is a descriptive (not pejorative) term referring to the spatial concentration and isolation of members of a racialized social group (in the case of Detroit, Black Americans).[9] While I was not drawn to Detroit for its "hipness" (nor were the neighborhoods I lived in "hip" at the time), Hyra's analysis is use-ful for reflecting on my own experiences as a white newcomer in a majority Black city with high rates of poverty, violence, and crime.

Hyra compares the way white newcomers and longtime residents don't just *discuss* but *experience* violence and crime in different ways. He notes that many white newcomers "described neighborhood car jackings, shoot-ings, and purse snatchings with laughter and jokes. They described crime as if it were something to brag about . . . It was as if they were proud to live in an area that was unsafe and edgy. It seemed that the neighborhood violence gave some newcomers to the area bragging rights and something interest-ing to talk about at parties."[10] Hyra contrasts newcomers "living the wire" with oldtimers "living the drama"[11] which Hyra references as meaning to "carefully navigate and cope with extreme forms of urban violence."[12]

Like some of the newcomers in Hyra's study expressed, I learned many new things and had many new experiences in Detroit, some of which are the result of living in a segregated city with high rates of crime and poverty. I learned it was better to leave our old vehicles unlocked so that anyone inclined to see if there was anything valuable inside could do so without breaking a window. I learned to walk in the street because sidewalks were so precarious, and you couldn't count on cars to stop at stop signs in vacant neighborhoods. I learned to identify the sound of gun shots from afar. I learned what it was like to frequently be the only white person in a room, or the grocery store, or in a lot of places.

I learned the positive and negative aspects of living in a neighborhood that city officials largely ignored. Our neighbor put in a new curb cut to his side yard—no need to ask permission, he explained, just chunk up the concrete with a sledgehammer and pour it yourself. Too often plagued by multi-day power outages, our neighbors rented generators and chained their dogs to them in the backyard to keep them from being stolen. Neighbors hosted massive community block parties for holidays like the Fourth of July, spreading out across vacant lots and streets without being bothered by authorities. I first encountered bulletproof glass at the fast food restaurant at the end of our block: it separated the workers and customers. My partner once was passed a counterfeit twenty dollar bill at the gas station nearby. One of our neighbors robbed another neighbor's house in midday, then tried to sell us a drum set he had stolen. Our house was never targeted: I surmise this is because we had three loud, large pit-mix dogs, and if you looked through the windows all you could see were secondhand couches and crammed bookshelves, nothing of value that might entice someone to break in.

Unlike some of the white newcomers in Hyra's study, I had enough knowledge and self-reflexivity that I wasn't "living the wire" in Detroit. But I also didn't feel like living in Detroit meant that I had to carefully navigate extreme violence. I wasn't "living the drama" either because violence didn't circumscribe my experiences or daily life the way it did for the boys in Harding's study nor the longtime residents in Hyra's. And, because of my newcomer status, it hadn't circumscribed my past either. Instead, I typically felt simultaneously safe and uncertain: uncertain because I *didn't* typically feel threatened by the crime or violence around me. I found myself continually trying to figure out how I ought to feel or respond, especially when situations came spatially close to home. For example, our neighbor a few houses down was shot and killed as he started up his car one morning—a contracted murder arranged by his wife, a detective I spoke with suspected. A young man walking down my street was shot and killed by an acquaintance after an altercation. I remember hearing the gunshot in the middle of a sunny afternoon, and after pausing for a moment to listen for more, peering out the front window. We later watched the fire truck pull up to wash away his blood. While playing out front with the neighbor kids one afternoon, half a dozen police cars came to a screeching halt in front of our house, and several officers feebly attempted to chase two young Black men on foot through our backyard. I noticed, as they ran closely past me, that these young "men" were barely teenagers. One was in his socks.

My personal feelings of safety contrasted with the knowledge longtime residents often tried to impart: warning me where I should and should not go, or what areas I ought to have an escort through to ensure my safety. One resident even refused to give me information about another potential interviewee because she didn't think it was safe for me to try to speak with him or go into his neighborhood. In reflecting on these experiences, I believe my privilege often protected me, and my naivete also gave me a false sense of safety at times. Like Hyra's newcomers, I didn't know what scenarios were actually threatening and what weren't because I had so little prior experience to draw on.

One particularly elucidating experience came during the first of several interviews with Jackie and her son Joe (both white adult squatters and heroin users) at their squatted house. They asked for payment up front, and after handing Joe the twenty-dollar bill, he left the house and came back a few minutes later. He flashed me a small black ball of heroin in his palm and asked, "Wanna party?" I balked. A rush of adrenaline washed through me and I felt my stomach drop. "No thanks," I replied and turned back to Jackie, sitting across from me at the table. She didn't react, just sipped her drink and waited for my next question. I tried to compose myself and keep my voice from shaking. I was terrified. I did my best to continue the interview, watching Joe out of the corner of my eye as he returned from the next room. He stood behind Jackie, occasionally chiming into the conversation for the next few minutes. But soon he began to bend forward in the most awkward way, practically nodding out while standing. I tried not to stare . . . wondering why he didn't fall over; he looked so off balance, as if he were about to topple onto the top of his head. I took a breath, feeling my heart return to its normal rhythm as I realized I could have knocked Joe over with a flick of my pen. He wasn't dangerous in that moment. Recanting this to my partner later at home, he laughed, being more familiar with the habits and practices of drug users than I.

My point in discussing this is to eschew any misconceptions about my status as a researcher for this book: there was no "going native" with the residents in my study in part because of the varied social contexts I participated in. Rather, some were more familiar and comfortable for me than others; Detroit's social geography is as varied as its spatial conditions. My position as a homeowner in Detroit gave me the most insight into the views of other residents who were variously invested in the city; yet I could never "live the drama" because my past experiences were so different from many longtime residents. Demographically I shared much more with a category of informal property users I call Lifestyle Appropriators (younger white newcomers) than those I label Routine or Necessity Appropriators (typically Black longtime residents). But I had very different views on the city than many other newcomers and wasn't "living the wire" either. More broadly, I think I probably made some poor decisions (with regard to safety) during my research but got lucky, and/or my privilege protected me where it may not have for others. I also may have felt scared in scenarios that were perfectly safe. Growing up as I did, mostly in and around Portland, Oregon, I had no preparation for a city like Detroit. Spending time and later living there brought new experiences and expanded understandings that I've described here to convey the sense with which I've really had to learn about Detroit to carry out this research. Harking back to my friend Fred's poetic introduction, I and many of us don't know what Fred knows, because we haven't shared his experiences. But when we listen and learn we can come to a sphere of shared understanding. This is a thread I trace throughout this book: that in attending to the problems in a city like Detroit, we ought to be learning from those who do know.

Acknowledgments

This book began as my dissertation project while working on my PhD in sociology at the University of Michigan. As such, it's difficult to identify the beginning of this project to enumerate all those to whom I am indebted. This list is, undoubtedly, unfinished. In graduate school, my advisor Sandra Levitsky and committee David Harding, Howard Kimeldorf, and Martin Murray were my ardent supporters and necessary critics. To Martin I owe additional thanks for early advising and collaboration that shaped my academic trajectory. The financial support I received from the Mary Malcomson Raphael Fellowship awarded by the Center for the Education of Women at the University of Michigan allowed me the time to get this research done. In the sociology department at U of M, my friends and mentors in the graduate program provided intellectual, emotional, and childcare assistance, especially Amanda, Charity, Dana, Danielle, Denise, Jonah, Laura, and Meagan. The administrative staff in the sociology department carried a heavy load of work to keep all of us on track in so many ways. Other scholars, including Debbie Becher, Jason Hackworth, Josh Akers, Jeff Morenoff, Alex Murphy, Jason Orne, Kevin Moseby, Diane Sicotte, Kelly Joyce, and Renia Ehrenfeucht, provided valuable feedback along the way. Kim Greenwell provided amazing editorial assistance. I am grateful to my UCP editor Naomi Schneider for her guidance, encouragement, and excitement with my work and to her editorial team for their assistance and patience with all my questions. Over the years and iterations of this project, I've benefited from the hard work of several undergraduate research assistants, but especially Heather Leis and Madeline DelVescovo. Reaching back even further, one could say this project began with my amazing professors at the University of Oregon who helped guide me toward graduate school, some of whom I now get to call my colleagues. Most importantly, I am grateful to the Detroiters who contributed their time, experiences, and knowledge to this book, many of whom I still get to call my friends. From them, and my time in the city, I have learned more than could ever fit into a book. I am ever thankful for my parents, Anna and Bill, and my brother Gabe for listening, asking questions, and flying all over the country to be with us when we needed them. Only other dog lovers will know how much I've appreciated the four mutts who have provided their patient presence through this journey, two of whom are still here to see this project across the finish line. I am grateful for my little love Mneme, whose impending presence in the world pushed me to meet deadlines, like defending my prospectus on her due date, and compelled me to focus on my research and writing so I could save time to hang out with her. And when I couldn't, I'm thankful for all the times when she would sit quietly on the floor in my office with a pile of books, refusing to leave and insisting she too was working on her "disserpation" so we could be together. This book—this whole dynamic project— really began with conversations outside of Chiles hall with my comrade Michael Brown. From bringing home massive sheets of paper for me to sketch out early patterns in my data, to debating the meaning of resistance while tinkering in the shop after bedtime, to reading drafts and picking up my slack at home, he continues to provide inspiration, to remind me why we do what we do, and to support me in every way.

Introduction

I followed Jerome down the crumbling sidewalk in his Westside Detroit neighborhood. The sidewalk narrowed where grass and weeds had won the fight with the concrete, leaving only a small tread left open from feet trampling through. On our right, we passed by several burnt-out houses with collapsed porches. Sandwiched in between the charred remains was a dingy white post-war bungalow. It sagged visibly in the middle, looking tired from struggling to keep up appearances amidst the disrepair. An elderly woman sat on the front porch, waving to Jerome and greeting us as we walked. He stopped and chatted with her for a moment before we continued.

"Here's the garden," he said. Jerome pointed up ahead to an entire city block, vacant of any homes but filled with brightly colored raised beds that were lined up neatly across the lots. A tiny orchard of young fruit trees filled another section. At the far end in a grassy area was a homemade projector screen—a large wood panel painted white—facing lawn chairs arranged in a semicircle. His neighbors—skeptical at first—love it. Jerome put local kids to work on these gardens, and hosted neighborhood meals from its bounty. He didn't mean to become a community organizer or a food activist, Jerome says. Instead, these gardens and community space grew from his frustration with the conditions of his neighborhood, overlooked by a municipality that does not have the resources for maintenance. Jerome was merely out one cold winter day trying to unclog the sewer drains at the intersection at the end of his block. He wanted to keep the street from flooding as the snow melted. His father sent his younger brothers out to help him, asking Jerome to keep them busy. Once the drains were clear he looked around and thought, "What else can we do?" His gaze settled on the vacant lots straddling either side of the intersection. He decided that they would clean them up once the snow thawed, and after they did that, Jerome kept adding projects to keep the momentum going. First some planter boxes, then a compost pile, next some fruit trees. Then he came home one afternoon to find some neighbors building the projector screen.

Jerome did not own any of these lots, nor did he and his neighbors have explicit permission from the owners to use them. Bank of America owned some, the city of Detroit others. Jerome looked up the owners online when he began to clean them up but had since forgotten where the lot lines of one owner began and another ended. *It's irrelevant,* he said, *because nobody minds.*

On the contrary, police officers often joined in, pulling up their squad cars to catch a glimpse of the game on the projector. Once, Jerome was interviewed for a panel on some of the promising aspects of urban agriculture in Detroit; many city officials were in attendance. Afterward, Jerome stood up and turned around to find Dave Bing, the mayor at that time, reaching out to shake his hand. Jerome grinned as he recounted Mayor Bing telling him: "You know, I've heard everything you've been doing . . . I appreciate what you're doing. Continue to do what you need to do, to do what you do." Jerome explained that to him, this meant doing things informally, without express permission, even when he was technically violating the law.

To people familiar with Detroit, this story is not surprising, so commonplace are various informal uses of property. Recently, much attention has been paid to urban agriculture that, in many contexts, proliferates without express permission. But community gardens are but one kind of technically illegal property use that shapes the city of Detroit and the lives of its residents. Squatting, blotting ("squatting the block"), demolition, scrapping, salvaging, and art projects are commonplace as well.

While a resident of Detroit for 4½ years, I conducted ethnographic research and sixty-five in-depth interviews, learning about and documenting these practices. I interviewed residents illegally using property to find out why they did it and what it was like for them. I interviewed their neighbors to find out how they felt about these practices nearby, and often discovered that they too were illegally using property in some form or another. I talked with city officials and local authorities to find out how they responded, both on the books and off, to illegal uses of property. Through this research, I discovered not only how prevalent these practices are, but how they influence the form of the city and the experiences of everyday life for residents. Neighbors I spoke with recalled decades of demolishing nearby drug houses together, stepping in to keep their neighborhoods safe when the city would not. A mother and her son showed me how they kept their squatted house warm in the bitterly cold Michigan winters despite not having electricity. Other squatters explained enjoying the process of building rain collection and heating devices (like furnaces out of 55-gallon drums) to get by without utilities. I met with longtime residents who refused to leave after their homes were taken via tax foreclosure, steadily paying the utility bills to keep the heat and lights on despite their now technically illegal residency. I learned how scrappers earn meager income picking through the remains of burnt houses or by dismantling pieces of old buildings and selling their finds at scrapyards. And I followed salvagers as they foraged through Detroit's decaying buildings, looking for everything from extra bricks to unique architectural pieces to use in home renovation or art projects.

In less eyebrow-raising form, but technically no less illegal, residents in my neighborhood a few miles from Downtown Detroit rounded up supplies to board up an abandoned commercial strip, painting the boards lively lavender and turquoise after affixing them to the building and cleaning up broken glass. In another neighborhood, a local artist helped children paint butterflies across abandoned buildings. Dotting lots throughout the city are informal play and parking spaces, unsanctioned community gardens, and de jure illegal art installations using empty land or abandoned buildings

What practices like these all have in common is that they are made possible in part by the illegal appropriation of real property—land, houses, or buildings. That is, residents occupy, take over, use, take from, alter, deconstruct, trespass across, or otherwise engage with real property that they have no formal legal right to. I call these residents "appropriators."[1] But, unlike many illegal activities, the laws and regulations surrounding these practices are poorly enforced and many of these practices have gained legitimacy in Detroit, in large part because of the positive effects they have for individual residents, community dynamics, and the built environment of distressed neighborhoods.[2]

The prevalence of practices that brazenly transgress property laws may be unthinkable in a different urban context, such as in booming cities where there is competition for urban property and authorities reliably uphold private property rights and enforce regulations. But increasingly, scholars are uncovering the ways that informality—the proliferation of illegal or effectively unregulated but commonly accepted/legitimated practices—shapes the form of the built environment and the everyday experiences of residents in the United States, from Los Angeles[3] to Philadelphia[4] to rural Texas.[5] It is productive for scholarship and policy to recognize the way informality shapes cities and spaces beyond the Global South, where squatter settlements and informal economic activities are common and have been well researched.

The informal practices that are the focus of this book violate laws of land and property ownership. This kind of informality needs interstitial, poorly regulated spaces in which to proliferate, which declining US cities like Detroit, Cleveland, Pittsburgh or Buffalo have in abundance. Urban decline or "shrinkage" is a process of urban change stimulated by global/regional drivers like economic shifts, demographic changes, suburbanization, political conflicts, or natural disasters. At the local level, decline manifests with decreasing populations and the resulting underutilization of housing and infrastructure, and diminished tax revenues.[6] In post-industrial Rust Belt cities in the United States, these changes leave behind vacant homes, abandoned garages, defunct factories, and empty lots. On, within, and through these spaces arise diverse informal practices in Detroit, undertaken by residents from varied backgrounds seeking to meet a plethora of different needs and desires. Poor residents take over property to meet daily needs like shelter and income. More stable long-time residents, like Jerome, use property without permission as part of their repertoire, developed over time, for negotiating the difficult conditions of the city. While more privileged newcomers to the city often occupy houses or land as a kind of urban pioneering adventure. These practices unfold against the historical backdrop of suburbanization, white flight, institutional racism, and the enduring spatiality of racial segregation.

Real property is a particularly salient element of both social and spatial dimensions of urban life, and purports to function very differently under conditions of growth versus decline. Under the former, property is in high demand, low supply, and often increasing in economic value (a central concern during processes of gentrification). In many growing urban spaces in the United States, private ownership of real property is a source of investment and stability, and a state tool for sociospatial control. But under conditions of decline, property is in abundant supply, holds little economic value, and is often a liability more than an investment. These conditions help to promote property usage that transgresses formal property laws and rights, as residents reimagine the physical environment of their neighborhoods.

In the United States, what I call "property informality" (informal practices that arise from the transgression of laws regulating real property—land, houses, and buildings) has been overlooked by researchers. Property law-breaking violates very deeply held American values about the sanctity of private property ownership. And our legal, regulatory, surveillance, and governance systems are staunchly committed to protecting private property rights as a kind of public good. Thus, in some ways, it is difficult to conceive of property informality as being at all prevalent in the United States.

At the same time, some legal scholarship has argued that property law violations like nineteenth-century homesteaders or civil rights protests have influenced the transformation of real property law over time.[7] Others have noted how informal practices can act as "law" when they are upheld and promoted by authorities.[8] In furthering our understanding of everyday life, studying informality also deepens our understanding of formal rules and norms, how they might change, and why they are sometimes not enforced. In Detroit, the illegality of practices such as squatting, scrapping, or gardening does not explain who participates, who does not, nor how neighbors or even authorities respond. Instead, many forms of illegal property use have achieved a level of legitimacy and are common among residents, in part due to the constructive impacts they can have for individuals and their communities. The sociospatial conditions of decline have altered the social relations of real property, and a different framework—one that decouples the law and legitimacy—is needed for understanding these practices.

This book borrows epistemological insights from scholarship on urban informality in the Global South to understand the sociospatial dynamics of Detroit. Focusing on *informality* rather than *illegality* illuminates facets of everyday life and the form of the city that elude the strict dichotomy of legal/licit and illegal/illicit. Using this framework reveals Detroit as a city whose form and content is comprised of an intricate interweaving of informality and legality: they depend on each other rather than one substituting for the other.[9]

Dominant approaches to managing urban problems have largely failed to tune in to the dynamics of informality in the Global North, particularly in the United States. Yet there are social costs to policymakers' and urban authorities' ignorance of the way that informality shapes daily life in cities and regions of the United States. In the context of decline, the consequences of this lag are significant for how new regulations and revitalization strategies reproduce longstanding urban inequalities. This book explains why property informality arises and how alternative ways of using and relating to property shape neighborhood conditions and community dynamics in Detroit. I elucidate the constructive impacts of property informality that have bolstered various practices' legitimacy among residents and authorities. I draw out the important, fine-grained differences in informal practices which, in the eyes of the law, are largely the same. These differences are consequential for the disparate ways in which new property regulations impact residents: formalizing the practices of more privileged newcomers while criminalizing and erasing the informal practices of longtime residents.

More broadly, this book contributes to sociological understandings of declining cities, informality, and property. First, I show how property informality is intertwined with formality across the social and spatial landscape of a declining city, identifying various alternative ways of using and relating to property that persist in the city. And second, I uncover how the interface of the formal and informal reproduces inequalities in ways that declining cities aiming to revitalize must confront. Scholarship on urban informality in the Global South over the past half-decade has produced a wealth of important knowledge about cities and urban life. Urban researchers in the United States should tune in to these epistemologies to inform our understandings of and possibilities for improving the conditions of declining cities in the Global North. Finally, this book reiterates the centrality and complexity of property relations for everyday life and calls us to critically engage with and challenge the liberal private property regime.

OUTLINE OF THE BOOK

This book unfolds as follows. Part I (chapters 1–3) provides an overview of the social and spatial conditions that lead to the concurrence of decline and property informality. In chapter 1, "Urban Decline and Informality," I introduce readers to the process of urban decline and explain how it impacts urban conditions, property relations, and everyday life. I contextualize this arena of research with reference to my case: Detroit. I discuss some of the obstacles of existing plans and policies that attempt to intervene in the problems of urban decline. Finally, I scaffold existing research on urban informality to explain my analytical framework and define my concept "property informality." I explain how the lens of informality can advance our understanding of declining cities in the United States.

In chapter 2, "Regulations and Enforcement," I present four main reasons why the conditions of Detroit—and other declining cities—are ripe for informal practices that transgress property laws. First, there is a plethora of property vacancy and abandonment providing spatial opportunity for informal appropriation. Second, there is essentially no functioning monetary property market in many neighborhoods in Detroit. Third, city authorities are overburdened, underfunded, and do not effectively or uniformly enforce property laws. And fourth, there is a good deal of need and other motivation among residents to construct alternative use-values for the vacant property that surrounds them. Together, these conditions undermine the liberal private property regime and mean that resident and neighborhood well-being is often harmed by the enforcement of legal ownership. Residents find themselves with opportunities for de jure illegal property use that carry little risk of punishment because it is effectively unregulated (meaning, existing regulations are rarely enforced and diminish in meaning).

In chapter 3, "From Illicit to Informal," I explore the way that these de jure illegal—but effectively unregulated—practices achieve legitimacy in Detroit. I interrogate this transition, uncovering why residents and authorities in Detroit frequently accept or even encourage practices that violate property laws in their neighborhoods. Detroiters in my study view illegal property use as legitimate when it conforms to a community-embraced norm rooted in an ethos of care, requiring that appropriators demonstrate care for both the property and the community. Together, chapters 2 and 3 provide empirical evidence for why informality—not illegality—is an appropriate framework to better understand urban life in the context of decline.

Part II of the book focuses on appropriators (informal property users) and how their informal property use is integral to the experiences of everyday life in a declining city like Detroit. In chapter 4, "Beyond Politics or Poverty," I argue that existing categories for understanding informal practices are not sufficient for capturing the diversity among appropriators in my study. I propose a typology of informal appropriation to make sense of the wide variation among appropriators and their practices in Detroit: Necessity Appropriation, Routine Appropriation, and Lifestyle Appropriation, highlighting how race, class, and place-based backgrounds are stratified across these types of appropriation. Chapters 5, 6, and 7 then explore in detail the different motivations, experiences, and material conditions of these three types of appropriation. Chapter 5 examines Necessity Appropriators who are poor, predominately Black residents of Detroit who rely on informal appropriation for meeting daily needs. These appropriators scrap metal to sell at scrapyards for quick cash and squat houses to secure adequate shelter for themselves and their families. Chapter 6 examines Lifestyle Appropriators who are predominately younger, white newcomers to the city who call their illegal occupation "homesteading," start large farms and gardens, and salvage materials from vacant properties for art or remodeling supplies. Chapter 7 examines Routine Appropriators, more stable, longtime residents of the city, who informally use property as a coping mechanism developed over time for navigating the harsh conditions of the city. These residents help tear down deteriorated, unsafe properties on their block, turn abandoned lots into extra yard space or parking, or remain as holdover squatters in their homes after foreclosure. These differences in the practice of property informality are reflective of residents' divergent wants and needs, and ensuing approaches to negotiating the obstacles and opportunities of life in a city like Detroit.

Part III of the book looks forward to consider how informal plans and formal policies unfold and intersect in Detroit. Chapter 8, "Surviving the City or Settling the City?" explores the planning-by-doing that appropriators embody with their practices. I use narrative analysis to uncover how appropriators understand the normativity of their law-breaking and how property informality is directed toward a future Detroit. As predominately longtime residents, Routine and Necessity Appropriators largely understand themselves to be the survivors of a failed city, whose legal violations are ethical because structural forces constrain their options otherwise. Their goals are primarily a return to urban norms and the comforts of a modern city—where they don't *have* to squat to find shelter or tear down drug houses because the city has failed its responsibilities. As newcomers, Lifestyle Appropriators utilize a pioneering narrative, in which they venture into the wild city and tame it with their appropriation of urban property. By settling down, they aim to continue their pioneering practices. This dynamic between old and new inhabitants echoes historical confrontations of settler colonization and mirrors contemporary conflicts arising from gentrification, warranting the question, Whose informal practices and visions for the future of Detroit will win out: longtime residents or newcomers?

Chapter 9, "Regulating Informality, Reproducing Inequality," examines how recent urban policies aimed at revitalization stand to impact informal practices and appropriators in Detroit. In seeking to remedy some of the deleterious effects of urban decline, local authorities envision and roll out new forms of property regulation that aim to be creative and locally responsive. I argue that these recent policies in Detroit are situated to formalize the practices common among more privileged Lifestyle Appropriators, while increasingly criminalizing and/or erasing the informal practices common among more marginalized appropriators. In other words, when designing long-term plans for revitalization, these urban authorities of the Global North handle informality by paving the path for urban pioneers to settle and legally claim the city. While at the same time, they are removing and further criminalizing the informal practices relied upon by poorer, more marginalized residents who pose an obstacle to revitalization.

"Lessons for Informality in the Global North" concludes the book by considering what scholars in Northern contexts can learn from decades of robust scholarship on informality and policy responses in the Global South. I critically examine common regulatory responses—titling and upgrading—and consider how the advantages or disadvantages of these approaches may play out in cities like Detroit. Both strategies are limited by their adherence to dominant models of property ownership and formal legal equality. I examine more progressive regulatory responses and demonstrate how states of exception, incremental enforcement, and expanding property rights could ensure more equitable access to property, the city, and its resources for residents, while also helping to progress city authorities' revitalization goals as well as longtime residents' stabilization goals. As cities across the United States and other Global North contexts grapple with the complexities of urban decline, the epistemological and practical insights garnered from research on informality in the Global South will prove valuable for understanding these cities and for effectively responding to the informal practices that arise therein.

PART I

Social and Spatial Context

1 Urban Decline and Informality

Cities like Detroit . . . now there's a phrase that may seem out of place to many readers. Detroit is often regarded as an exemplar of post-industrial ruination, Black poverty, and economic collapse—a place so extreme and tragic that no other city could possibly come close to mirroring the post-apocalyptic conditions of America's Motor City. But as a declining city, Detroit is one of many scattered across predominately the Midwestern and Northeastern United States. Decline is a process of urban change involving significant decreases in population, often upward of 20 to 30 percent in the United States. Buffalo, Cleveland, Detroit, Pittsburgh, and St. Louis have lost more than half their populations, and Baltimore and Philadelphia lost nearly one third. Smaller cities like Camden, as well as many cities outside the Northeast and Midwest such as Richmond and Birmingham, have also lost significant population.[1] Recent research estimates that from 2015 to 2025, globally, 17 percent of large cities in developed regions and 8 percent of all large cities will experience population decline.[2]

The current state of Detroit is often reductively blamed on the collapse of the auto industry.[3] But instead of having a singular stimulus, migration out of certain urban centers in the United States is the result of a complex

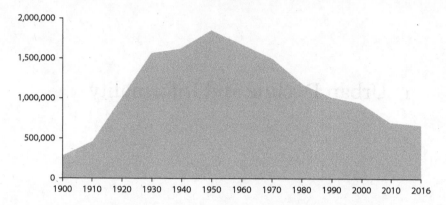

Figure 1. Change in Detroit's population over time. Source: Detroit Future City 2017, 15.

tangling of historic (and ongoing) economic, demographic, spatial, and political shifts like deindustrialization, shrinking family size, suburbanization, white flight, and institutional racism. Thomas Sugrue's seminal *The Origins of the Urban Crisis* details how these conditions played out in creating contemporary Detroit, but notes that "the differences between Detroit and other Rust Belt cities are largely a matter of degree, not a matter of kind."[4]

In the United States, urban decline is associated with the rise of a host of problems that vary in degree and form depending on local context.[5] Strained economic conditions and shrinking tax bases leave few resources for remaining residents and municipalities, who struggle to maintain the infrastructure and built environment constructed for significantly larger populations. Declining cities tend to suffer from high levels of vacancy; property abandonment and blight; high crime, jobless, and unemployment rates; low property values; and poor service provision. Histories of racial conflict and white flight are common among declining cities, resulting in stark racial segregation between majority Black cities and their majority white suburbs, or even within the cities themselves.

Since Sugrue's book, Detroit has been shaped by a host of other factors which have exacerbated its decline. From 2000–2010, many households that could fled to the inner suburbs, leading to a 25 percent population loss during that time.[6] The Great Recession decimated an already sick

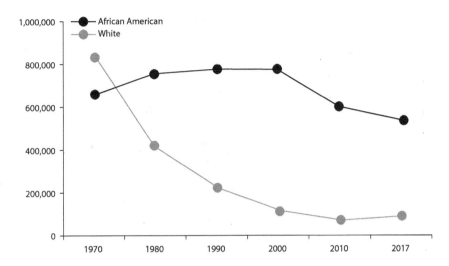

Figure 2. Change in Detroit's Black and white populations over time. Source: Detroit Future City 2019, 14.

city, ravaging deteriorated neighborhoods with even more foreclosures and tipping many others from somewhat-stable to distressed. Bankruptcy and Emergency Management in 2013 signaled hitting rock bottom. Figure 1 shows the decline in Detroit's population over time. Figure 2 shows the rise in the percentage of Black residents and decline in white residents in the city over time. And Figure 3 shows the concurrent dramatic rise in low-income households in Detroit as these population shifts take place.[7]

Detroit is not unique, but it is a particularly stark example of a declining city and thus a useful case through which to study what is really a broader, historical, global process of urban transformation. Since the 1970s, scholars have increasingly attended to the phenomenon of urban decline,[8] but only since around the mid-2000s has shrinkage become "a new master framework for a broad range of empirical studies."[9] Research has well documented how decline comes about as a process of urban change and various planning responses to decline. But there is still a gap in scholarship about what life is like in these cities.[10]

The key point, however, is that despite popular presentation of Detroit as a one-off city that declined because of the loss of auto manufacturing in

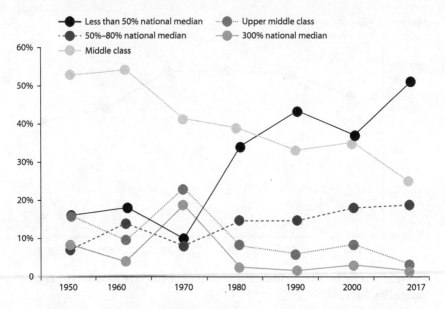

Figure 3. Change in household income in Detroit over time. Source: Detroit Future City 2019, 14.

America, it is instead a particularly lucid example of the global process of decline or "shrinkage." The instigators of this process are not unique to America's Rust Belt. Rather, we can expect that regions across the globe will continue to grow and decline.

WHY DO WE NEED TO STUDY DECLINING CITIES?

Much urban research has focused on conditions of urban growth. Theoretical approaches to understanding what cities are and how they change have focused on the way increasing populations create competition over urban space. Urban ecologists view the form and dynamics of cities as the product of natural competition over urban space, where the "fittest" economic actors seize control over prime locations, relegating less powerful actors (like the poor) to less attractive or desirable spaces (such as neighborhoods near environmental hazards). Political economists have explained cities as created through struggles between entrepreneurs and institutional actors, who want to make money by investing in and developing urban space, and those who are concerned with their quality of life within urban space (residents). From this perspective, cities are imagined as sites of contestation and power struggles over scarce urban space (property), as both populations and capital grow.

Essentially, predominant theoretical frameworks for conceptualizing what the city is and how social relations within urban areas play out suppose that cities are places wherein competition over urban space results from increasing populations and rising demand for property. The resulting dynamics between classes, social groups, entrepreneurs and investors, city authorities, and the proliferation of different uses of property are explained by various power struggles over high-demand urban space. In this context, *property* is urban space carved up by law, assigned to public or private owners, and regulated by zoning codes and lot lines. And in cities with growing populations, there is increasing demand for access to urban space (property). Those with more political and economic resources tend to "win out" in struggles over this resource.

But in declining cities—or even distressed neighborhoods within otherwise stable or growing cities, like the South Side of Chicago—there is *decreasing* demand for urban space. Developers have little interest in property that does not guarantee a return on investment. Residents who wish to leave the city are often unable to sell and may resort to abandoning their properties. Municipalities struggle to fulfill the responsibilities for maintenance and care of property that private owners have left behind. In this context, property becomes a liability more than a high-demand resource. What explains, then, the form of the city—which residents and what functions are able to exist in different areas of the city? And how does this sociospatial form influence residents' experiences of daily life therein? In a declining city it is not, as urban ecology or political economy frameworks presume, competition or contestation over urban space.

In Detroit, it does not take the "fittest" or most powerful economic actors to gain formal, legal access to property. Architectural theorist Andrew Herscher argues that in Detroit, property has become more significant for what residents can *do* with it than for how much investors or property speculators can *profit* from it.[11] Nor does accessing urban property require legal right—informal (de jure illegal) uses of property are able to flourish, giving even Detroit's poorest residents access to urban space. Property laws diminish in salience for regulating sociospatial dynamics, and informal metrics for assessing legitimate uses of urban space gain traction.

One important reason for studying informal uses of property in a declining urban area is to understand how property relations change. Property relations—understood in a Marxist sense as how we relate to land once it is property, and how that relationship mediates our interactions with others around us—are typically regulated by law, delineating who has legal right to access, control, and benefit from property (urban space). While sociologists haven't often explicitly studied property, some legal scholars consider property law to be a dynamic institution that is social in nature and reflects community values. As such, violating property laws can have both acquisitive and communicative impacts—helping residents gain access to property (a valuable resource) and conveying problems with existing formal, legal arrangements of property rights, access, and control.[12]

POLICY AND PLANNING FOR DECLINE

Despite shifts in how property is valued and used by residents in Detroit, local planners and policymakers still largely adhere to a market-based approach to remedying urban decline, trying to encourage investors and legal private ownership, and stimulate various forms of development.[13] While growth and decline are linguistic antonyms, they are not inverse processes in the urban context,[14] which complicates attempts to remedy urban decline by trying to shift the process in reverse and stimulate growth. Growth builds upon a geographic area, densifying and expanding the infrastructure, footprint, and built environment, all of which are not easily "unbuilt." The durability of housing, infrastructure, and other real estate means that there is an asymmetry in the trajectories of growth and decline: they don't look the same coming down as they do going up. Like growth, decline is spotty and uneven, happening at different paces and scales within a geographic area, and is inextricably linked to processes of growth and decline at other scales and in other regions.[15] At the city-scale, we often speak of growth or decline, but the rate and trajectory of population change varies across neighborhoods (Philadelphia, for example, has some neighborhoods with similar sociospatial conditions as Detroit).

Since the post-WWII era, urban planners have been dealing with the hollowing out or "donut effect" that the rise of the suburbs has had for many urban centers. And planning agendas have relied on models of growth to inform revitalization strategies for distressed urban centers.[16] That is, urban policies and plans have sought to tackle decline by strengthening economic competitiveness and promoting economic and population growth.[17] Local governments adhere to this market-based approach as well, but the lack of reliable property law enforcement in places like Detroit undermines confidence in the potential economic value of property.[18]

Early approaches to solving the crises of urban decline *without* relying on growth models involved grand schematics for "right-sizing" the city.[19] The idea is that if the city could be shrunk back down to a scale appropriate for the remaining population, then the burdens of infrastructure costs, blight, and vacancy would cease, and the city would once again be able to take care of itself. Right-sizing requires areas of the city with high vacancy rates to be cut off from city services and turned into green space. Residents in such areas would be encouraged and provided support to move to denser neighborhoods so that services like road maintenance, utility provision, policing, public transit, and trash pickup could cease. However, as a top-down approach, right-sizing has met many obstacles to implementation, most significantly from residents who do not want to be forced from their homes and moved into an area of the city that is to be "saved" while their old neighborhoods are left to "return to nature." Collective memories of slum razing and displacement during urban renewal give residents legitimate cause for concern.[20]

The logic behind the idea of right-sizing is that there is an appropriate population density that can enable a city to support itself and overcome problems related to urban decline. Take, for example, the following map of Boston, Manhattan, and San Francisco all nestled into the footprint of Detroit that began circulating around 2008. It visualizes the idea that Detroit's "problem" is that it is too big for its current population.

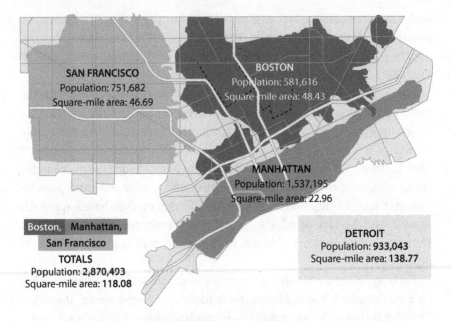

SAN FRANCISCO
Population: 751,682
Square-mile area: 46.69

BOSTON
Population: 581,616
Square-mile area: 48.43

MANHATTAN
Population: 1,537,195
Square-mile area: 22.96

Boston, Manhattan, San Francisco
TOTALS
Population: 2,870,493
Square-mile area: 118.08

DETROIT
Population: 933,043
Square-mile area: 138.77

Figure 4. Footprint of Detroit. Redrawn from Dan Pitera, University of Detroit Mercy. Printed in John Gallagher, "Detroit: Land of Opportunity: Acres of Barren Blocks Offer Chance to Reinvent City," *Detroit Free Press*, December 15, 2008.

But this idea of needing to "right-size" declining cities by shrinking them down like a too-big T-shirt in the wash to improve local conditions is challenged by comparing a city like Portland, Oregon, to Detroit, Michigan. Both have comparable populations and square-mile footprints, with an average density of 4.7 (Detroit) and 4.3 (Portland) thousand residents per square mile.[21] In contrast to Detroit, Portland is constantly lauded for its smart, comprehensive planning schemas and overall livability. Such a comparison reveals that Detroit and other declining cities' "problems" are not as simple as the ratio of population size to square miles. Instead, it is perhaps the *direction* of population change (intersecting with the economic stability of remaining residents) that is a more accurate root of the problem: Detroit's population has declined nearly threefold since 1950, while Portland's has nearly steadily increased during this same time period.[22] The term "decline" linguistically points toward 1) the process of population decline that is caused by and causes a variety of social problems, and 2) the decline in quality of life associated with this population decrease. The latter is impetus for more comprehensively understanding the former: if population decline were associated with a return to idyllic small-town comforts for remaining residents, this urban process would not be so pressing for social scientists and urban planners to understand.[23]

Decline poses such a problem in part because there exists no tried and true model for how to accommodate the convergence of economic crisis and population drop in a way that does not call on the growth machine to save the city.[24] Even the logic of planning for population shrinkage is viewed as a threat or taboo.[25] Ideologically, planning for decline counters historically rooted notions about the normativity of geographic and economic expansion. But perhaps even more troubling is the realization that urban decline is not a short-lived condition to be "recovered from"[26]—it is a byproduct of multiple historical shifts, global processes, and even natural disasters that are not easily controlled. For municipal actors, policymakers, and urban planners to imagine something other than a strategy of growth requires new models of urban life that are situated within and take seriously the conditions of decline and can accommodate the unique processes, social dynamics, and spatial conditions therein.

Toward this end, this book borrows the lens of informality from its rich history in urban studies of the Global South and trains it on Detroit. After introducing this epistemological framework, I interrogate the conditions of Detroit's decline that call into question dominant understandings about how urban property functions and demonstrate how these conditions promote and give rise to what I call *property informality*.

INFORMALITY AND URBAN PROPERTY

Early ethnographic work on informality in the Global South focused on documenting and defining the phenomena, by studying squatters in Rio de Janiero's favelas[27] or the informal economy in Peru.[28] More recently, scholarship on informality uses case studies of squatters or unregulated economic activities to illuminate other social issues, such as the politics of informal practices;[29] possibilities for social change;[30] struggles to redefine citizenship;[31] and gender relations.[32] Until very recently, informality was not recognized as being at all prevalent in the United States, and this lack of engagement with Southern scholarship has left gaps in our understanding of how informality is interwoven with housing, work, community, urban change, and property.

Throughout Southern scholarship, informality has been defined in various ways, often related to and depending on the practices being studied. More recent research has deployed two different conceptual frameworks for understanding informality, what Ananya Roy calls "economies of entrepreneurialism" and "political agency."[33] That is, researchers often study informality as a mode of entrepreneurialism, wherein actors produce and circulate goods and services outside the boundaries of formally regulated economic activities. On the other hand, informality is commonly viewed as an assertion of political agency by impoverished actors—"groups of population whose very livelihood or habitation involve violation of the law"[34]—who influence the socio-political realm via what Asef Bayat calls "the quiet encroachment of the ordinary."[35] Both these approaches—economies and politics—counter early problematic conceptualizations of informality as a condition of poverty.[36] Moreover, some scholarship has evolved to synthesize both—informal practices are part and parcel of the "habitus of the dispossessed,"[37] simultaneously everyday economic survival strategies but also a political refusal of the exploitative conditions that threaten poor and/or oppressed populations.[38]

Building on prior frameworks, I operationalize property informality as practices that 1) violate or are denied the protection of property-related laws and regulations, and 2) have achieved a level of social legitimacy such that they are no longer viewed as illicit, despite their illegality. My definition draws from other widely adopted understandings of informality that focus on informality's relation to the state. Manuel Castells and Alejandro Portes explain informality as a process (in their case, economic activities or income generation) "unregulated by the institutions of society, in a legal and social environment in which similar activities are regulated."[39] Relatedly, Edgar Feige defines informal economic activities as "those actions of economic agents that fail to adhere to the established institutional rules or are denied their protection."[40] The fact of their illegality or noncompliance with the regulations/laws of the state, however, does not alone mean practices are accurately labeled *informal;* social legitimacy plays a role as well.

In further developing the concept of *informal,* Castells and Portes[41] examine the complex relationship between legal and illegal, and licit and illicit *processes of production* and *final products.* They argue that different permutations of these facets result in formal, informal, or criminal activities. Informal activities must have a *licit* final product, even if the process of production is *illicit.* Although Castells and Portes's writing referenced informal economic practices, the schema is aptly applied to informal housing as well. As a poorly regulated or unregulated *process of production,* self-built housing is de jure illegal. But, the *final product*–shelter— is largely considered socially legitimate. As such, self-built housing can be understood as *informal* because of the combination of an illegal process of production with a licit final product. On the other hand, the making of methamphetamines, for example, is an illegal process and results in an illicit final product, rendering it (and other aspects of the drug economy) *criminal* according to Castells and Portes's schema.

Scholars from a variety of disciplines urge us to reverse the typical directionality of epistemological insights (e.g., north to south) and consider what the North can learn from the South.[42] Yet researchers in the United States (and other Global North contexts) have generally been slow to adopt the lens of informality to make sense of economic, housing, or urban development practices, even when studying practices that may fit these definitions of informality. For example, there is a wealth of scholarship on squatting in the Global North.[43] Here too these de jure illegal activities have gained a level of acceptability and are often tolerated in part due to widespread notions that the provision of housing is a socially legitimate pursuit.[44] Many studies in the United States investigate economic practices, variously termed "underground,"[45] "survival strategies,"[46] "hustling,"[47] or "making ends meet."[48] Some such research documents the way that illegal or unregulated economic practices like recycling or under-the-table businesses can gain legitimacy if they are in line with dominant narratives about personal work ethic and self-sufficiency.[49] Thus, this existing research on squatting and economic practices may "fit" with widely adopted definitions of informality—as unregulated/illegal but socially legitimate.

Relatedly, a body of scholarship on "do-it-yourself" (DIY) urbanism examines informal interventions into everyday life that urban actors carry out to improve their neighborhoods/cities. In the context of increasingly neoliberal and austere urban governance regimes that have decreased service provision, residents take up government's role of improving urban spaces. These practices range from library boxes in front yards for neighbors to swap books to pop-up beer gardens or movie venues to more organized activists using guerilla tactics to paint much-needed bike lanes. DIY urbanism is often viewed as a form of civic engagement by middle-class or hipster urbanites who value creativity and spontaneity in their neighborhoods. But scholars have warned against the "glib superficiality in the rising fervor for pop-ups" and urge a more serious consideration of the equity and spatial justice issues at stake in urban informality.[50]

With regard to the United States, scholars have surmised that this lacuna in research is perhaps due to unfounded perceptions that informality is unlikely amidst what is arguably one of the world's most deeply entrenched legal and governance regimes.[51] That is, scholars may be relying on unreflective notions that informality couldn't possibly be pervasive in the United States because our society is governed by the rule of law. At the same time, this view is somewhat surprising, given that socio-legal scholarship has long noted that in everyday life actors negotiate, avoid, resist, or reinterpret the law in a variety of ways.[52] Meaning, the presence of deeply entrenched juridical ideals, laws, institutions, and regulatory mechanisms does not mean that the law "on the books" translates neatly into everyday practice. In fact, as Castells and Portes emphasize, formality and informality go hand-in-hand, rather than one replacing the other.[53]

Rather than precluding the presence of urban informality, the comprehensive legal and regulatory capabilities in the United States may mean that informality presents in ways that differ from other contexts. Adopting Castells and Portes's definition of informality, urban scholars Vinit Mukhija and Anastasia Loukaitou-Sideris's edited volume uncovered various informal practices across an array of US cities.[54] Here, too, many of their chapters can be conceptually divided according to those focused on informal economic activities and those involving the informal use of space, e.g., for parking, housing, gardening, or various other activities (though some practices cross this boundary). Colonias near the Mexico border in

Texas and California—self-built housing on illegally subdivided land—are arguably the most well-researched examples of informality in the United States that explicitly use this framework.[55] Research on colonias illuminates the widespread presence of housing informality in one kind of US context—the urban periphery; the obstacles to formalization; and the way that informality in the United States reflects and reproduces inequalities.[56] Other recent scholarship in the United States investigates a very different urban context, studying informality in Los Angeles.[57] In South Central LA, for example, Jake Wegmann finds that densification occurs through unpermitted renovation or construction.[58] In part a response to a lack of affordable housing and the prevalence of single-family homes on spacious lots, residents divide existing homes into apartments, add on unpermitted apartments to the back of their homes, and construct new structures, or even park RVs or trailers in their backyards. These additional dwelling spaces provide affordable housing for friends, family, or tenants, and often extra income for homeowners. Both these examples—the peri-urban fringe of Texas or California, or dense high-cost LA—demonstrate the way informal uses of land/property in the United States respond to local sociospatial, political, and economic conditions.

This recent attention to the dynamics of informality in the Global North is promising. But it also requires careful consideration of how we conceptually adopt this framework to better make sense of urban development, housing, and economic activities in contexts like the United States. For example, Noah Durst and Jake Wegmann conceptualize informal US housing as noncompliant (actors violating laws or regulations such as by squatting), non-enforced (state wielding its power to decide when to enforce laws or regulations), and deregulated (when the state withdraws from regulating certain activities).[59] This typology helps us consider how informal housing practices exist in varied relationships to the state in the US context.

Also seeking to improve conceptual clarity, Richard Harris proposes a typology of what he calls "modes of informal urban development," a heuristic tool to help identify the commonalities and differences across various instances and types of informal practice.[60] Rather than creating discrete categories, Harris suggests a continuum of modes of informality that vary according to "the extent to which a regulation is violated, the seriousness of consequences, and the number of people or regulations involved."[61] This tool helps situate the informal practices in this book in a schema that can link informality in the North and South.

At one end of Harris's continuum is "latent" informality, which refers to the possibility of practices being in violation of laws/regulations. For example, formerly rural self-built housing that is incorporated into a suburban municipality *becomes* informal (i.e., non-compliant) after this geographic expansion of a municipal boundary takes place). As a relatively isolated instance of informality, recent squatting in Portland, OR, can be considered "diffuse": these are individualistic, weakly coordinated, geographically dispersed practices that are largely hidden. But as practices grow in number and coordination, they cross a threshold into being "embedded." Embedded informality describes practices which become organized or common within a particular social group and are characterized by cooperation, physical concentration, and popular legitimacy (perhaps more akin to some of the squatters in cities like London or Amsterdam). As these dimensions grow, informal practices cross another threshold into "overt": when the number and visibility increase such that authorities cannot help but take notice. The final threshold is crossed as overt practices grow in number and impact, becoming "dominant": wherein informality comes to "shape the mode of the state governance itself,"[62] as Ananya Roy argues is the case in much of the Global South.[63] The informal practices in this book sit somewhere between the modes "diffuse" and "embedded," as number, cooperation, concentration, and visibility vary across three dimensions: 1) the geography of the city of Detroit and sociospatial conditions of vacancy, abandonment, and blight; 2) who participates in informality; and 3) what kinds of property informality residents engage in.

In comparison to other studies of US informality, this book is unique in that it focuses on a wide variation in practices and participants. Roy has noted that, even in the Global South, informality is not limited to the slum or deproletarianized labor.[64] Instead, she explains that even illegal urban projects by powerful actors that are sanctioned by the state are *informal*, and argues that informality can be understood as a "flexible strategy wielded differentially by different social classes in the context of urban inequality."[65] Urban informality as a "flexible strategy" is evident in Detroit in the wide range of practices that proliferate—from scrapping metal from abandoned industrial sites, to salvaging old doorframes or molding from vacant houses, to squatted houses and gardens—as well as in the wide variation in the type of actors participating—from hipster suburbanites new to the city, to poor residents who struggle to get by day to day, to long-time residents who labor to keep up their neighborhoods amidst decline.

Given this variation, it is not useful to focus on informality in Detroit as *either* economies *or* housing, nor as a survival strategy by the poor or DIY interventions by the middle class. Instead, understanding the significance of informality for urban life in declining US cities requires shifting away from the focus on *actors* or *practices* and focusing on their common thread—the informal use of real property. Roy contends that informality is "a mode of the production of space that connects seemingly separate geographies of slum and suburb."[66] Extending this idea, we can conceptualize *property informality* as a mode of producing the sociospatial form of declining cities in the United States. As such, we must consider the conditions of real property in cities like Detroit.

Real property refers to land, houses, and other buildings, and in the urban context, these provide the *space* for informal practices to take place. Typically, in the United States, these spaces are highly regulated by property laws that give individual owners exclusive rights to control their property, nuisance laws that influence conduct and property conditions, lot lines and property boundaries, local policies like zoning ordinances, and even longstanding customs. Private property in urban areas allocates power, creates and reflects inequalities, and adjudicates access to urban space. Because real property is spatially rooted, it mediates relationships among individuals in a given proximity as well as their relationships to the resources of the city. Legal rights to property in highly sought-after, gentrified neighborhoods afford access to the resources therein: quality schools, retail choices, safe spaces, efficient transit, etc. In highly segregated, disinvested neighborhoods or spaces of concentrated disadvantage, residents are hindered by the limited resources proximate to the properties to which they have access.

Many property laws and regulations are created to protect the economic value of real property (like a house) and to protect an individual owner's right to control and benefit from their property (economically and otherwise, e.g., calling a house *home*). When the legal and economic incentives that help to regulate property are diminished, practices that violate these laws rise in prevalence in part because the state no longer effectively enforces them. Furthermore, as chapter 3 demonstrates, in Detroit these practices often gain legitimacy and acceptance among residents. Property law violations that are effectively deregulated and socially legitimate conceptually shift into the realm of *informal*, and formal law is insufficient for understanding how squatting, scrapping, gardening, and the like shape neighborhood conditions, community dynamics, and everyday experiences in Detroit.

Classic conceptions of *space* emphasize the way the spatial form (e.g., the planned and regulated city) influences the everyday experiences and practices of residents/actors who then, through praxis and struggle, reshape the sociospatial environment.[67] The spatial conditions of declining cities (of vacancy, abandonment, lack of surveillance, and poorly enforced regulations, etc.) shape the experiences of daily life for residents. In Detroit, for example, residents interact with the spatial environment— with *property*-in different ways than under conditions of growth and highly regulated property. They live in houses without legal right; they fence in lots they do not own; they paint and affix boards to houses without permission from owners; they take materials from or even tear down properties they have no legal right to. The characteristics of these practices influence relations among residents (both those who engage in property informality and those who do not) and neighborhood conditions, which, in turn, influence how new informal practices arise or take shape. Property relations—both formal and informal—may appear to be *dyadic* (existing between a person and property) but are always actually *triadic* because access and use of real property—which is spatially fixed—influences the relations among others, especially those who are proximal.[68]

Thus, property informality is integral to *producing* the sociospatial form of declining cities like Detroit. Informality is not just a survival strategy or lifestyle practice, it is a way of shaping and reshaping the built environment of the city and social relations therein. Durst and Wegmann note that housing informality in the United States is geographically uneven, varies greatly by location, is interwoven with formality, and is very hidden.[69] Similarly, Detroit is not *only* an informal city. Rather, Detroit is a territory with undulating, interwoven patches of formality and informality scattered unevenly across the city. This may be different than informality in other regions; or it may be surprisingly similar. Johannesburg, for example (as another city with a history of racial conflict and oppression, and a hollowed-out urban core surrounded by wealthy suburbs), has a very intermixed terrain of formality and informality where (as one example) Sandton—known as the richest square mile in South Africa—is one mile from Alexandra, a large shanty township.

Because the process of urban decline is spotty and uneven, thus also are the spaces wherein property informality can arise. While city-wide, different neighborhoods have reputations for their varying levels of stability and vacancy, residents often colloquially use "the block" as a unit for assessing conditions. One block may be a neat row of large stately homes, seemingly fully occupied if a bit rusty around the edges; the next may have several vacant lots and decaying empty houses interspersed between occupied homes; and two blocks further only two houses remain.

We cannot think of Detroit as *only* an informal or formal city. It is both at the same time. In a context like Detroit, property informality is one dimension of the way the city takes shape. Formal urban planning still operates, perhaps in even more intense form than growing cities, as wave after wave of urban authorities roll out their approach for "fixing" the city.[70] In recent years, new property laws and regulations, strategic plans, and zoning ordinances have been deployed to try to improve urban conditions in various ways. Thus, also consequential are the interactions that take place between informality and these new top-down formal property regulation schemas. Tensions and conflicts arise between new regulations and persistent, enduring modes of informality. This interaction shapes residents' experiences, neighborhood dynamics, and—perhaps most significantly—the way that longstanding inequalities develop and are reshaped. Interactions between formal and informal are happening even if urban authorities do not recognize them as such, but the consequences are far-reaching and significant, especially for the well-being of poor residents.

In cities of the Global South, Roy argues that informality can be understood as a mode of urban planning because laws and policies take shape in response to and are influenced by informality.[71] But we don't yet know enough about urban informality in the United States or other Global North contexts to be able to keenly assess the way the interaction between the informal and formal may create problems or bring benefits for informal actors. In the United States, seemingly all that must be done to address informality is to enforce already existing laws and regulations, thus likely threatening informal actors in ways that differ from some Global South contexts where gaps in legal frameworks or different property laws may be at least somewhat enabling rather than prohibitive. A wealth of research has uncovered various policy responses to urban informality and the problems and possibilities therein.[72] But even prior to the creation of "new" responses to informal practices, the details of how local enforcement takes place; doesn't take place; or takes place conditionally matter a great deal to the development and persistence of informality.[73]

Curbing property informality in Detroit does not necessarily require devising new laws or regulations; existing ones just need to be applied and enforced. This could be a justification for not needing to study US informality, but I argue it is precisely this possibility that makes studying informality in America's Motor City all the more pressing. The legal framework to curtail these practices already exists, making it possible for urban authorities to repress property informality if so desired, having potentially dramatic consequences for the well-being of residents.

In the following chapters, I will show that residents in Detroit face little risk by appropriating property to which they have no legal right, and that counter to the perceived pejorativity of property law-breaking, property informality can have positive impacts for individuals and communities. Detroiters are variously motivated to take advantage of available property and reap these benefits. Some residents struggle amidst problems like unemployment and poverty and take advantage of property for shelter or to scrap for income. Other longtime residents are frustrated with the decline in municipal service provision and take it upon themselves to board up or demolish properties or repurpose the vacant spaces around them. Surrounding Detroit are suburbs full of disaffected millennials struggling amidst rising housing costs, enormous student debt, and an inhospitable economic landscape that doesn't even provide them meaningful work post-college. Many of these young adults yearn for alternative lifestyles that are made possible with access to "free" property. Given the confluence of these conditions in Detroit and other declining cities, it might be more appropriate to ask, "Why *don't* we see more property informality?" than "Why *do* we see this happening?" And in fact, it may be the case that we don't see more informality—or haven't yet—because we simply aren't looking for it. Focusing on the legality of urban activities actually obfuscates a salient mode of negotiating the constraints and opportunities of declining cities: informality. The categories legal and illegal and their relative normative and pejorative connotations cannot accurately identify informality, which violates the law but achieves legitimacy. As Henry, a Detroit resident and urban gardener explained, "There's no sense of the law to enforce it . . . And there's no sense of law so it doesn't seem illegal . . . it just seems as another option for something you can do."

2 Regulations and Enforcement

There is a dynamic relationship between local conditions and informality, as residents navigate these conditions in various ways to meet needs and desires. In high-cost LA, informal housing "hangs off" of existing structures as buildings and lots are subdivided to meet demand for low-cost housing.[1] In sprawling Phoenix, Arizona, lower income residents who lack transportation and disposable income use informal place-making strategies to make suburban developments better fit their needs.[2] Along the peri-urban fringe of Texas, land is subdivided and sold to families to self-build their housing.[3] The conditions of decline are conducive to the particular form I analyze in this book: *property informality*, which involves the transgression of formal private property rights through illegal appropriation.

Detroit and other declining cities are often referred to as structurally disinvested ghettos[4] or spaces of concentrated disadvantage.[5] But we should consider that "sites of metropolitan innovation often emerge at the very sites of metropolitan degradation."[6] The presence of property informality in declining cities makes perfect sense when all the pieces of the puzzle are arranged. Local spatial, economic, and political conditions coalesce to make property informality not only possible, but often advantageous for individuals and communities. Decades of population decline has left a plethora of vacant property, providing abundant opportunity for informal occupation and deconstruction of real property. Lack of demand for property has bottomed out property values, such that there is essentially no functioning property market in many of Detroit's neighborhoods. Disinvestment and the movement of jobs out to the suburbs have left a dearth of economic opportunities and high unemployment and poverty rates in the city. Decreasing tax revenue, aging infrastructure costs, and thousands of municipal-owned properties mean the city is without the resources to effectively regulate property and enforce property laws. Nor is there significant push to do so for the thousands of devalued, abandoned properties. Against this backdrop, authorities selectively enforce property-related regulations. This combination of widespread opportunity and lack of enforcement or pushback by the state leaves much real property use in Detroit effectively unregulated, a key feature of informality. In this chapter, I outline the intertwined spatial, economic, and political conditions characteristic of Detroit and other declining cities that undermine the liberal private property regime and simultaneously encourage the growth and proliferation of property informality.

VACANCY AND ABANDONMENT

By 2014, Detroit's population decline had resulted in 78,506 blighted, vacant buildings[7] and over 20 square miles of occupiable vacant land owned by the city (roughly the size of Manhattan) within its 139 square mile footprint.[8] In the post-war years, white flight, racial conflict, and technological and economic changes began a process of depopulation and deterioration for Detroit.[9] This was exacerbated by rampant foreclosures during the recession, the effects of which are salient today.[10] Built for its population peak of almost two million in 1950, Detroit had about 677,116 remaining residents as of July 1, 2015.[11]

In cities like Detroit, many property owners seeking to leave the city are unable to sell because there is so little demand for property and instead take a financial hit and walk away from their homes or businesses, leaving them to foreclosure by the bank if they had a mortgage or by the city for tax delinquency.[12] Within these conditions, profit-seeking landlords

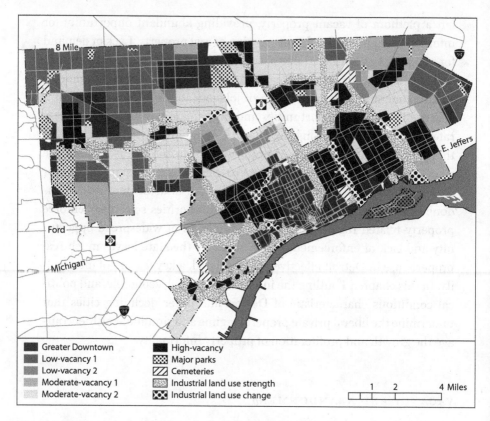

Figure 5. Vacancy rates and land use in Detroit. Source: Detroit Strategic Framework 2012, 234.

purchase cheap properties to rent out but make few repairs and let them deteriorate over time.[13] Homeowners who have stayed often find it hard to maintain their houses in the face of plummeting property values and a bleak employment environment.[14] As a result, much of Detroit's housing stock is in poor condition even prior to becoming vacant, and empty properties are further deteriorated by scrappers.

At the street level, vacancy rates and property conditions vary greatly from block to block and between different neighborhoods.[15] Figure 5 and Table 1 show the variation in vacancy rates across the city of Detroit. Vacant property—land and buildings—is scattered about the city, thus also are informal uses of these properties, making them "diffuse" and often

Table 1 Vacancy Rates in Detroit in Figure 5

Category	Rate of Vacant Land Parcels	Rate of Housing Vacancy	Percentage of City Land Area
Greater Downtown	32%	21%	5%
Low Vacancy	7%	16%	26%
Moderate Vacancy	22%	26%	33%
High Vacancy	56%	30%	17%

SOURCE: Detroit Strategic Framework 2012, 236–239.

disconnected from each other.[16] More stable areas like Midtown or some parts of far northwest Detroit have few vacant houses or lots and look like stable neighborhoods in many other cities with older housing stock. Small post-war bungalows or modest four-squares tightly line the streets, aging and outdated but occupied and cared for by residents. The withdrawal of municipal services is evident across the city as streetlights have long gone out, sidewalks are crumbling, and cavernous potholes make driving feel like one is dodging obstacles in a video game. But in these more stable neighborhoods there may be only a handful of vacant lots on a block, and residents often work strenuously to keep empty houses looking occupied to prevent further blight.

Other neighborhoods, like those surrounding the city airport in northeast Detroit, look like a war zone. The city lacks the funds to demolish all the decaying properties, leaving vacant, blighted houses littering the blocks. Charred remains of houses or buildings sit precariously, waiting for the next storm to crumble them into a heap. Debris spills out across overgrown, used-to-be sidewalks [See Photos 1 and 2]. Mildewing personal belongings and furniture—the collateral damage during evictions—are littered across front lawns, curbs, and driveways.

The near east and west sides of Detroit are commonly referred to as "urban prairies" because streets are often empty except for a few remaining houses [See Photo 3]. Depending on one's vantage point, the area might look like a quiet country setting, its true urban identity revealed only by old defunct streetlamps stretched across the waist-high brush that mark

Photo 1. A deteriorated, fire-damaged house in Detroit; the house next door has melted siding from the heat of the fire. Photo credit Michael Brown

Photo 2. A scrapper (circled) searches through the rubble from a fire-damaged building in Detroit. Photo credit Michael Brown

Photo 3. The "urban prairie" stretches out in front of three houses in Detroit. Photo credit Michael Brown

where an alleyway used to run. These urban prairies were the product of past administrations' targeted demolition funds, leaving large swathes of vacant land that the city often compiles and holds in anticipation of future redevelopment projects.

In other neighborhoods, variation in vacancy is visible from block to block or even from house to house [See Photo 4]. The mansions of the historic Boston Edison district are quite intact, even if a bit run-down, with houses either occupied or stringently closed up and heavily surveilled. But a walk down the street one block over reveals large well-kept homes backing up to Boston Edison and facing these, smaller houses showing major signs of disrepair. On one lot, a tree grows through the collapsed frame of a house, blackened from a fire.

These varied and spotty conditions of vacancy mean that there is a lot of opportunity for property informality spread out across the physical

Photo 4. Varying levels of deterioration across three houses in Detroit. Photo credit Michael Brown

geography of the city. But across the neighborhoods I visited throughout this study and during my time as a Detroit resident, what seems to remain regardless of the level of vacancy is a nostalgic desire for community and proximal human relationships, as though the connections between some neighbors left with the auto plants back in the 1970s.[17]

PROPERTY MARKET AND ECONOMIC CONDITIONS

In cities experiencing population decline, vacant land is increasing, while demand for property and property values have decreased. Detroit's property values have fallen a staggering 78.76 percent in today's dollars since their peak in 1958,[18] such that there is no "market" for property in many neighborhoods. While the collapse of the housing market in 2008 called into question the widely held belief that property is always a stable source of wealth, generations of Detroiters had watched their properties plummet in value long before the Great Recession. The Great Recession hit Detroit hard, just as it did many other regions. But residents note that the foreclosure crisis only murdered an already sick city; that is, it exacerbated a weak property market and sped up rising vacancy rates but did not introduce conditions that were not already rampant across the city. From 2007–2010 alone, Detroit's average house value dropped 40 percent, and from 2000–2010 the city lost over 25 percent of its population.[19] According to the census, the median value of owner-occupied housing (arguably some of the highest-valued property) in Detroit from 2011–2015 was $42,300 (compared with $178,600 nationwide);[20] but the median home sale price in 2015 was only $19,070.[21] Over 26,000 foreclosed properties were open for bids starting at a mere $500 in October of 2015 through the county property auction.[22] Property in Detroit is not always a reliable source of wealth and stability but rather a tenuous foundation for residents or, increasingly, a liability for the city, which must take on the responsibilities of ownership that are abandoned along with the properties.

Classical economic theory would suggest that when land is in abundance, its price would fall until market activity picks back up. But this hasn't happened in Detroit, in part due to complications like tangled property titles and mortgage lenders' refusal to give loans for very inexpensive properties. The weak property market in Detroit has several repercussions that are influential for the spatial conditions of the city and the prevalence of property informality.

A weak property market contributes to the proliferation of atypical property sales and title transfers. In part because of obstacles to obtaining mortgages for purchasing low-valued properties (and/or when buyers have poor credit or low incomes), declining cities see an increase in less conventional forms of property sales and title transfers,[23] including seller-financing, quit-claim deeds, un-recorded familial inheritance, or even informal handshake deals. Research has identified these as a kind of housing informality that persists in the United States.[24] Another important dynamic is the tangling of property titles that can happen when properties don't go through a proper probate process or when they are transferred informally. There may be multiple claimants to the property, or heirs may be far away or have died. Detangling these titles can become arduous and expensive to resolve and results in a kind of "freezing" of the property from a legal standpoint. Without any institutional oversight to ensure that title transfers are clear, legitimate, and recorded, these unconventional methods for transferring property ownership can exacerbate obstacles of regulating urban property and make it difficult for these properties to enter a formal property market.

Residents in my study frequently recalled frustrating experiences trying to locate legal property owners. Rita, a homeowner who squats several lots to farm, recalled trying to find the owner of one of the lots to try to buy it:

> I looked at the tax records and found the name on it and then tried to locate the person . . . I might have looked him up online . . . He was friendly and he was like, "Oh yeah that was a long time ago . . ." He was laughing at it . . . he just completely thought that it was gone and he couldn't really explain to me exactly what happened but he said, "You won't be able to get that, it's just kind of stuck in the system. And I don't have it . . . I don't own it anymore." But his name was still on it. And you know that's not the first time I've encountered that sort of thing.

The property market conditions in Detroit have reduced the economic incentives attached to property ownership, giving city authorities little reason to expend their tight resources to protect such low-valued property and increasing the burden on city authorities to decipher confusing, unclear, or inaccurate property records. These conditions make it harder for the city to hold property owners liable for the care and maintenance they are legally required to uphold. Deferred maintenance and negligence increase the likelihood that a property will need to be demolished, an expense that ends up falling on the city.

A collapsed property market and economic problems combine to produce a host of obstacles for homeowners and renters in declining cities. Because macro-level economic changes such as deindustrialization are central to processes of urban decline in the United States, these cities often have too few opportunities for formal work, and high unemployment, joblessness, and poverty rates. From 2011–2015, only 53 percent of Detroiters age sixteen and above were in the labor force, 40.3 percent of Detroiters were living in poverty, and the unemployment rate was 24.9 percent (compared with about 63.7, 15.5, and 8 percent, respectively, nationwide). During this time, median monthly household income in Detroit was $2,147; compared with $4,490 in the United States.[25]

Lack of economic opportunities leaves many Detroiters looking for ways to save money, make money, or get by from day to day.

Several factors make homeownership in Detroit cost prohibitive and negatively impact the rental market. It is technically possible to buy a house in Detroit for as low as 500 dollars,[26] but these houses are in very poor condition and require significant rehabilitation and investment. Even property owners who use and care about their properties are often hard-pressed to invest in sufficient maintenance and upkeep. Property maintenance becomes a risky investment because of low property values citywide. Further, cities often raise tax rates to make up for shrinking tax revenue as residents leave the city. In Detroit, property tax rates are twice the US average[27] and, adding insult to injury, properties are notoriously over-assessed—often upward of 50 percent, especially for low-valued property.[28]

While being a property owner in Detroit can be economically burdensome, renting can be as well. Combined with these dire economic conditions, Detroiters experience a surprisingly unaffordable rental housing market.[29] Despite abundant low-valued property, from 2011–2015 an average of 58 percent of renters in Detroit were rent-burdened (spending more than 30 percent of monthly income on rent) and 37 percent were extremely rent burdened (spending more than 50 percent of monthly income on rent).[30] Other shrinking cities across the Rust Belt have similar conditions with respect to affordable housing,[31] and many also have closed their housing voucher waitlists.[32] Homeless rates in Detroit in 2013 were estimated at 22.6 per 1,000 people (compared with 1.97 nationwide).[33] These trends indicate both a high demand for access to affordable housing as well as the inadequacy of the current housing landscape to meet the needs of poor residents in declining cities.

From the landlords' side of things, high taxes and a low-income rental market make it most profitable to purchase cheap properties and "milk" them: minimally maintain them, not pay property taxes, and let them go through tax foreclosure.[34] Affordable housing options are not always available, and/or may be in very poor condition, just as squatted houses are. Residents may find themselves faced with the option of paying to rent a run-down house or illegally (but freely) occupying a house that may be in comparable condition. Photo 5 shows two houses, one more deteriorated than the other, but both of which resemble many squatted houses.

Photo 5. Houses in Detroit similar to those that squatters often occupy. Photo credit Michael Brown

The blighted, vacant built environment becomes a resource, either for finding housing or for generating meager income (by scrapping) [See Photo 4 on page 36 where a scrapper combs through rubble]. While poverty is not the only motivator of informal property use in Detroit, it is a significant condition citywide. Part 2 of this book will discuss these varied motivations in more detail.

UNDER-RESOURCED, OVER-BURDENED MUNICIPALITY

Where is the city in all of this? Why doesn't local government step in to secure vacant property so that it is not used without permission; hold property owners accountable for their run-down properties; or demolish blighted, abandoned properties that threaten residents and neighbors? The short answer is that city authorities and municipal agencies in Detroit are overwhelmed by few resources and snowballing responsibility for urban property. In many respects, Detroit's local government is like many others—increasingly strained with few resources to cover municipal expenses. Nationally, cities have neoliberalized their local governments, meaning that city personnel and services have been reduced and their functions privatized, motivated by the belief that for-profit industry is most well-suited to efficient service provision.[35] But Detroit and other declining cities are impacted from both sides: decreasing population reduces tax bases and thus municipal resources while also increasing municipal responsibility for urban property as it is abandoned by owners or taken via tax foreclosure. These are mutually reinforcing conditions that are difficult to disentangle.

Detroit's dire conditions are evident in its recent crowning as the largest city to ever undergo bankruptcy.[36] Detroit's bankruptcy was the outgrowth of decades of mismanagement and corruption, amidst failed schemes to overcome the pernicious effects of white flight and deindustrialization that resulted in the accumulation of debt. Over the years, layoffs and reduced oversight have exacerbated the problems of urban decline, particularly with respect to how property is regulated in the city.

While unclear property records can result from the combination of poverty, low property values, and informal/unconventional title transfers, these conditions are exacerbated by an underfunded municipality that cannot maintain accurate city records more generally. Finding out who actually owned an abandoned property or vacant lot in Detroit was surprisingly difficult throughout most of my time in Detroit because of antiquated and confusing processes surrounding city records. For example, as of 2013, many of the city's tax records were reportedly still kept solely on 3x5 index cards.[37] In a bankruptcy-related document, it was recommended that the city "urgently"[38] overhaul their technology systems (including that of property information and assessment),[39] in order to increase accuracy, efficiency, and save the city money.[40] Unclear or inaccurate records make the liabilities and responsibilities of legal ownership more difficult and costly to enforce.

Detroit's tight budget is in large part due to decades of decreasing tax base as residents and businesses fled the city. But raising property tax rates to make up for decreasing tax bases in declining cities shifts the burden to residents, who often struggle to keep up with this rising cost. In Detroit in

2011, only 53 percent of property owners in the city paid their property taxes: the city was owed $131 million that year.[41] For comparison, from 2006–2016 the US average tax collection rate was 95 percent; Philadelphia's was 88 percent.[42] In declining cities, tax foreclosure has arisen as a strategy for tackling blight and abandonment, allowing municipalities to more easily take control of abandoned properties rather than having to go through the costly and lengthy process of eminent domain. However, in cities like Detroit, tax foreclosure also affects longtime homeowners who have struggled to keep up with their rising taxes and over-assessed properties. The tax foreclosure timeline in Detroit is supposed to take three years, but until recently, residents could be delinquent on their taxes for upwards of seven years before the city completed the foreclosure process.[43] This lag and the disparity between policy on the books and its implementation on the ground has meant that a homeowner in Detroit may *think* her property has been foreclosed and move out, but the city has not yet taken possession, thus leaving the property unsupervised. Or, conversely, at times the city has foreclosed a property, but the occupant is unaware or refuses to vacate.[44] Thus, the transfer of legal title via foreclosure contributes to unsupervised vacant properties available for informal occupation and to holdover squatters when occupants of foreclosed properties refuse to move out.

In Detroit, the properties transferred to municipal ownership via tax foreclosure are predominately worth less than the accumulated tax bills owed,[45] so this transfer of ownership does not change the lack of demand for the properties—they are overwhelmingly a liability for the city. Through tax foreclosure (over 160,000 between 2002–2017[46]) and targeted application of nuisance abatement lawsuits, the city is the largest property owner in Detroit, owning over 80,000 properties in 2016.[47] However, lack of funds and personnel often makes securing these properties difficult, and ensuring they remain as such impossible—even the fire department is not always able to board up properties after a fire, as they are legally required [See Photo 6].[48]

Detroit's budgetary problems also impact service provision for residents. Increasing off-loading of service provision in many cities (again, in line with this trend to neoliberalize local governments) means that residents often begin to step in where the government leaves off. In Detroit, for example, residents often mow city-owned lots that are not properly

Photo 6. An example of a fire-damaged house in Detroit left open and unsecured. Photo credit Michael Brown

cared for, they may board up vacant houses nearby, or they may act together to prevent illegal dumping on vacant lots. In her book *DIY Detroit,* Kim Kinder details how residents get by in a "city without services,"[49] studying these practices that are similar to what other urban research calls "DIY urbanism" or "guerilla urbanism"—the informal interventions into urban life or local conditions undertaken by residents aiming to improve their city.[50] This lack of sufficient municipal service provision bolsters the rise of property informality, as residents navigate the difficult conditions of daily life in Detroit.

DIMINISHED PROPERTY LAW ENFORCEMENT

The city's tight budget means it is ill equipped to enforce various property-related laws and regulations. It is technically unlawful for homeowners to leave their vacant properties open and unsecured. The city can issue citations to owners whose properties are a "nuisance," but the city rarely collects on these fines. In 2013, for example, the department that handles nuisance citations and building code violations reportedly had $50 million outstanding accounts receivable owed.[51] Police officers can cite or arrest property appropriators for violations like trespassing or vandalism, but seldom do so. City officials are permitted to evict squatters in city-owned property but cannot afford the court costs.[52] The city's inability to adequately handle these issues means that property owners who walk away do so with little to no repercussions,[53] and appropriators face little risk for their activities.

Mirroring the conditions of the city overall, the police force—commonly a key agent of property-law enforcement—is severely underfunded and overburdened. Detroit's police force has undergone severe cuts in staff and funding, losing 40 percent of their workforce over the last ten years.[54] In 2011, Detroit only "cleared" 8.7 percent of reported crimes.[55] In 2012, Detroit was considered the most violent city in America, with the highest violent crime rate for cities with over 200,000 people and a violent crime rate five times the national average.[56] In 2013, the average response time in Detroit for "priority one" 911 calls was fifty-eight minutes.[57] Stories abound of residents waiting two hours for police to respond to 911 calls or of the police just never showing up. Detroit's police force is overwhelmed by high crime rates, is underfunded, and suffers from low morale. Up until 2013, they had experienced a high turnover rate of police chiefs—five in the previous five years—and have been forced to rely on aging and inadequate equipment.[58] Officers in my study reported not being able to respond to 911 calls because available squad cars would not start.[59] These conditions mean that calls about illegal property use like squatting and scrapping in the city of Detroit are very low priority for police officers.[60]

Compounding the lack of sufficient resources is that property-related laws can be confusing (particularly those pertaining to squatting) and difficult to enforce when legal owners are absent. If the police can ascertain that a person has broken into a property illegally, that person can be charged with several criminal offenses, such as trespass, breaking and entering, or intent to harm. However, if a resident calls 911 in Detroit to report that someone has illegally broken into a vacant property, it falls into the category of low-priority because it is not considered life threatening.[61]

Therefore police are rarely able to get to the scene of such a break-in quickly enough to ascertain that the person entered without permission and is therefore trespassing. If a squatter has the chance to set up residency—which may include, for example, moving in personal possessions, having mail sent to the property, or having the locks changed—then the police cannot immediately prove that a break-in has happened nor establish that the person is occupying the property illegally. Without the ability to judge if an occupant has broken into a property or entered without permission, the issue becomes a civil matter. Only the legal owner (or agent of the legal owner) of a property can try to evict an occupant through civil court. Given that many owners of vacant properties have given up and walked away from them, it makes sense that they are not willing to nor interested in spending the time and money to go to court to pursue an eviction.

While not entirely an issue of enforcement, the idea of "squatter's rights" serves to bolster the confidence of some illegal occupants and can strengthen their perceived legitimacy among residents. Many resident witnesses and appropriators in my study expressed belief in the existence of some sort of hazy "squatter's rights" in Detroit, which is a widespread misinterpretation of the doctrine of Adverse Possession.[62] In Michigan, in order to claim adverse possession of a property, one must demonstrate that they have been in "actual, visible, open, notorious, exclusive and uninterrupted possession of a property that was hostile to the owner and under cover of a claim of right for a fifteen year period."[63] This means that the squatter's presence must have the hallmarks of ownership, meaning they maintain and/or improve the property, they may pay property taxes, and the like. The act of squatting must also be done so visibly and openly that the original owner could have taken notice of the occupation and asserted their right to the property. Adequate property maintenance and paying taxes are sometimes even difficult for legal owners in Detroit to do—much less illegal occupants—for a continuous fifteen-year period. And, a squatter must have documented proof that they met all these requirements. The fact that I never came across a single successful adverse possession claim during the course of my research attests to this obstacle and also reflects the fact that one cannot make an adverse possession claim again the government, which is now the largest property owner in Detroit. In interviews and conversations, residents' belief in "squatter's rights" in the city was frequently traced to Detroit's now-defunct Nuisance Abatement Program, which provided a legal avenue for residents to claim, fix up, and gain ownership of abandoned properties (discussed more in Conclusion). This program (linking back to the role of enforcement for the production of informality), was largely regarded as poorly administered.[64]

Local government's inability to reliably enforce property-related laws impedes improvements to Detroit's formal property market. Investors or potential homeowners are likely to hesitate if they cannot be assured that their financial investments in property will be protected. Legal violations like trespassing, vandalism, or arson are costly for property owners. Deteriorated housing and increasing blight and vacancy can compromise the quality of neighborhoods and community well-being. Research shows that Americans expect government to protect not just their economic investments in property but their emotional, labor, and time investments as well.[65] Detroit's local government has not been doing any of these, decreasing residents' confidence in government's ability to improve the conditions of their neighborhoods.

SELECTIVE ENFORCEMENT

City-level conditions and constraints impact the reliable legal regulation of property in Detroit. During interviews and casual conversations, many authorities reiterated how a lack of funds and resources pose significant obstacles for their ability to carry out their jobs from day to day. But the way that officials respond to property informality cannot be reduced to simply a lack of resources. Authorities selectively enforce laws in accordance with their own understandings of what is good for the city.[66] This selective enforcement is key to understanding the rise of informal practices,[67] as government agents balance not just resource constraints but also political and personal considerations.

Evidencing the constraints of time and resources, a city bureaucrat named Quentin, who oversaw thousands of city-owned real estate, initially didn't even want to take time to speak with me because he was so overloaded by his work duties. After months of frequent emails and phone calls, I finally managed to land an interview with him. He invited me into his office, and said, *You've got thirty minutes. Go.* Quentin was busy. So busy that he multitasked through much of our interview, sifting through mounds of paperwork on his desk and occasionally typing away at his ancient computer. Quentin, a Black lifelong resident, dreamed of a better Detroit but had little hope for realizing such a transformation. Quentin opened up a bit more after we discovered we had mutual friends.

I asked Quentin if he ever encountered squatters in city-owned property and how he dealt with such a situation. Quentin sat back in his chair, crossing his arms. He sighed and explained that he no longer had the resources to ensure that every city-owned property had been vacated and properly secured. He gestured around his cramped office and said, "I mean right now it's an impossible task . . . there's not enough money, there's not enough resources, there's not enough people. We just basically put out fires now (short laugh). I mean that's it." Because of constrained budgets and a high volume of city-owned properties, calls made to the city to report illegal property use were very low priority. He explained there is little he can do even when he finds out there are squatters in a property:

> But now we don't have any money for evictions anymore, so I mean we can try and rob Peter to pay Paul and worst-case scenario when people are just really out of control in the neighborhood, I'll evict somebody every now and then, but for the most part, there's nothing we can do.

Clarence, a Black firefighter and lifelong Detroit resident, also faced constraints in his line of work. Sitting at the bar in his basement rec room, I asked questions about how often squatters started house fires trying to stay warm in the winter and what his encounters were like with scrappers who like to sift through rubble after a building fire (which provides easier access to valuable metals that are hidden within the walls). Clarence explained that the police are frequently even unable to respond to calls from him or other firefighters. He stood up behind the bar and comically acted out what would happen if he tried to involve the police with a scrapping incident. He held up an imaginary walkie-talkie to his mouth:

> *Uh yeah Central Office this is Squad 5 . . . I got a scrapper right here . . . He's yanking everything off this house and putting it in a god damn grocery cart . . . Will you please send me a scout?*

Squad 5 we have no scout available . . . is there any danger to the citizens in the area?

Uh, well the citizens are sitting here smoking cigarettes and having a beer with [the scrapper] . . . there's no danger.

Squad 5 please stay the fuck off the radio until you get a good run

Clarence set down his imaginary walkie-talkie and looked at me and laughed, then said seriously, "Yes ma'am, you're not going to get any help . . . nobody's going to, I'm sorry."

While constrained budgets and resources are certainly a pervasive issue for all city employees trying to effectively do their jobs, it's not the only factor preventing authorities from intervening. In addition to facing resource constraints, many authorities did not feel they should interfere with activities that they viewed as having a positive impact for residents or the city. Frank, a white police commander and lifelong Detroit resident explained,

> It's just that nobody really cares, so they don't worry about it you know. I mean really, if I had the resources . . . if I had more police than I have, if all of a sudden, I had like a thirty percent increase in police resources, I certainly wouldn't use them to go in there and encumber people to tear down urban farms and gardens on a technical violation of ownership you know.

Dean worked for the city, handling issues related to Detroit's 40,000 vacant lots. A white man in his early thirties, he was a recent college graduate of a prestigious university who was new to living in and working for the city. We met at a café in Downtown Detroit, where he spoke in a low voice as if hesitant to have others overhear our conversation. I wanted to know how his office responded to illegal uses of city-owned lots. Dean explained that his ability to respond to illegal uses of property was constrained by inadequate resources. But also, he believed that residents taking over vacant lots can help keep them in the city precisely because it deters negative activities from taking place on their block. Recalling past conversations with residents who want a vacant lot that is not available for purchase, Dean explained,

> "I tried to couch it in terms like, 'I don't suggest this and this is not legal, but some people have just fenced in the lot . . . and I can't recommend that you do that, but you wouldn't be the first one to do it . . . But I didn't tell you to do that and that would be illegal.'"

Rather than try to enforce the law at all costs, Dean encouraged using vacant lots because he believed it was more beneficial for the city.

Another key point to consider with respect to how Detroit police officers and other city authorities respond to illegal property use is that most of these officials are also Detroit residents. They know all too well how difficult the conditions of life in Detroit can be and have dealt with these practices in their neighborhoods. As one police officer, a Black lifelong Detroit resident named Cedric, told me, "you're going to have squatters, might as well be good ones." Residents and local authorities recognize that the illegal use of property can benefit the city and consider these benefits more important than the legality of the practice. Similar to other research, officials in Detroit have ethics that are shared with residents about what kind of property use ought to persist, even if it conflicts with full enforcement.[68]

LINKING REGULATIONS, ENFORCEMENT, AND INFORMALITY

In declining cities like Detroit where vacancy rates are high, property values are low, and authority surveillance, regulation, and intervention are spotty at best, illegal uses of vacant and abandoned property can proliferate. As residents have left the city, they leave behind property—land, houses, and buildings—that are of little economic value and that have become a liability for local government. Fewer residents mean a shrinking tax base and inadequate funds to properly surveil or secure all the property that is abandoned. The abundance of low-valued property creates opportunity for illegal uses that ultimately overwhelm resource-strapped municipal actors, who also choose to selectively enforce laws and regulations. The result is that many de jure illegal uses of property become effectively unregulated by the state, a key feature of informality.

Because population decline, property vacancy, weak economic conditions, low property values, and castrated municipal surveillance and regulatory capabilities reinforce each other, they are often co-present in declining cities. Other regions in the United States experience some, but not all, of these conditions, which influences the extent to which property informality (informal uses involving the transgression of property laws) is able to proliferate. For example, some sprawling cities experienced high foreclosure rates post-recession, and some suburban residential developments were even halted midway, leaving vacant homes often owned by banks.[69] Media reports of squatters in properties outside of Las Vegas, Nevada or Fort Lauderdale, Florida, for example, demonstrate that in contexts wherein vacancy rates rise, informal property usage like squatting may arise as well.[70] But in cities where municipal oversight is more robust, police forces are equipped to respond to calls about squatters, and when property values are higher, banks or other legal owners have an economic incentive to pay for eviction proceedings. Vacant property in recently developed suburbs may be newer and in better condition than declining cities where vacancy has been on the rise for decades, thus leading nearby residents or homeowners to be less likely to tolerate or accept squatters and still yearn for "legal" neighbors (and, attracting legal occupants may be easier than in cities like Detroit). Thus, because we do not see all of these conditions in areas like the suburbs of Las Vegas, for example, it is harder for property informality to persist, to spread, and to influence community dynamics as it does in cities like Detroit. Even within Detroit, the extent and severity of these conditions vary across neighborhoods, leading to a spotty patterning of informality across the city. Amidst other urban conditions—growth, gentrification, or sprawl, for example—residents partake in different modes of informality.

What the coalescence of these conditions means for residents and appropriators is that the law does not act as a useful or relevant arbiter of the kinds of property use that helps or harms a neighborhood. Property appropriators in Detroit are well aware of the fact that they are unlikely to be penalized for violating property laws, especially (as the next chapter will demonstrate) for practices that have positive impacts for the community. Thus, Detroit's vacant property becomes an opportunity for all matter of practices that require or are facilitated by access to property. Residents use urban property for finding shelter, earning income, growing food, pursuing artistic projects, or facilitating community engagement. Urban space is a resource, and Detroit is giving it out for free.

3 From Illicit to Informal

The conditions of declining cities like Detroit undermine the liberal private property regime and, as I will demonstrate in this chapter, mean that resident and neighborhood well-being might even be harmed by the enforcement of formal legal ownership. Chapter 2 showed that laws regulating the appropriation of real property in the city are not reliably enforced; this is the first feature of informality.[1] These conditions influence residents' everyday perceptions about property law violations, and residents in distressed neighborhoods in Detroit frequently accept, embrace, or even promote illegal uses of property in their neighborhoods. This is the second key feature of informality: that de jure illegal practices gain acceptability or, put differently, informal practices produce a socially licit product and thereby shift from being illicit to legitimate.[2]

In Detroit, residents encourage squatters to move into abandoned properties that they believe should be protected and preserved, and consequently also gain another neighbor. Scrappers, salvagers, or demolishers help to clean up the built environment by "recycling" materials from blighted houses or by tearing down unsafe structures. De jure illegal gardens pop up on lots previously littered with old tires, bedbug infested mattresses, and that were overrun with weeds. Buildings, houses, and

Photo 7. A deteriorated building and vacant lot in Detroit with a "Please No Dumping" sign. Photo credit Michael Brown

lots—like in Photo 7—are repurposed in ways that may be technically illegal, but residents in my study overwhelmingly supported their presence because of the positive impacts they have for the social and physical conditions of distressed neighborhoods.

In part because they are so poorly enforced, property laws stop being a sufficient arbiter of the kinds of property use that helps or hurts a neighborhood. Legal owners in declining cities often cause harm by neglecting their properties. But squatters may help by caring for property and providing neighborly presence. To understand how squatting, scrapping, gardening, and the like impact daily life and community dynamics in Detroit, we have to look beyond the law.

This chapter uncovers how the second key feature of informality—social legitimacy—has come about in relation to de jure illegal property use in Detroit. When property appropriators adhere to what I call an *ethos of care*, demonstrating care and concern for the property and the community, de jure illegal property use is frequently accepted and even promoted by neighbors or other community members. Police and other authorities are less likely to intervene or attempt to quell them, and property informality positively influences neighborhood conditions.[3] This chapter draws out the processes by which property law violations can achieve legitimacy and acceptability among residents in my study, and thus elucidates why *property informality* is an important framework for understanding everyday life, community dynamics, and the form of declining cities like Detroit.

INVERTING THE OWNERSHIP-CARE NEXUS

We know from chapter 2 that city authorities are often unable to respond to property law violations, and these city authorities admit that a lack of resources isn't the only reason they don't always enforce property laws. Unreliable enforcement undermines the law, but this alone does not explain why residents would defy deeply held beliefs about the normativity of property ownership. Private ownership of real property is a particularly valorized legal relationship in the United States.[4] Historically, only property owners could vote, and today homeownership is a hallmark of the American Dream.[5]

Undergirding the firm belief in the good-ness of private property ownership is a presumed relationship between private ownership and individual and societal benefit. The inferential link being that private ownership generates care for property—I call this the "ownership-care nexus." Reflecting this logic, a well-known allegory "The Tragedy of the Commons" argues that private property is the "solution" to the overuse and resource degradation that ostensibly takes place when land is held in common.[6] Private ownership is valorized because it is presumed that only private owners, in seeking to secure their property as a long-term investment, will ensure that property (whether it be a house, a farm, a factory, etc.) is protected from damage and maintained for future productive use, thereby protecting it as a social good.[7]

These ardent commitments to private property ownership as an individual and collective good are not just historical phenomena, nor mere ideology. Much research demonstrates that homeowners (owner-occupants) tend to better maintain properties than renters (nonowner occupants)[8] and that homeowners are more likely to be engaged with neighbors and community organizations.[9] According to the ownership-care nexus, homeowners' interests in protecting their individual investment in property induces them to be more active in maintaining the physical and social conditions of their homes and neighborhoods than renters. While it is unclear if these outcomes are causal, it is also significant that neighborhood residents overwhelming *believe* that only the financial investment of property ownership could evoke maximum demonstrations of care and social engagement. Research shows that residents tend to advocate for the presence of homeowners in their neighborhoods because they believe that, as residents with an economic *and* emotional stake in property, they will be better neighbors than renters.[10]

But in Detroit, this ownership-care nexus has been compromised. Many property owners (including the city) have abandoned possession of and responsibility for their properties, leaving behind high levels of vacancy, deteriorated buildings or overgrown lots, and a gutted tax base. This process has had pernicious effects for remaining residents. First, many Detroit residents have watched dozens of neighbors depart over the years, whether it be because of foreclosure, eviction, to try anew in the suburbs, or in search of better economic opportunities and safer (and for some, whiter) neighborhoods. Remaining residents are often desperately seeking community and neighborly presence. But they can't rely on the unlikely arrival of new home-owning neighbors, so the legality of neighbors' relationships to property diminishes in concern: residents just want good neighbors.

Clarence, the firefighter, said regardless of the legality just "give me a good neighbor . . . It's better for the neighborhood . . . to have more presence and he's maintaining the property." Because city service provision is so poor, and police and emergency medical service response times are so long, residents often rely on each other for rides to the hospital or for watching and securing their block. As Carlos, a white resident who squatted his home until purchasing it at auction, explained, "I mean, I would call my neighbor before I'd call the cops because he could be there a lot quicker and I'm sure he's got a gun." Didi, a white homeowner who blotted (from "blotting"—a colloquial term for "squatting the block") several lots adjacent to her house, commented on the increased presence of illegal gardening in her neighborhood: "I don't think there's any negative thoughts about it for certain because it was really quite bad. It was really very, very down and when people started moving in and farming, it just did good for the neighborhood."

Second, high levels of vacancy and few eyes and ears on the street mean more interstitial spaces where undesirable activities take place. Frank, the police commander, said these happen

> all the time. Anywhere from little nuisance issues like knowing that a particular house is a smoke house where the crackheads go to use their dope, to where its being sold out of a particular location, to where it's sporadically being used in attacks on people . . . So there's a variety of bad things that can happen in an abandoned property . . . Dumping trash, you know it starts out bad and sometimes it attracts other negative issues.

The conditions of Detroit reveal fissures in the presumed normativity of private property ownership: when neither economic incentives of future benefit nor the pressure of laws and regulations can induce legal owners to care for property, many do not. Detroiters can't rely on legal property owners to be good neighbors, nor to demonstrate the kind of care and solicitude they seek on their blocks. The idea that property ownership begets care doesn't track with many Detroiters' everyday experiences. Many are angry with and blame the property owners who have long since abdicated their responsibilities to not only their properties, but to the city as a whole. This has undermined remaining residents' ideological commitments to the ownership-care nexus (or, at least, its applicability in Detroit given current conditions).

LEGITIMATE PROPERTY LAW-BREAKING

In other contexts, property law violators are predominately viewed as criminals or thieves. And conversely, property owners might be considered victims of the deviant criminal activities of squatters or scrappers: people who commit theft, vandalism, or trespass to appropriate property that does not belong to them. But in Detroit, the moral directionality of these actions is inverted. Because residents are angry with and blame the property owners, who have long since abandoned not only their properties but the whole city, space is created therein to view residents who appropriate these properties as morally blameless. Not only are illegal appropriators not necessarily denigrated for their actions, but if they demonstrate care and concern for the property and the neighborhood, then their actions begin to fill some of the spatial and social holes created by negligent property owners.

A Black lifelong resident named Ted, who lived in a neighborhood with a lot of squatters and urban gardeners, laughed when I asked if he would ever involve the police with regard to these activities. "No. No," he said, "I'm really happy to see that type of thing is going on . . . versus car chases, men chasing women down the street . . . all type of crazy stuff was happening over there so I would rather see [squatting and gardening] than anything else." Ted and other residents find that the increased neighborly presence can deter other negative activities. In a separate interview, Ted's girlfriend Ashley, a Black lifelong Detroiter, echoed a similar point:

> [Vacant properties] give the dope dealer a chance to find him a house to sell out of . . . If somebody going to jump in [and squat], let them jump in . . . that's more eyes around the city . . . if more of these abandoned houses was taken over, the less chance of something to happen because it's more people that *seeing* in their neighborhood.

Remaining residents in Detroit want good neighbors who care for their properties and contribute to the community. When legal ownership proves ineffective at bringing this about, residents renegotiate the right to property in a way that is most useful. Instead of viewing private ownership—a legal right to property—as a necessary condition for evoking responsible care, care becomes a necessary condition for the informal right to appropriate property.

The law acts as a moral barometer, such that illegal practices are predominately viewed as illicit, bad, or harmful. However, when illegal activities gain legitimacy among a social group, they shift from being illicit to being informal.[11] One way this transition takes place is when actors pursue illegal methods for legitimate ends. In other contexts, for example, squatters who are viewed as deserving housing provision by the state are considered justified, like homeless families with young children.[12] Informal economic activities have gained legitimacy if they are in line with dominant narratives about personal work ethic and self-sufficiency.[13] The goals of securing home or work are legitimate ends to pursue. In this case, property appropriation—which is de jure illegal—becomes informal if appropriators demonstrate the kind of care and communal solicitude typically associated with property ownership. Care is a legitimate outcome of a property relationship, even if not brought about legally. By accepting or promoting property appropriation that aligns with an *ethos of care,* Detroit residents positively influence the social and physical conditions of their neighborhoods.

AN ETHOS OF CARE: ASSESSING THE INFORMAL RIGHT TO PROPERTY

Property law violations have often been associated with a breakdown of collective efficacy: broken windows, trespassing, or vandalism signal disorder and apathy amongst neighbors and invite more crime.[14] However, historical examples also illustrate what I find here: that illegal appropriation of property can contribute to visible and social order.[15] In my research, residents express ideological adherence to a loose set of normative ideals about how one ought to relate to property and the community, which characterizes and guides their responses to illegal property use in their neighborhoods. I call this an ethos of care. According to Detroiters in my study, the illegal appropriation of real property is considered ethical, appropriate, beneficial, and even necessary so long as appropriators demonstrate care and concern toward the property and the community. There are many ways in which appropriators can adhere to an ethos of care and thereby contribute positively to a neighborhood. Squatters might care for a property by fixing it up, cutting the grass, and keeping garbage off the lawn. Blotters and gardeners might plant vegetables, flowers, or build a fence that deters illegal dumping. Demolishers or scrappers might burn or tear down a dangerous property that concerns residents. Salvagers might improve other areas of the block by reusing materials from a blighted, vacant home: bricks from an old chimney repurposed as a firepit for neighbors to enjoy or a bench made from scrapped lumber. Photo 8 shows a lot which was repurposed as a garden with community space and a vacant building that was artistically decorated.

Photo 8. An example of art and urban agriculture in Detroit. Photo credit Michael Brown

This ethos of care exists between and among appropriators and residents, so I draw on data from both to illustrate how the ethos of care works. Appropriators "offer up" care in part because it is one piece of their complex justificatory narratives for violating property laws[16] and in part because embracing an ethos of care is a tactic they employ to aid in the longevity of their practices by smoothing over any opposition and gaining other residents' support. Residents at the same time "require" care from appropriators in exchange for their support, so that residents do not mount opposition to illegal property appropriation in their neighborhoods. This dynamic is evidenced in the following quotes from an appropriator and his neighbor.

Allen, a white newcomer to the city, called himself a homesteader. He illegally occupied a house and land, farming a dozen adjacent lots. Selling his produce at farmer's markets provided him just enough income to scrape by. He interpreted his illegal actions, saying: "I felt no harm in [taking the house], I feel no harm in taking these lots and doing something great with them . . . You've lost your rights, sorry, but you know if you're not going to take care of your property, it's not yours anymore." Allen felt justified in his actions because he demonstrated stewardship, which the legal owner was not doing.

When asked how she felt about Allen squatting the house next door in a separate interview Ashley, who was his neighbor at the time, replied:

> If it was me, I probably would've did it too . . . because what was going to happen to that house? Nothing . . . So my thought was, it's really making it better because we don't need all these abandoned houses. So much is happening, people being found dead in them. So that was actually a plus, because I don't have to worry about staying next to an abandoned house. Somebody is in there and he's a nice neighbor you know. If I had a problem I could knock on his door—hey I need help, you know, he's there.

Ashley countered Allen's (illegal) presence with the absence that would have otherwise been: his presence helped overcome some of the challenges she and her neighborhood faced because of vacancy and the deteriorated built environment. Being a good neighbor, then, was part of how Allen secured the ability to occupy his property and make a living from farming.

As a rubric for assessing illegal appropriation, this ethos of care takes two forms: requiring care and neighborly presence for occupation and requiring that deconstructors[17] enact care by making the neighborhood cleaner and safer, and not further damaging certain properties. Just as prior research finds both physical and social benefits of owner-occupancy for neighborhood conditions, this ethos of care requires fulfilling obligations to both the physical property and community. In other contexts, researchers have found that squatting can gain legitimacy,[18] but I find there is also support for informal property uses that not only don't entail *occupancy* but that tear down properties rather than improve them. The desire to remove troublesome vacant properties isn't new, but finding support for it outside the formal economy or policy-arena is unprecedented in previous research.

Informal Occupation

When assessing property appropriation that involves occupation (like squatting or gardening), resident witnesses' primary concerns are if the occupier is fulfilling an ethos of care by using and maintaining the property, contributing to the community, and refraining from negative activities (like gun violence or drug use/sales).

Resident witnesses Paul and Violet, both white lifelong Detroiters, told me about the squatter who used to live across the street from them. Paul gestured toward the house and explained, "that house was occupied by a man named Fred when we got there. Fred was a squatter . . . he was a good neighbor. If you needed something, he'd be willing to help you, he was quiet, he took care of business." When the legal owner died and her heir wanted to move into the house, Paul said, "I was sad to see him go, and the people who moved in were good for nothing homeowners . . . they've been a problem ever since they've been in the house." For Paul and Violet, the legality of occupation was not primary, but rather that Fred upheld the two components of the ethos of care: he cared for the property because he "took care of business" and contributed to the community by being "a good neighbor" who was "willing to help you."

An integral part of this ethos of care requires that occupiers refrain from engaging in undesirable activities. Henry, a white resident who grew up in the suburbs (and used to informally garden in the city), described this requirement:

> Now if they're engaging in criminal activity then I have a problem with that. Like as soon as I have gangbanger kids coming through or like, you know, they're stealing the copper out of that house then there's a problem . . . But if your goal is to just find shelter, find a home and go with the motions and like, live and develop the home and . . . just take advantage of the space that you have, then I think that's good.

A Black lifelong Detroiter named DeAngelo who squatted a house echoed a similar perspective about squatters:

> If they ain't got a place to go, if there's a house that's just there . . . they shouldn't have no problem with it you know as long as there ain't no drug selling, chaos, fighting and you know cutting up . . . I don't think there should be no problem . . . if you going to try to fix the house up or something like that.

DeAngelo holds occupiers like himself accountable to an ethos of care by requiring a social obligation—no "cutting up"—and a physical obligation—

that they "fix the house up." Alondra, a white lifelong Detroiter and city authority affirmed this point saying, "Some of the squatters have also been the scrappers of the home, and also used if for illegal activity, and they're not really living in the home ... But then I've seen squatters who, you know it's their house, they're planting stuff ... that's great, I love that. And I feel like this is a person that's really invested in the neighborhood, in the community."

Squatting on vacant lots is supported and encouraged if the practices signal investment in the community. Henry explained, "So there's this idea of changing a space [where] the lawn is super tall and you're pulling syringes out and you're turning it into a garden and you're mowing the lawn and planting flowers and ... verifiably making the space better." Improvements to vacant spaces enhance the neighborhood by cleaning up unsightly blight but sometimes also because they are intended for communal use, such as a garden or an outdoor movie projector screen. Detroit resident and Police Commander Frank said, "It's a positive use of the land if a neighbor decides 'well I'm gonna cut the grass next to me,' and he cuts it and puts a picnic table and a swing set on it, I just can't get mad at him you know?"

Property appropriators know that enacting care is what other residents who witness their practices will require of them. Therefore, adhering to the ethos of care is also a tactic that appropriators use to help them carry out their illegal practices. John recalled an interaction with a neighbor when he and his friend Rob (both white newcomers in their twenties) first started squatting:

> I think it would be different if I were in here like dealing crack or something, it might be a different response you know. One neighbor pulled up and was like, "What are you guys doing in here? Are you squatting?" I said, "Yes we're squatting," ... And she was like, "Well thank you for being honest, are you selling heroin or crack?" and I was like, "No, we're not selling heroin or crack, we're going to fix it up," ... and she's like, "Okay," and then drove off.

By asking if they were going to sell drugs, this neighbor sought information that helped her assess what kind of presence John and Rob would be in the neighborhood. Telling her that they were going to fix up the house conveyed that they would be caring for the property and intended to have a positive influence in the neighborhood. Many residents contextualize the appropriateness of these practices within the broader conditions of the city. Samantha, a Black resident who moved to the city several decades ago to run a nonprofit, expressed her support of squatting in this way:

> Squatting in, in a city where the unemployment rates are so high, you know I see people on the street begging who . . . you know it could be my grandmother. How is this possible in a city with so much surplus land? Squat. That's what I say . . . It may not be legal, but who cares when you're cold and hungry? Who cares about the law at that point?

This context is important for understanding how the ethos of care materializes. Rather than challenge the legitimacy of private ownership altogether, residents recognize how squatting can respond to and alter the conditions of the city and how informal occupants can demonstrate care in ways that may look very different than suburban ideals of white picket fences and carefully manicured lawns. White lifelong Detroiter (and occasional informal demolisher) Chuck explained,

> I have no problem with squatters. None whatsoever. First thing you have to realize in the city of Detroit and a lot of cities now—you leave a house vacant long enough and it's gonna get destroyed and now you have nothing. So I personally have no problem with it as long as the tenants are acting like neighbors and not idiots. You're cutting your grass, you're taking out your trash, you're protecting the property. So no, I have no issue; matter of fact, I encourage it.

Informal Deconstruction

The requirements for upholding an ethos of care are more stringent for deconstruction practices, such as scrapping or salvaging materials from empty properties, or burning or tearing down blighted houses. Deconstructors are not expected to occupy property, but instead they enact care when they clean up and salvage materials from a property or when they burn or tear down blighted, dangerous houses to get rid of a neighborhood hazard. Deconstructors must not further damage properties that could be easily restored and used again. Similar to occupiers, there is both an obligation to invest in the physical environment (by cleaning it up), as well as the expectation of positive social impact (by making it safer) for the community.

Appropriators who salvage usable resources, tear down properties, or who scrap saleable materials adhere to the ethos of care only if they deconstruct a property that is already decayed beyond likely repair. Salvagers are considered justified because often these materials are put to good use to improve other parts of Detroit, commonly nearby if not on the immediate block. Many residents who salvage do so from very nearby their homes. They watch properties over time and gain a sense of when a property has "tipped"[19] beyond repair or when it is clearly no longer maintained or utilized by the legal owner, thus allowing salvagers to adhere to an ethos of care if they choose to take materials from it. Old tiles may be reused to improve a bathroom or bricks repurposed to outline a pathway through a resident's garden. Salvaging and scrapping put to good use the ruins of the city left behind by negligent property owners. Salvagers, scrappers, and resident witnesses extol the virtues of recycling the city, rather than leaving blighted properties to be demolished as trash.

Fern, a white longtime Detroiter and homeowner in a very blighted neighborhood, said he and his wife were able to rehabilitate their dilapidated house almost solely by using salvaged materials. He reflected on the boundary between harming and caring: "I feel better about it once the house is down and I'm like, okay I made the right decision. You know like I don't want to be stealing wood from a house that's going to be saved, but if it's clear that it's not going to be . . . I think I'm saving it from being demolished." Fern thinks it is better to use salvageable materials before they are demolished by the city and thus wasted. Allen, the self-identified homesteader, used the words "save," "reclaim," and "recycle" throughout his interview to talk about scrappers and salvagers who take left-behind metal from buildings or wood from old houses.

Scrappers—who take materials to sell for income—can be understood to be helping clean up the city. Jackie, a white woman in her fifties from the suburbs who squatted with her adult sons and occasionally scrapped materials for income, explained, "Who wants to look at all the shit, you know what I'm saying? . . . I think we're doing the city a favor personally." Ginnifer, a white city authority who moved to Detroit a few years prior, even recalled a time when she hoped scrappers would come to clean up a property near her house: "I'm like, not in my backyard, not this ugly shit. I'm going to get a scrapper . . . I'm like what's wrong with you people, it's metal, like get it out of here you guys!" Salvagers and scrappers who adhere to an ethos of care benefit the neighborhood by helping to clean up blight, by using salvaged materials to improve other houses or lots, or by selling materials to scrapyards where they may be reused.

Deconstructors who demolish deteriorated properties demonstrate care for the community by making the streets safer. Many blighted houses are opportunities for unwanted criminal activity, are structurally precarious, and left wide-open and easily entered by curious passersby or neighborhood children. As such, when deconstructors tear or burn down such structures, they care for the neighborhood by protecting residents from potential harm. Lamar, a Black lifelong Detroit resident, started helping his neighbor tear down a blighted home on his block fifteen years ago and continued this practice ever since. He said,

> I feel what I'm doing is right. It's helping the neighborhood and it's keeping kids safe . . . They won't be able to go up in them houses and then falling through the floors or the house caving in, because they don't know no better. They see something like that as a playground.

There is an informal boundary operating that elucidates the tenets of this ethos of care. Once a property has decayed due to neglect by the owner or has been torn apart to such an extent that the likelihood of someone rehabilitating the property is nil, then deconstructors are considered to be *caring* for a property by recycling salvageable parts or demolishing it. William, a white artist from the suburbs, salvaged materials to use in his art. He explained how the boundary between care and harm influenced his practices:

> Well most of the houses that I go in are already ransacked or I guess if I went into a house that didn't have evidence of scrapping or didn't seem clearly abandoned, I probably wouldn't take anything, you know? . . . Right, or it's just like, oh well it caught on fire and they haven't been back in three years or you know the downstairs is wasted and the windows are smashed up, but there's still some stuff in the attic. Like I'll pretty much take anything then . . . It's, it's long been neglected.

Resident Ashley clarified this boundary for scrapping:

> That's where the boundary line comes in because it's a right way and a wrong way to scrap . . . I figured stealing from somebody is wrong. Or if somebody move out the house, as soon as they move out, you go scrap out that house, which is wrong, because that landlord was probably going to rent that house out. So here you go, you going to tear the house up. So he's like "Aw forget that," and here we go stuck with another abandoned house.

Bond, a Black lifelong Detroiter, scrapped for income. He explained how his practice is guided by his sense of responsibility to both the property and the community. He only went in "burned houses" that "should've been torn down anyway" and would never "mess" with an occupied home because "they ain't doing that good, I ain't doing that good neither . . . they would've been doing worse than me if I took what they already had. So I wouldn't do that."

Theo, a white resident, even referenced the law while advocating for certain kinds of deconstruction:

> We've got laws, and the laws are supposed to prevent functional property from becoming unfunctional due to illegal [activities]. Now when you've got like a burned down house or something like that, hey go on in there, scrap the shit out of it you know. When you got something that's like messed up, go pull everything of any value out of it and like put it to some use somewhere. Like that seems like a good thing and for there to be any economy around that, that seems like a good thing.

Just as with informal occupation, Detroiters in my study often referenced the conditions of the city to help explain their support of informal deconstruction. In further articulating her sense of when scrapping/salvaging is appropriate, blotter Didi reflected,

> Um it depended. If the house was vacant and it was already a piece of junk, I didn't think nothing of someone coming and taking it, taking something if they needed it . . . because you know some people are out there, they're so poor and they just, they can't get jobs you know what I mean?

The conditions of Detroit complicate the relationship between homeownership and neighborhood benefit. Here, residents do not rely on promoting ownership as a strategy for improving their neighborhoods, because in their experience legal ownership does not necessarily beget the kind of responsible care for property that they seek. And, conversely, responsible care can be found among property appropriators. Thus, instead of championing legal property ownership to improve the conditions in their neighborhoods, residents look for care to determine the informal right to property.

CONTEXTUALIZING THE ETHOS OF CARE

An *ethos* can be understood as the prevailing tendency of beliefs and aspirations across a given community. Translating these beliefs into practice is complex in a number of ways that are important to consider: 1) not everyone agrees with this ethos of care; 2) there may be disagreement as to what constitutes "care"; 3) there are limits to residents' abilities to enforce an ethos of care in practice; and 4) race impacts how we assess and interpret others' actions.

First, there were four people—three resident witnesses and one institutional actor—I interviewed who expressed alternative views and did not explicitly support illegal property use in their own neighborhoods. The local context is significant for understanding these alternate views. These residents all lived in (relatively) more densely populated blocks: one lived in Hamtramck and three lived in several historic districts across the city. Their property values were higher, and they had hope for increasing value in the near future. Authorities were also more likely to intervene in these areas: Hamtramck is a two-square mile city almost completely surrounded by the city of Detroit that has its own police force, and these historic districts often pay private security companies to patrol their neighborhoods. In these four interviewees' neighborhoods, the legal and economic regulation of property is more instrumental than in other areas of Detroit.[20]

Interestingly, these perspectives vary across neighborhoods and are flexible. One of these resident witnesses, Black lifelong Detroiter Francine, had recently moved to her (more) stable neighborhood after she was the last remaining resident on her block in a very vacant and distressed neighborhood in southwest Detroit. She supported the idea of useful or constructive illegal property use in her old neighborhood, but not her new one. Another, Nina, a white lifelong Detroiter, refuted any constructive dimension of illegal property use on her own stable block, yet frequently helped to board up, paint, and clean up vacant properties on adjacent blocks with much higher levels of vacancy—engaging in property informality herself in an effort to improve the conditions of her neighborhood. These examples illustrate the influence of local context for understanding under what conditions residents accept or condone property informality in their neighborhoods, and when they continue to view these practices as illicit.

Second, there was also some discord over the extent to which squarely illicit activities could be aligned with "care." Bobby, a Black lifelong Detroiter and a former drug dealer, used to squat vacant houses from which to sell drugs. Recognizing the tenuous presence his enterprises had on a given block, he deployed "good neighborliness" as a tactic for quelling any opposition from neighbors who might have disagreed with his illicit enterprise. Not only did he and his crew put in some minor effort to keep a house looking presentable, such as by cutting the grass or cleaning up trash, but they also made sure all drug traffic came down the alley behind the house instead of the street out front. Going even further, Bobby often made sure residents' driveways were shoveled in the winter or gave them money for home repairs or other gifts to smooth the way for their presence on the block.

When I interviewed Bobby, he was no longer selling drugs, having narrowly avoided prison time for a felony conviction due to a technicality in court. But he still recalled the presence of his squatted drug houses as positive for neighbors—he himself thought he was abiding by an ethos of care—because he helped them with personal expenses, led actions to clean up and maintain the block, and showed a modicum of concern for neighbors' well-being. He also believed himself to *not* be complicit in the negative aspects of drug use and economy—he just provided a service; it was up to others to partake of those services or not. To what extent residents actually valued the presence of Bobby and his drug houses is unclear since I was not able to interview any of these former neighbors. Perhaps they begrudged having such an illicit enterprise in proximity and demanded profuse demonstrations of neighborliness as a tax. In very distressed areas of Detroit, it is hard to *avoid* drug houses popping up in vacant property, thus it is possible that residents reluctantly accepted Bobby's presence because (mirroring police officer Cedric's comment about squatters in the previous chapter), *You're going to have drug houses . . . might as well be good ones . . .* Overwhelmingly, however, residents in my study reported drug houses as *not* according with an ethos of care. More often, "good neighbor" squatters or property demolition were the antidote to vacant structures potentially ending up as drug houses.

This leads to the third point to consider: there are forms of property appropriation that do not conform to an ethos of care, and residents are often limited in their ability to curtail these harmful practices. Most commonly, scrapping and salvaging perceived as "theft" have had a widespread negative impact on the city, and residents are vehement about the problems these forms of deconstruction have caused. Deconstructors who do not adhere to an ethos of care harm properties that are still being used or that are intact enough that they could be used again. One resident who runs a nonprofit in Detroit had his organization's iron fence stolen, the gutters torn off their facility, and their heating units ripped from the roof.[21] Another resident told of the air-conditioning units stolen from the Department of Human Services office in northwest Detroit.[22] Others fear leaving their homes empty to go on vacation because scrappers might break in and do thousands of dollars' worth of damage pulling copper pipes from the walls or the aluminum siding off of their home. Residents expressed that among the biggest problems facing Detroit are scrappers and salvagers who steal from houses that are still lived in or from businesses or churches that are still used and arson that destroys stable properties.

In seeking to address illegal appropriation that does not fulfill an ethos of care, residents employed a variety of tactics to try to remove unwanted squatters or deter harmful deconstruction in their neighborhoods. Residents may hang curtains in empty houses or park their car in the driveway to make the house look occupied. In one neighborhood, residents had constructed a text-alert system, so that they could try to intervene when harmful scrapping was taking place nearby. If unwanted squatters move into a property, residents often call the utility company to get illegal hookups shut off, making it harder for squatters to remain.

Neighbors may try to track down the legal owner of the property to request that they evict a squatter (which is usually unfruitful). Some Detroiters may also board up houses they feel should be preserved in order to deter scrappers.[23] Or residents may directly confront appropriators and explain "the rules," in essence trying to teach appropriators how to adhere to an ethos of care. Cedric told me about confronting a few young squatters who moved onto his block: "I went down there and told them, 'Why you in the house?' And they said, 'oh we renting the house,' . . . but I said, 'I know you don't because . . . the bank owns it [and] you got illegal hookups,' but I told them to cut the grass.'" And now? "They're cutting the grass," he told me with satisfaction.

Fourth, and finally, it is important to remember that how residents assess the ethos of care in practice is likely shaped by the perceived race and class backgrounds of appropriators (even though this was not made explicit in interviews or observations). Voluminous research demonstrates that prejudice shapes how residents and authorities interpret the legality of people of color's behavior (especially young Black men).[24] In this case, it is likely that Black appropriators are held to a higher bar and/or scrutinized more closely for their adherence to an ethos of care than white appropriators.

THE INFORMAL RIGHT TO THE CITY

Property laws are used to regulate access, use, and control over urban (and rural) space. Private ownership is valorized for the presumption that by carving up space into legally owned parcels, individual owners will care for these spaces and protect them for future use. But in declining cities like Detroit, residents engage in pragmatic rearticulations of the right to property, wherein practices that are in line with an ethos of care gain legitimacy, despite their de jure illegality. This kind of appropriation is, to Henri Lefebvre, a more legitimate claim to the space of the city, rooted in use and habitation rather than abstract law and exchange-value.[25]

In some sense, this rearticulation happens because, quite simply, the law stops being a sufficient arbiter of whether or not property appropriation helps or harms residents and communities. What are the implications of this? As this chapter demonstrates, relationships among neighbors and the conditions of one's block are often shaped by property informality in Detroit. Informality is intricately woven with formality and legality, as homeowners may encourage squatters to move into a vacant house on their block or may illegally take over lots nearby. Some urban farmers straddle informality and legality, owning some lots but not others. Some appropriators use the former as an avenue for the latter by illegally occupying property at first, then purchasing it later on. Similarly, salvagers often use informally acquired materials to improve the properties they legally own. Poor residents may use scrapping to maintain legal ownership of their homes or stay current with rent.

These informal practices shape neighborhood and community dynamics by negotiating access to proximal property via positive obligations of care. This is an implicit recognition of the social nature of the institution of property, countering pervasive liberal interpretations of property as a bastion of individuality and exclusivity.[26] Grounding access to urban space in care for property and communal solicitude provides a different way of relating to neighbors and other residents, one which considers the import of one's actions for the community as a requirement for continued appropriation. This is (perhaps unfortunately) not a radical re-visioning of social relationships. Residents in my study frequently affirmed the value of homeownership—both for the neighborhood and as a disciplinary mechanism for owners—while simultaneously championing "good" squatters or other appropriators. Rather than abandoning belief in the value of homeownership altogether, residents seem to recognize the contextual obstacles to private property ownership as the cure for their neighborhoods and thus rearticulate a right to property in a way that is more pragmatic given the often-harsh conditions of some areas of Detroit.

And, while the ethos of care exists ideologically and frequently in practice, there is still much illegal property use that does not conform to an ethos of care, and residents are severely restricted in their ability to do much of anything about it. Many residents frequently encounter and must deal with illegal uses of property that are detrimental to neighborhood and community well-being; illegal property use *also* causes many problems, and residents are eager for solutions. But the axis of differentiation between harmful and positive practices is not formal legality. The obstacles posed by harmful illegal property use is perhaps why media stories abound that portray squatters as the scum of Detroit or scrappers as vultures preying on the city's carcass.

The rest of this book deals with those informal uses of property that do generally align with an ethos of care. These are the practices that often go unnoticed either because they are not topics of contention or concern at community meetings nor the focus of local news reports. The stories in this book are, perhaps, not as exciting as the former squatter on my block who, angry with the property owner who returned and demanded she move out, plugged all the drains and left the water running, flooding the house and causing catastrophic damage for a structure of that age and condition. I do not focus on the scrappers who shimmy up light poles and daringly remove transformers, risking death by electrocution for a few hundred dollars' worth of copper. I have passed over the hipsters filling houses with flowers to call attention to the possibilities of beauty amidst blight. These make for great news stories and often dominate discussions of illegal property use in Detroit, creating polarized understandings of these practices. But these are the exciting and exceptional, not the everyday.

This book is instead about ways of getting by, of making a life, and building community in a declining city with an abundance of vacant property. Using the lens of informality, I retrain our collective eye toward the constructive, purposeful, creative, and necessary ways in which property occupation and deconstruction in Detroit bolster neighborhood vitality, enable individual and family survival, and fulfill personal goals and desires. In doing so, these residents recreate possibilities for themselves and the city and contribute to the way the urban environment of Detroit is shaped—literally. They tear down and build up property in Detroit. They move into houses and protect the structure as it protects them. Who lives where, who does what with this or that, or how residents interact with the built environment and physical geography of Detroit are frequently not in accordance with property titles, permits, lot lines, or zoning codes. To understand social life in Detroit—and other declining cities—we have to understand how property informality works alongside more traditional property arrangements and regulations, to shape the sociospatial landscape of the city. Toward these ends, the next section

examines the mundane and routine ways that longtime residents negotiate an increasingly deteriorated and vacant urban environment; how
impoverished residents take advantage of these conditions to ensure their
survival from day to day; and how newcomers see possibility in Detroit's
sociospatial landscape to create lives that overcome the alienation and
monotony of mainstream culture.

PART II Informality in Everyday Life

4 Beyond Politics or Poverty

Appropriation, to Henri Lefebvre, is a claim to urban space rooted in use-value and social connectivity.[1] There is a great deal of variation among appropriators in Detroit and the use-value claims they make through their informal practices. Appropriation is undertaken by residents from many different backgrounds: newcomers and longtime residents; those who are very poor, poor, stable, or more economically privileged; white and Black; young and old; male and female; individuals or families. Appropriators also have varied uses or goals in mind—income, shelter, yard space, "the good life," art projects, remodeling, etc.—that shape the material conditions of appropriation. For some, appropriation is carried out dangerously, with limited resources; others have many resources that promote safety and comfort. Existing scholarship has tended to conceptualize poverty or politics (resistance) as the primary motivator for informality, but these themes don't capture the complexity of informal property appropriation in Detroit.

This section of the book delves more deeply into the kinds of property informality common among different appropriators and how these practices shape their everyday lives. Part I of this book focused on the social and spatial context in which de jure illegal uses of property arise and how they can positively shape community and neighborhood dynamics. These findings counter prominent views that, because illegal practices violate formal norms and subvert the rules (laws) that attempt to prevent social problems, illegality is necessarily pejorative. Because the practices in this study can be beneficial, residents often accept or advocate for them, and they transition from illicit to legitimate. The ethos of care outlined in the previous chapter operates across the various practices and types of appropriators in the city.

Appropriators tend to violate the same property-related laws: committing trespass, vandalism, or theft. But the laws violated do not capture important differences across appropriators and their practices. With the aim of making readable a landscape that is hidden and complex and to capture and make sense of these important differences, this chapter introduces a typology of appropriators in Detroit. I categorize the informal property users in my study as Necessity Appropriators (NAs), Routine Appropriators (RAs), and Lifestyle Appropriators (LAs). These categories reflect patterns in how race, class, and place-based backgrounds relate to different motivations for appropriating property in Detroit, and how they manifest with very different materials conditions that appropriators live and labor under (such as how property conditions impact their safety and comfort, and how they experience their practices). This typology shows that different social groups frequently use the same modes of informal appropriation (occupation and deconstruction)—and violate the same laws—as solutions to different social problems.

The process of typologizing is often used in sociological research to increase our understanding of complex social phenomena. A typology is often a first step toward making sense of new or under-studied phenomena. David Snow and Leon Anderson describe creating their typology of street homelessness as "a basic cognitive process that makes the world more manageable by reducing and ordering its complexity."[2] This process involves identifying similarities among empirical observations such that they can be grouped; then articulating the differences between these groups; and trying to understand where these differences come from and why they arise. Consider the stark differences in how these appropriators talk about squatting.

Marsey, a Black lifelong Detroiter in her forties who has squatted with her children to secure housing, said,

> Most of the time, squatting comes from a circumstance. It's not a desire and people get it twisted and when you're placed in a circumstance situation you have to address your issue. You just do what's best for you to do at that time to get through to the next phase, but every person who ever squatted, it had to be because that was the choice that was available. For damn sure it wasn't, 'oh I have enough money to go live in New York.'

To Marsey, squatting is something one only chooses from among very limited options for housing. This is a common orientation among the category I call *Necessity Appropriators:* that informal property use is a strategy for meeting pressing needs. On the other hand, Gavin, a single white newcomer in his thirties, explained,

> [Squatting] allowed me to come into better touch with my true self. It was like right where I needed to be to like uh, to self-actualize . . . I left an apartment, which I could afford. I left my own business, which made more money than I knew what to do with. Like I gave up all those things to go do this.

Gavin, like other *Lifestyle Appropriators*, chose squatting from among a variety of housing options and wanted to be doing so. Appropriators have different resources available for them to meet their diverse needs and goals, reflecting different backgrounds and motivations.

In the case of Detroit, there is a shared sentiment that gathering materials from vacant properties to use in one's art projects is different than gathering materials from vacant properties in order to sell them for income and pay the electricity bill. But there is no existing framework that sufficiently parses out these differences to better understand how informality based in need versus desire manifests or impacts individuals or the city. Such a framework is increasingly necessary in the United States because widening income inequality, decreasing real wages, and the expansion of various forms of debt mean that many young adults from middle-class backgrounds are downwardly mobile and may find themselves pursuing informal means to achieve goals that previous familial generations found attainable (like homeownership or meaningful work).

INEQUALITY ACROSS INFORMALITY

In the United States, most research on the informal practices of urban dwellers has been variously termed do-it-yourself (DIY), insurgent, guerilla, or everyday urbanism. Countering top-down urban planning approaches, this research draws attention to the diverse ways in which residents envision and implement changes to their environments in response to various problems or unmet desires, from lack of public space to slow and ineffective bureaucracy. But some recent scholarship has cautioned privileging the DIY practices of more well-off, creative-class type residents.[3] These are residents who have the time, resources, and desire to engage in practices that may include "whimsical"[4] endeavors like knit-bombing, which involves knitting sleeves for features of the built environment like light poles or bike racks; guerilla interventions like painting bike lanes or creating speed bumps to slow down traffic; turning parking spaces into "parklets" for the duration of the meter to create mini-public gathering spaces; to larger, more permanent endeavors like self-built skate parks.[5] Some of this research has been criticized for what urban scholars Vinit Mukhija and Anastasia Loukaitou-Sideris call its "glib superficiality"[6] and/or has been conceptualized as ways in which middle-class urbanites dally in a kind of new-age civic-mindedness.[7] DIY practices are often fun, creative, and unique—making for interesting research and reading. But serious criticisms have honed-in on a lack of attention to the underlying inequalities that shape who participates in DIY practices and how and with what impact or response by authorities.[8]

The survival strategies of the poor are largely absent from this DIY scholarship in the United States, despite some of these practices being similar to those carried out by middle class residents. For example, urban gardens may serve the food-needs of poor residents but the social/recreational desires of more economically well-off participants. Scholarship has been perhaps overly concerned with the resistant or political potential of the middle-class/creative-class DIY-ers and less with the survival strategies of the poor, whose practices are often eschewed as reactionary, piecemeal, and self-interested, or, alternately, ascribed a kind of political intentionality that is not embraced by the practitioners themselves.[9]

Scholarship on informality in other contexts has developed more nuanced frameworks over time for grappling with diversity among informal practices and in what ways informality is significant. Early scholarship on informality in the Global South often conflated informality with poverty or marginality—it was a condition of the poor who were forced to rely on informality to survive. This brought a pejorative connotation to informal actors (like squatters, garbage collectors, or day-laborers). As informality scholarship developed over time, focus shifted to understanding informality as an assertation of agency amongst the poor, a political strategy for ensuring survival.[10] When formal channels fail or are inaccessible, denizens pursue informal avenues to meet their needs. Studies of squatting in Global North contexts tend to use a social movement framework to understand the political goals and transformative potential of squatters who often have divergent motivations.[11] More recent scholarship recognizes that even powerful actors can engage in informality, such as when wealthy mafia illegally built shopping centers on government land in Mumbai[12] or state authorities influence informality via the enforcement (or not) of regulations.[13] Research has shown the way that informality refracts class power and various forms of inequality, but existing conceptual frameworks are limited.

For making sense of property informality in Detroit, these interpretive frameworks overemphasize the role of need for some appropriators; overemphasize the power of others; and are too liberal in their ascriptions of resistant or political intentions among informal property users. In her co-edited volume on informality in Latin America, Brodwyn Fischer reflects this tendency to dichotomize informality: "Portraits of the informal cities that focus only on their pathologies, or their transformative potential, can easily miss their constitutive role in extant urban cultural and power relations, the settlements' functional vitality in the here and now."[14] In seeking to make sense of informality in a Global North context, urbanist Ryan Devlin argues that we need to more clearly consider how social class and informality intersect and manifest with very different solutions and experiences.[15] In New York, for example, Devlin explains that Uber and "dollar vans" (mini-vans that shuttle residents through the city's outer-borough neighborhoods) both arise in response to a similar urban problem—that of inadequate access to transportation. But as informal solutions, they "exist in very different worlds":[16] their significant cost differences attract users from different social classes, and provide disparate levels of comfort and efficiency. He concludes that informal solutions to urban problems arise very differently for poor versus middle/upper class residents.

By creating a typology of informal appropriation in Detroit, this chapter suggests a more fine-tuned and productive way to understand the significance of informality for individuals and communities. Studies of informality and resistance need to consider the way that background, motivation, and resources intersect with individual's goals for the future and the opportunities they are presented with. It's a kind of trajectory analysis that recognizes the impact of the force and angle of a projectile to understand where it will land.

TYPOLOGY OF APPROPRIATION

If informal appropriation in Detroit were a spectrum, Necessity Appropriation (as an urgent survival strategy) would sit at one end; Lifestyle Appropriation (as an enjoyable, desirable practice) would be at the opposite end, with Routine Appropriation bridging the two (as a getting-by or making-do strategy that is less urgent than Necessity Appropriation but less enjoyable than Lifestyle Appropriation). Across all three categories, appropriators engage in forms of *occupation* and *deconstruction*. Occupation involves taking over land or housing by, for example, squatting in vacant housing or gardening on vacant lots. Aesthetic practices like art installations may also involve property being occupied by the art, even if the artist comes and goes (or leaves altogether). Deconstruction refers to practices that tear down or take away pieces of property by demolishing blighted structures, taking metals to sell at scrapyards, or taking usable materials for other building or art projects.

NAs are predominately very poor longtime residents of the city. In my study, they are overwhelmingly Black and tend to be over the age of 40 (not including their children). Education levels vary; some have college degrees, others GEDs. Many in my study have struggled with various crises, such as unemployment, drug addiction, custody battles, personal violence, or the death of a child. In my data, there was a tendency for NAs to be single mothers with children or single male adults. NAs informally take over property to fulfill urgent needs for survival. They squat to secure shelter or scrap metal from blighted buildings to earn meager income.[17] For NAs, property informality tends to be risky and difficult, and/or these appropriators endure extremely substandard housing conditions.

RAs are also often Black longtime residents of Detroit, but they are more economically stable than NAs. RAs informally use property as a coping mechanism developed for navigating the harsh conditions of the city over time. These residents help tear down blighted, unsafe properties on their block and turn abandoned lots into extra yard space or parking. They might remain as holdover squatters in their homes after foreclosure. These residents typically begin to informally use property out of frustration that local authorities are not doing their part to take care of the city. For RAs, appropriation tends to be burdensome of their time, labor, and sometimes money; but some RAs come to enjoy their practices (or elements of them) and how they have taken shape over the years.

Finally, LAs are predominately white, younger newcomers to the city who are motivated by dissatisfaction with the cultural ideals of mainstream America and seek alternative lifestyles. These appropriators often call their informal occupation "homesteading," start large farms and gardens, and salvage materials from vacant properties for art or remodeling supplies. There was a tendency for LAs to be single male adults or male-female couples. LAs enjoy appropriation and have actively sought it out. Property informality for LAs tends to be more comfortable and less risky or burdensome than it is for NAs or RAs. LAs tend to have enough economic security and other forms of capital such that they have alternate options, allowing them the ability to "opt out" of appropriation at any time.

The labels for each category are used to best capture the way appropriators talked about their own practices but should not be read as reductive of the complexities of the individuals in this study. Other research shows that even recyclers in the Global South pursue their informal practices as both a survival strategy and to cultivate a certain lifestyle.[18] My use of the term "Lifestyle" is not flippant: while I am critical of LAs, their struggles for "the good life" and feelings of alienation are very consequential. Similarly, using the term "Necessity" is not to diminish the agency of these appropriators; E.P. Thompson argues that scarcity can never be the explanation for any human life and that we must instead explore the question of what do people do when hungry?[19] Despite their varying motivations,

Table 2   Overview of Property Informality Practices in Detroit

Mode of Appropriation	Informal Practice	Description of Practice
Occupation	Survival Squatting	Occupying houses or other buildings to fulfill an urgent need for shelter
	Holdover Squatting	Remaining in a formerly owned/rented home after it has been foreclosed
	Homesteading	Occupying houses or other buildings for fun/ adventure, typically with the intent of purchasing the property in the future
	Blotting ("squatting the block")	Using vacant lots for yard space, community fire pits, art projects, or even just parking
	Agriculture	Growing food, plants, etc., on vacant lots for eating, sharing, and/or selling
Deconstruction	Scrapping	Taking materials (primarily metals) from buildings to sell (mainly to scrap yards) for income
	Demolition	Tearing down deteriorated or unsafe · structures that are deemed a threat
	Salvaging	Taking materials from buildings for personal use such as house renovation or in art projects

all appropriators in my study demonstrate creativity, resourcefulness, and a refusal to accept problematic social conditions; they cannot be reduced to their unmet needs or desires. While all the appropriation practices in my study can be interpreted as acts of defiance that poke holes in hegemonic social structures and relationships, I refrain from ascribing or denying a resistant mindset among appropriators because it is not necessary nor productive for considering what their practices can teach us.

Table 2 is an overview of the different informal practices in my study that are examined in-depth in the rest of Part II of this book. This table shows the variations in informal practice within both modes of property appropriation (occupation and deconstruction) that this book examines.

Table 3 shows how many appropriators from each category engaged in which kinds of informal practice. This table shows that different social

Table 3 Distribution of Property Informality Practices across Categories

	Number of Each Category Participating in Each Informal Practice								
	Forms of Occupation					Forms of Deconstruction		
Category	Survival Squatting	Holdover Squatting	Homesteading	Blotting	Agriculture	Scrapping	Demolition	Salvaging
Necessity	10	0	0	0	0	5	0	1
Routine	0	4	0	4	3	2	4	2
Lifestyle	0	0	8	4	12	0	2	14

groups/classes sometimes use the same mode of informal appropriation (occupation and deconstruction)—and violate the same laws—as solutions to different social problems. That is, NAs, RAs, and LAs may all trespass when they occupy houses, but this occupation fulfills different goals: avoiding shelter living, negotiating foreclosure, or fulfilling a desire for adventure. LAs may take a section of steel coil to use in an art project; NAs may take that same material to sell for income.

As these tables show, I make an analytic distinction between "scrapping" (taking materials to sell for income, typically to scrapyards) and "salvaging" (taking materials for personal use) and find that an ethos of care operates within each category to demarcate acceptable ways of engaging in these practices. However, in Detroit, the term "scrapping" is often used to refer to either of these deconstruction practices when they do not adhere to an ethos of care. Thus, study participants sometimes made a distinction between salvaging and scrapping that is different than the analytic distinction I make. In interviews, "scrapping" was commonly used pejoratively and "salvaging" positively. This is likely because salvagers are often more economically stable residents pursuing artistic endeavors or improving the properties they own, while scrappers are predominately poor residents (also sometimes substance users) desperate for income who occupy a structural position more likely to violate the ethos of care. This distinction relies on prejudiced notions about illegal property users and thus was not useful for analyzing the characteristics of the practices themselves. Photo 9 shows an abandoned library where a salvager in my study took materials to use in art and building projects. Conversely, Photo 10 shows the abandoned industrial building where a scrapper in my study found steel and copper material: two highly desirable materials that scrappers sell for income.

There were no NAs in my interviews engaged in agriculture. I had encounters with many longtime residents of Detroit who were farming or gardening, but my participant observation data did not capture enough of their individual stories or backgrounds to be able to categorize them according to this typology. It is possible that agricultural practices are less common among more economically marginalized and unstably housed residents because agricultural practices entail significant up-front and ongoing investments of labor and resources to be fruitful. For residents

Photo 9. A salvager searches for materials in an abandoned building. Photo credit Michael Brown

Photo 10. A scrapper searches for material in an abandoned industrial building. Photo credit Michael Brown

who struggle economically or who don't know how long they will be able to reside in their home, this kind of longer-term investment may not be as desirable.

TYPOLOGIES IN EVERYDAY LIFE

This typology, as an analytic tool, disentangles and simplifies what is experientially and spatially complex to be able to understand the landscape of informality in Detroit and the experiences of residents. Property informality in Detroit can be very hidden and difficult to identify, and therefore this typology is illuminating in several ways. First, a key feature of informality in Detroit, as in other case studies, is that in everyday life these practices are very much interwoven with formal uses of urban space, and they occur in very spatially interspersed ways. Appropriators were scattered across the city and living in areas with residents who were not (to my knowledge) appropriating property. That is, informal and "law abiding" residents live in proximity with each other; and appropriators often engage in both formal and informal uses of property. A homesteader may live across from a homeowner who might blot (a colloquial term for "squatting the block") the lots next door and use them for extra parking space. Around the corner may be a squatter who has scrapped the remaining saleable materials from a blighted home, before helping neighboring homeowners tear it down to prevent children from playing in the unsafe structure. This typology makes visible the different ways that appropriators engage with property: informality does not encapsulate the entirety of their being in the world. They are residents who informally use property in some ways and formally in others.

Second, this typology also helps us start to see the way that informal appropriators interact differently with each other and the space of the city. Many LAs have congregated on different blocks or neighborhoods throughout the city, drawn in by shared networks, common goals, and communal ideals. As some of these practices have gained increased visibility and acceptability, other proximal longtime residents have joined in. Where in other cities one has to vie for available property in areas with certain cultural features (like a city's gayborhood or university district), in

Detroit, LAs can fairly easily join others in like-minded practices because of the availability of vacant property to take over and use in many neighborhoods across the city. In areas where informal occupiers have gravitated, some homesteading LAs have encouraged homeless Detroiters to squat nearby to share resources and knowledge. While spatially dispersed, many NAs come together to share strategies over meals at soup kitchens or community meetings across the city.

Third, this typology helps us understand some of the ways that appropriation can change over time for appropriators. These categories are not always static nor entirely discreet in everyday life. For example, there are nonprofits in Detroit that could be said to have started out as Routine Appropriation by their founders. The Heidelberg Project (a multi-block art installation using found objects and abandoned property) and Blight Busters (a blight deconstruction and neighborhood improvement organization) are two such examples.[20] Both were started by longtime residents (Tyree Guyton and John George). They leveraged these practices to help the city and help themselves (by creating meaningful work and income). In these cases, in part due to an injection of resources (such as funding, time, and/or knowledge), these RAs were able to transition the ways that they navigated Detroit's cumbersome conditions into formal organizations. As such, their practices shifted from burdensome strategies (Routine) to desirable practices they wanted to continue (Lifestyle). But it's not only RAs whose practices change or shift into other categories. Many LAs in my study expressed becoming invested in their neighborhoods and communities over time and began participating in practices like demolition to clean up their block, acting in ways that arise from routine negotiations of life in Detroit.

Other shifts from one category of appropriation to another were less common. Scrapper/squatter Grant, profiled in chapter 5, is perhaps the only interviewee who could be said to represent the transition from Lifestyle Appropriation to Necessity Appropriation. His initial forays into squatting in Detroit were part of his lifestyle as a youth, exploring the city and using drugs recreationally. But once he became addicted to heroin, appropriation became a survival mechanism for him. There were no examples in my data of NAs who came to enjoy or desire their practices the way LAs do, perhaps because the ability to transform appropriation into a lifestyle pursuit takes a certain distance from necessity that NAs do not have. The closest is perhaps NA squatter Rhiannon (also in chapter 5), who was later able to purchase her squatted house to provide a stable home for her children. But there are other important elements to how these practices can change over time and how the future is envisioned with regard to appropriation. These are discussed in chapter 8.

Finally, this typology makes clear that it is the confluence of a variety of factors, such as socioeconomic status (SES), place-based background, and life experiences that shape how different appropriators understand and navigate the city through informal appropriation (explored further in chapter 8). These categories do not map precisely on to different demographic characteristics; for example, not all LAs are white, and not all NAs are from Detroit. This typology reveals that while these categories are shaped by factors like whether one is a longtime resident of Detroit or a newcomer, and while there are tendencies across categories (such as NAs and RAs tending to be older and Black), these alone are not explanatory of the differences between categories.

For conceptual clarity, I delve into these categories separately in the next three chapters. To convey what these practices are like, I present vignettes of select appropriators who can be understood as representative of the three categories. Each account is organized to uncover what motivated appropriators to informally use property, how they went about it, and what the conditions were like for them. Taken together, these vignettes illustrate how appropriators' backgrounds, resources, and needs/wants (goals) intersect, shaping not only the material conditions of their appropriation but also their experiences of and views on their practices. Scholars attempting to grapple with the complexities of urban decline have called for deeper understandings of the way decline influences social life.[21] Property informality is one of these ways, and thus an in-depth engagement with the details of everyday life for appropriators is necessary for filling this gap.

5 Necessity Appropriators

Necessity Appropriators (NAs) are motivated by the urgency of daily needs and to ensure their survival. For them, informal property use is a means for getting by that turns the obstacles of Detroit into opportunities. For example, while the multifaceted correlates of urban decline have coalesced to create a bleak employment environment in Detroit (an obstacle), these conditions have also produced a plethora of abandoned buildings that residents can scrap (an opportunity) to mediate this obstacle. NAs in my study overwhelmingly expressed that they did not want to be engaged in practices like squatting or scrapping but confronted limited options for meeting their pressing needs for shelter and income. Even though appropriation is an assertion of agency, NAs testified experiencing a lack of choice regarding their informal practices.

As Table 3 showed, the NAs I interviewed primarily engaged in squatting and scrapping. Squatting for shelter and scrapping for cash is a rough existence that requires a great deal of work. The harsh conditions of life for people surviving by these means are indicative of the constrained options and dire situations that motivate them. Squatters often lack access to essentials like electricity and running water. Scrappers are referred to as "pancakes" by local firefighters, who all too frequently are tasked with trying to pull someone out of the rubble of a building that collapsed on them. NAs lack the economic capital that would enable them to significantly improve the quality of their informal practices as Lifestyle Appropriators do. What NAs *do* have are broad networks of family and longtime friends from their neighborhood or church, who they commonly reference as aiding their appropriation in various ways—whether by identifying houses to squat or helping with clean up and repairs. But, because many NAs prefer not to be squatting or scrapping and thus do not wish to maintain these practices, many find a way to make do with minor adjustments or few investments in order to allow these practices to suffice "for now." When NAs deconstruct property (typically by scrapping), it is often much riskier than when LAs or RAs deconstruct property because the materials they tend to look for are different, and their level of desperation motivates them to take greater risks. The conditions of appropriation for NAs are harder and more dangerous than they are for RAs or LAs.

The vignettes here are chosen as representative of the category Necessity Appropriator. For each, I have drawn out selections from interviews that illustrate two main points: 1) NAs are motivated to informally use property to meet urgent needs and to ensure their survival and 2) the conditions NAs experience while informally using property are difficult, risky, and frequently lacking even basic comforts associated with life in a metropolis in the Global North.

T.J.

T.J., a single Black male in his fifties, had been squatting a house on the west side of Detroit for nearly three years at the time of our interview. T.J.'s experiences illustrate his constrained options, substandard living conditions, and his lack of desire or ability to substantially invest in improving his property.

T.J. was tall and gregarious, with thinning grey hair pulled back in a ponytail. I frequently found him at a soup kitchen surrounded by a table full of other hard-up Detroiters as he doled out advice like a social worker. He carried a billfold with business cards of social service agencies, soup kitchens, shelters, and lawyers. T.J. liked to tell how his basketball career was thwarted after an injury in high school, but he was grateful that instead he graduated from college in Michigan. T.J.'s troubles started several years ago after losing his job at a factory. He could not afford a legal divorce from his wife, so he did not qualify for housing assistance and was biding his time until he was eligible for social security.

After separating from his wife, T.J. asked his daughter if he could live with her. She had been sharing a house with a friend and their combined eleven children. T.J.'s daughter told him that she was moving to Florida. She had been in a rent-to-own contract with the property owner, but the house was falling apart, so she didn't want it any longer. Besides, the owner had stopped coming by to collect rent, and a tax foreclosure notice had been posted on the door several months prior.[1] T.J. moved into the property as his daughter, her friend, and their children moved out. Subsequently, T.J.'s son, his son's girlfriend, and her daughter occasionally stayed in the upstairs of the house. T.J. explained how he felt about squatting:

> I really don't see any benefit outside of just having a roof over my head and not being completely homeless . . . And it's, it's something that I thought I'd never be doing because like I say, I have always worked, even when I was in high school, I have always had a job . . . So I've never had that to worry until the economy hit. Hey, I just got caught up in the system like everybody else . . . and now I'm seeing how people were living. So I'm going through what they was going through now, you know, so. It's just a way of living right now . . . It's nothing to be proud about or to really even talk about you know, but it's, it's real.

If he were not squatting, he told me, he would probably be bouncing between friends' couches and a homeless shelter but acknowledged how hard the former can be on relationships. For T.J. and other NAs, squatting is chosen from among constrained options for housing.

The outside of T.J.'s house looked like any other occupied house on the block. It was a small post-war bungalow, its white siding now dingy from years of neglect. There were plastic chairs on the front porch (covered in snow as it was the middle of winter) and what looked like flowered bedsheets hanging over the front windows in lieu of curtains. For a while after moving in, T.J.'s friend lived in the basement and kept the utilities on using his social security check to pay the bills (which were still in T.J.'s daughter's name). But after his friend moved out and the utilities were shut off, T.J. borrowed a key from a friend to illegally turn on the water, and he paid a guy to illegally turn the electricity back on. T.J. said that the guy took the lock off the box, switched the electricity back on, then put the lock back on so it didn't look like it had been tampered with. There was no furnace, so T.J. heated the house with a few space heaters. He warmed bath water on the kitchen stove since the house lacked a water heater. In his basement, a busted pipe constantly leaked water onto the concrete floor, filling it up like an icy swimming pool.

T.J. had learned to time when the meter reader from the electric company made his rounds and—during the winter—waded through nearly three feet of ice-cold water in the basement to unhook his electricity, so the meter would stop running and his illegal hookups would remain undetected. In his affable style, T.J. recalled the last time this happened:

> I was standing in my dining room, shivering, cold, 'cause I had got in that cold water and I'm chillin' cause I got to go back down and put the power pack back in so I can cut all the power back on in my house when they leave ... So I couldn't just take off my clothes and get out the cold so I'm standing up there and I'm shivering and I'm going, "Oh please, come on, hurry up, go back to ya'll truck, hurry up, hurry up."

T.J. laughed but then added seriously, "And that ain't funny, but that's how my lights are still on today."

T.J. made changes to the house to make it more livable, but he clarified that "I'm not spending no money into this house, really, you know." When he moved in, it was infested with cockroaches and bedbugs, and he had to clear out mountains of trash left behind by his daughter's household. He shook his head as he described the space:

> Yeah, it was bug-infested and [there's] a ledge around the top of our ceiling. And when I first went in there I looked up at the ledge and it was black, you know ... that little room was painted white and I seen that black stuff up there and I said, "It ain't supposed to be like that." I could tell it wasn't painted or nothing. But then when I looked at it closer, it was roaches.

He told me how before he was able to save up the money to buy a "bug bomb" for the house, he slept on three folding chairs pushed together in the middle of the room so the bedbugs could not reach him. Even then, he said, "I bug bombed it about five times and I still haven't got rid of all the roaches. The only way I got rid of the bed bugs is I threw everything out."

But T.J. could not afford more substantial investments to his property that would make it more comfortable or livable, like a water heater or the services of a plumber to fix the leaky pipe. T.J. survived by selling his $180 per month in food stamps for cash and eating at two different soup kitchens in the city. He often hung out at these soup kitchens all day long, especially in the winter. An outgoing guy, he enjoyed the company of others, and the warmth of the dining room. But also, the bus system in Detroit is deplorably slow and unreliable, such that it was not worth it to him to try to get back and forth to either of the soup kitchens for multiple meals each day.

DEANGELO

DeAngelo was a single Black man in his late forties who, when I met with him, had been squatting a very dilapidated property on the west side of Detroit for over four years. Prior to that he was at the Salvation Army for three years and the Detroit Rescue Mission for several years before that. A lifelong Detroiter, DeAngelo had been chronically homeless for at least a decade from what I could piece together of his story. He chose squatting over the shelter, and like T.J., endured very substandard living conditions.

We sat on his front porch drinking warm soda on a hot summer day, and DeAngelo explained why he left the Salvation Army and began squatting:

> For peace of mind. You know just not being around other folks. In a shelter, you're around a hundred guys all the time . . . you know and chaos always a problem. So now I got a peace of mind you know. [Here] I can get up when I want to you know. They (the shelter) put you out at six in the morning no matter where you got to go. But you know sometime you be tired, you don't want to get up at no six in the morning . . . they throw you out.

DeAngelo complained about the strict rules at the shelter—rules about what time he had to be checked in at night, rules about not drinking, and expressed simply that "I like to have my freedom." DeAngelo desired more peace and safety and the ability to make personal decisions for himself. But for DeAngelo, squatting a house was the only alternative to living in the shelter. His "nephew"—a younger male friend—now squatted with him. DeAngelo compared his squat to the shelter, saying, "The only thing is they have water, you can take showers there and stuff like that . . . I just, I prefer to be in a home you know." I asked DeAngelo how he found this particular house—what made him decide to start squatting here? He shrugged and explained,

> I had to leave [the shelter] so you know I was walking down the street and I just happened to look to this way and I came and looked at the house, the door was wide open . . . you know so I walked in, a lot of trash and everything. So I just grabbed a shovel and just started cleaning it all up . . . And ever since then I've done some things up in there . . . I have three beds and different little different things and fine-tuned and stuff like that. And I've been here ever since.

Despite his work of "fine-tuning" as he put it, DeAngelo's squat was another example of particularly rough living conditions. His small house was one of only four still standing on a block that used to have around twenty-six houses. Across the street were several lots filled with waist-high grass and overgrown weed trees. His porch was crammed, but organized, with folding and camping chairs, several barbeques that he used for all his cooking, and some milk crates. The faded front door had peeling wood veneer and a handwritten sign tacked on that read, "Private Property: Keep Out."

Inside, the space was dark and cramped. Many of the windows were boarded over, and the front living room was set up like a one-room house. DeAngelo had used salvaged materials and his own labor to improve his property. He had put down some scraps of carpet on the floor and covered over the broken windows to keep out the elements—some with plastic and others with boards. He had a few paint gallons sitting outside that he was planning to use to fix the chipping paint on the walls inside after he scraped them. But DeAngelo's lack of resources left him without the ability to substantially improve the conditions of his house. After showing me around the house he added self-consciously, "I was gonna fix all of that up, yeah I was just going to try to fix up and gonna do the best I can to you know make it livable, a more livable home."

DeAngelo did not have any utilities hooked up. I asked how he got by without having electricity or water. DeAngelo explained,

Well, I probably got used to it now . . . I might go to church to take me a shower and uh I got flashlights, I got about twenty flashlights and I got candles you know, it'd be lit up in here you know at nighttime, so I just use candles and flashlights. Everything is battery operated, I buy batteries . . . you know like I don't have no lights and that.

DeAngelo also sometimes showered at his mother's house and bought bottles of water and soda for when he woke up thirsty at night. When I asked about heat in the winter, DeAngelo explained, "I had a kerosene heater and I got about a thousand blankets on the bed." He laughed and pointed to the kerosene heater sitting near us on his porch, but he explained, "I just used it a couple times and some kind of way it stopped working [but] I didn't really care about the kerosene cause I lit it up that time and it had the walls all smoked up and everything." DeAngelo relied on local charities and soup kitchens for food. His mail was sent to his father's house nearby.

He earned money mainly by "hustling"—scrapping and doing odd, under-the-table jobs. His last consistent job was passing out handbills on front stoops. DeAngelo said he held this job for nearly six years, until he could no longer handle walking six to seven hours per day—often in the winter without adequate cold-weather gear—and only making twenty-five dollars each day. Most recently, DeAngelo helped a man down the block clean out a building, working from 9am to 8:30pm, for which he was paid thirty dollars. After talking with me, he was heading to help him clear out the debris from another building. DeAngelo explained that his biggest obstacle was unemployment, and that if he could find a job "I would just get me a place, you know another place you know and I have my light and gas and everything on you know . . ." Like other NAs who squatted, DeAngelo would have prefered a more comfortable living situation if he had the means to procure it.

LESLIE

Many of the NAs in my study who squatted were single mothers with children, like Leslie. Leslie, a Black single mother of two in her forties, had lived in Detroit since the age of five. Her case illustrates the adept skills appropriators developed to help them navigate their informal practices, but, like other NAs, despite this savviness she very much felt she had no choice but to squat. She lacked extra economic resources but had help from family members that enabled her to make her squatted homes more livable.

Leslie and I talked at the soup kitchen where I first met her and where she and her children ate many of their meals. Leslie's perfectly manicured nails strummed the chipped melamine table where we sat. The rest of her was carefully put together as well; she stood out at the soup kitchen. Her young son sat patiently next to us, picking at the food on his tray and playing with Leslie's cell phone.

Leslie considered herself a squatting advocate and wanted others to be informed about how to occupy properties "the right way." She offered advice to others at the soup kitchen, ranging from how to select an appropriate property to how to manage relations with the neighbors to how to create a fake rental agreement to show curious authorities. She explained how squatting had been a key stepping-stone for sheltering her and her two children on and off throughout the four years prior to when we met.

After a difficult divorce, Leslie planned to leave Detroit and so resigned from her job. However, she quickly found herself in a custody battle and was unable to leave the city but could not find a new job. Lawyer fees drained her savings, and she found herself homeless. Leslie's sister's home on the east side of Detroit was being foreclosed by the bank, and her sister had already moved out of the house, so she suggested Leslie and her children move in since it was vacant. She commented, "I had no choice at the time. So, um I went in, and I moved in and uh it was, it was a hard thing. It was something I was not proud of. But because it was my family's home, I did feel very comfortable there and I did have family in the neighborhood, so I felt secure."

Leslie spoke in a low voice and was careful with her words as she explained how she felt about squatting:

It wasn't my first choice so of course I didn't feel wonderful about it. But I did feel a sense of relief, once I was in the situation, once I had the knowledge and knew what it was that I was doing. So, you know, but if you wanna put a feeling on it, in some way you do feel like a failure, in some aspects, you know especially as being a parent and a provider. But you know you have to keep going. You have to keep living and I thank God that I've never been put in a situation where my kids were in danger and there was no drugs around them, and you know there weren't nobody looking for me . . . Never had any abusiveness or anything like that going on. So I prided myself that if I do the right thing, be careful and just not let all that other influence come into my situation that I would be okay . . . I was never proud of it.

It was important to Leslie that she never resorted to sex work nor had to stay with family members who were involved with drugs and other illicit activities that she didn't want her children to be around. Squatting allowed her to keep them safe and not "compromise my virtues," as she put it.

Her sister's old house, the first she ever squatted, was in decent shape since it had recently been occupied. She explained, "I would say it was semi-secure where it still had the locks and the doors and the windows, but there was one window that was broken and the roof was horribly bad, horribly bad. When it rained it'll come through." Family members who lived nearby helped her get her gas and electricity turned on illegally. Her sister had removed the furnace and water heater to sell when she learned of the foreclosure, so Leslie heated the small home with the gas oven in the kitchen and some space heaters. Leslie noted with pride that the house was always warm, saying, "You would come in there any day or night and you would never know that I didn't have a furnace in my house." No one bothered Leslie and her children for the year they lived there, including the bank that had foreclosed on the property.

During that time, Leslie was still unemployed and had been visiting the soup kitchen (where she and I met) for meals with her children. Here she recalled learning of a program where one could take over an unoccupied house and gain ownership of it—a misinterpretation of the city's defunct Nuisance Abatement program (discussed further in Conclusion). She decided to move her children out of her east side neighborhood, where drugs and violence were all too commonplace. Leslie wanted to find a home to squat where she might want to stay, in case she could in fact get the title to the house in her name. She and her children stayed in a shelter for about six weeks while she searched for another property to squat.

On her way to church across town, she frequently drove past a large home in a much more stable neighborhood. Through a church member, Leslie learned that the elderly owners had passed away, but their daughter didn't want the house, so it was vacant. The front of the house was secure, but Leslie found a window in back that was broken: "When I went into the home it was totally trashed, it was, it was a humongous mess inside there. But it had clothes and it had furniture and it had all types of stuff that was very, very usable." She decided to move in:

> So, I went about the business of saying, "This is where I'm going to stay." I don't know, I just felt like nobody's gonna bother me so that's what I did. I went in there in broad daylight, I had the papers—I printed the papers down for the taxes just in case somebody called the police on me, you know. I was like, well this my house. I'm just moving in it, I'm cleaning it up. I also know that the Detroit police cannot put you out of a house. That's not their jurisdiction so I wasn't worried about any of that. I cleaned that house up. I bought bags and bags of trash bags. They were contractor's bags, so they cost me a lot of money. I ended up throwing away about 100 bags of trash.

At that time, squatting was a civil offense, so Leslie knew that the police were not allowed to throw her out unless they knew she was trespassing. She had done her research and gathered documentation she felt made her occupancy look legitimate (the tax records). A few days later a police officer stopped by to check on a reported problem. She told him, "This is my house I'm just cleaning it up." She changed the locks, boarded up the broken window in the back, and a family member installed new wiring in the house (the electrical had been torn out by scrappers). Here too Leslie had to get the utilities turned on illegally. I asked if she was ever worried that the utilities would get shut off. She responded, "Somewhat yeah, somewhat, but not so much because I'd just have it turned back on again." Despite her keen abilities to procure what she needed for herself and her children, she still attested, "And you know, I'm not saying this to say that everybody should do this, but, I was, I felt like I was in a situation where I had no other choice."

Leslie lived there for about three years until she was able to move into a subsidized apartment. She lost custody of her older daughter during that time, which substantially cut the child support payments that she had relied on for income. At the time of our interview, Leslie and her son were doubled-up with a relative. Leslie's residential history was littered with bouts of squatting interspersed with short-term subsidized apartments and even several shelter stays.

MARSEY

Marsey was a Black single mother of nine children in her late forties. Like Leslie, Marsey highlighted the importance of having a place that was comfortable and safe for her children, and she worked hard with few resources to make livable spaces for them. Marsey seemed to maintain enough formal work to get by, but squatting enabled her large family to avoid the detrimental impacts of overcrowding from time to time.

At the time of our interview, Marsey was renting a small brick bungalow but had no reliable transportation. Before giving her a ride to work, we shared some French fries at a diner in Midtown while she told me how she first ended up squatting. Marsey explained that she had had a relatively stable upbringing. She was in the military, graduated from college, and used to own a home in Detroit. But after she came home to find her eleven year old son brutally murdered, she came unraveled. For several years, she used drugs and was very transient, often squatting in houses frequented by drug users and sex workers. After getting clean and struggling to regain custody of her eight living children, she rented a two-bedroom apartment for $650 per month. An acquaintance told her of a vacant home next door—the owner had passed away. Marsey recalled, "And so she said, instead of paying $650 to stay in a two-bedroom flat, it would make just good, better sense to go around to this house and try to get it in your name and fix it up and pay the taxes."

So Marsey visited the empty property and decided to move her children into the five-bedroom, two-bathroom house. For squatters like Marsey, informal occupation comes from the need to secure appropriate housing for her large family, which does not mean that Marsey's housing quest is a mere "lifestyle" concern. Living in a two-bedroom apartment with nine people is classified as unstably housed or being "at risk of homelessness" even according to federal definitions (which tend to be more restrictive than academic or social service agency definitions).[2] Research has documented the negative effects of over-crowding for individual and familial well-being, such as unsafe living conditions, increased stress, and decreased educational attainment among children.[3] When large families squat to find adequate space for themselves, it is a strategy to avoid the ill-effects of overcrowding and highlights the lack of affordable housing that can accommodate large families.

Marsey explained that this first squatted house was not in terrible condition because she moved in before scrappers could do any significant damage. Marsey was savvy. She did some research and found out that the woman who had owned the house had indeed died, no heirs had claimed the property, and that it was in its first year of tax delinquency. At that point in time, this meant that she likely had about two years before the property would be foreclosed.[4] Marsey slept in the house for a few days to see if it felt safe before moving in with her children. Then she and her children cleaned up the house and had mail sent to it. She says they were able to get water and electricity turned on legally by presenting a fake rental agreement and proving residency with the mail. It was important to Marsey to make certain changes for the sake of her children: "You know you have to make it livable. You have to make it homey. You know you have to make it safe. You have to make it comfortable. You have to change the locks. You got to decorate. You got to make it a *home.*"

Marsey and her children lived there for about two years before Marsey got behind on the utility bills. After the water was shut off, a family member reported her to Child Protective Services, and her children were once again temporarily removed from her care. She said she had to move into an apartment—a legal residence—to get them back. After regaining custody, she once again found a large house to squat and moved in her children. This house was in a much more stable neighborhood in Detroit with large, upscale homes. Marsey wanted a nicer, more comfortable space for her family. But after only a few days, the police came to the door demanding to see a lease. She showed them a fake one that she had made, but still they arrested her, and she spent three days in jail before being released. Marsey says she received an apology from the police department for their mistreatment of her and her children during that incident. But ultimately, she decided the house wasn't worth the effort and found a new place to squat in a less desirable neighborhood.

Marsey's residential history was littered with mentions of Section 8 housing, subsidized apartments, squatted houses, doubling-up with grandma, and so on. I deciphered that she had squatted on at least three separate occasions with her children. At the time of our interview, Marsey was employed but struggling to stay abreast of the bills, rotating paying them monthly to try to avoid utility shutoffs. She and her children had been living in the house in Northwest Detroit for about a month, but she was late with the rent and had already received an eviction notice from the landlord. Where she and her children would be in the next month was up in the air once again.

RHIANNON

Rhiannon, a white woman in her mid-thirties, was the single mother of five children. I first met Rhiannon at a meeting of residents organizing to impede tax foreclosures in Detroit. She had ridden to the meeting on her bicycle, but it was snowing by the time we left, and the sun had set. We put her bicycle in the back of my truck, and as I drove, we talked more about how she had come to be squatting in Detroit. Rhiannon recounted her story very frankly.

After filing charges against her abusive husband, she moved into a domestic violence shelter for nine months with her three youngest children and during that time gave birth to a baby. She said that when her time at the shelter had expired, she was forced to move out. The other shelters were full as it was the middle of winter. Rhiannon found herself living in her old minivan with her four young children and her teenage daughter.

Like many other squatters, Rhiannon told how she "shopped around" to find suitable housing for her family. She researched houses listed as coming up for sale at the Wayne County Treasurer's yearly property auction. She selected twelve houses and visited them to see what kind of condition they were in. Her requirements for the house were that it have doors, windows, and enough bedrooms for the kids. While squatting was only preferable among limited options, NAs like Rhiannon made a host of concerted decisions to procure the best scenario for themselves and their families.

We pulled up to a brick home in a relatively stable neighborhood not far from Downtown, where Rhiannon and her children had been living for about six months at that point. It was dark outside and none of the streetlights were working, but lights from inside the other houses on her block indicated they too were occupied. The house Rhiannon had finally settled on met her requirements for doors, windows, and bedrooms, and also had a fireplace—a bonus because they were able to have a warm space immediately when they moved in. She said the house was "completely trashed," and she had worked hard to clear out the left-behind garbage and debris.

Because Rhiannon no longer had her minivan, she and her teenage daughter took turns gathering wood for the fireplace from vacant lots nearby, using the bicycle and trailer they used to transport the younger children. Rhiannon, like many other squatters, paid someone to hook up the electricity and water illegally. Most squatters reported spending around fifty dollars to have this done, and many had to incur this expense several times a year if the illegal hookups were discovered and turned off by the utility company.

Rhiannon had benefitted from becoming involved with a network of local activists, who provided valuable resources throughout the years I've known her. About two years after we first met, I found out Rhiannon was temporarily living in a shelter because her water had been shut off, and Child Protective Services found out. She was required to move to a shelter or have her children removed from her care. After living in the shelter for a few weeks, she successfully raised the money, using a crowd-funding website, to turn the water back on and moved her family back into the squatted house. With the help of local activists, she was also later able to resist being evicted from the property when an absentee investor who bought the property found out she was living there, and eventually she even got the title to the house in her name.

JACKIE AND JOE

NAs were not all poor, native Detroiters (though in my interviews they overwhelmingly were). Some were folks, like Jackie and Joe, who moved to Detroit because they couldn't get by elsewhere and saw Detroit as a viable option. Their case is also a further illustration of how substance abuse creates obstacles that residents turn to appropriation to mediate.

Jackie was a white woman in her fifties who had been addicted to heroin for several decades. I met with her and her younger son Joe, who was twenty-five, one hot summer day. I pulled up to their squatted Detroit house in my old grey pick-up truck, and Jackie stepped out onto her front porch while I parked. She motioned for me to come inside as she said, "I hope no one steals your truck!" I looked up and down the desolate street, which could have been a quiet country lane except for the paved road pock-marked with deep potholes and wondered nervously if she was serious.

Jackie was very welcoming. She gestured for me to take a seat at the table in the dining room of her squatted house. Jackie was a small woman who had her blonde hair in two very thin braids each time I saw her. Her arms were thick and swollen, abused from decades of heroin injections. I offered her and her son Joe semi-cold drinks I had brought, and she began to tell me their story. Jackie's husband died of cancer about a decade earlier, and she subsequently lost their suburban home to the bank. After that, she and her three children moved in with her parents in a distant suburb of Detroit. But her continued drug use strained her relationship with her parents, so she moved out. She and her two adult sons left, but her teenage daughter still lived with Jackie's parents. Jackie explained that they ended up squatting in Detroit because "I couldn't afford to live out there in the suburbs you know, and then my car broke down and that was it." Jobless, carless, and needing to be walking distance to available drugs, Jackie and her sons (also heroin users) began squatting a house on the east side of Detroit, where many suburban residents trek to buy drugs.

In categorizing Jackie and Joe as NAs, I make an assertion about drug use: that for those suffering from addiction, it's not merely a lifestyle choice. In my study, many who suffer from addiction came to rely on appropriation to survive because they found themselves with few other options for getting by. Appropriation followed their drug use. On the other hand, recreational drug use was prevalent for some LAs (discussed further in chapter 6); it was part of how they spent their newfound free time while squatting. But drug use by LAs did not hinder their options for survival as it did for NAs. I asked Jackie if she wanted to get clean. She replied, "No,

I don't like pain," referring to the pain of detoxing from heroin. While she said that she wanted to continue using heroin, she did not want to be squatting or even living in Detroit, preferring to return to the suburb where she grew up.

Joe, on the other hand, still envisioned a future without heroin dependency. He said in five years he'd like to have his own apartment and landscaping business.[5] However, from the several interactions I had with them, it became apparent that Jackie needed Joe right there with her. She often criticized him, scoffing at the idea of Joe getting clean or having a stable job. They both reported that the other brother was "crazy"—unpredictable, unreliable, and sometimes violent. He would often disappear for days at a time. But their life was hard and required a good deal of physically demanding work to make it from day to day that Jackie, in her frail state, could not have managed on her own. Jackie and her sons survived and purchased drugs by panhandling and selling scrapped materials to scrap yards, though the latter was only possible for them when they had access to a vehicle. Both Jackie and Joe declared adamantly that they had never engaged in sex work.

With pride, Jackie explained that she had cleaned up their squatted house, hung curtains, and took care of it. But they had no spare money and little desire or ability to substantially invest in improvements. This house was the second they had squatted since moving to Detroit. It had no electricity, heat, or running water. I asked how they made it through the cold winter months—in Michigan, temperatures dip well below zero often for weeks on end. Jackie gestured around the small dining room where we sat and explained, "You get a room like this size right here and you got thirty candles going and you got a few people in there you'd be surprised it'll get like fifty degrees." At night, everyone huddled together to sleep. Every few days, her sons filled up a large cooler with water from their old squatted house a few blocks away that was in much rougher condition but still had running water. They told me how they used to walk a few miles to Belle Isle (an island in the Detroit River that used to be the center of summertime recreation in the city) to wash their clothes and bodies in the public showers, but the showers had since been turned off. Using their only resource—their own labor—Jackie and her sons made their squat as livable as they could.

GRANT

Grant, a white man in his forties, grew up elsewhere in Michigan but moved to Detroit about twenty-five years ago. He was tall with a long beard and credited his large stature with helping to keep him safe while scrapping. His story illustrates a quintessential way that urban informality shapes the lives of marginalized Detroiters; it is an opportunity for shelter and income but also creates difficult, often extreme hardships. We sat on the front porch of my house in Detroit late one evening. He smoked cigarettes while he talked, always looking slightly past me.

Grant's entry into squatting and scrapping started as adventuresome practices in his youth (akin to many LAs), when he and his friends would venture into Detroit in search of drugs. But these were fleeting, sporadic practices: crashing in an empty room in an industrial building or exploring vacant factories and collecting unique items like old gears from defunct assembly lines. But as Grant's drug use shifted from recreational to full-blown addiction (and as the market price of metals increased), scrapping for income funded his addiction, and squatting often kept him off the street during periods of instability. Exploring Detroit in his youth paid off: he knew the buildings and where to find what he needed.

The first time Grant scrapped was because a friend of his needed money and wanted to use Grant's truck, so Grant agreed. He explained, "We went in and he pulls out some big chunks of copper and brass and we go driving out of there and we went to another scrapyard and sold it, you know for a couple of hundred dollars. And I'm like damn, you know." His motivation for scrapping was the income: "Oh the money, it was great. I mean one day, I made three thousand dollars, you know pulling out some copper lying in an abandoned building you know. Yes, it wasn't hard to make a hundred dollars a day if you had a truck. So that's good money."

As his addiction intensified, squatting became a larger part of Grant's repertoire for getting by during times of instability. He guessed that he had squatted in about fifteen different places while he was in-between housing, but the longest he ever squatted at once was about one month. He cringed and noted, "It was terrible. It was wintertime and there was no heat." They had no running water or electricity, just a barrel in the living room that they burned wood in. "You just smell like smoke all day," he told me. To avoid squatting he often rented meager rooms, doubled up on friends' couches, or lived with various girlfriends.

As with many other examples, from payday loan establishments to groceries from quickie marts, those who are poor and most desperate for money often pay more for things they need. This even operates in the scrapping economy through after-hours scrapyards. Grant explained how these work: "You know it'll be a Sunday [when the scrapyards are closed], you need to get your dope, you'd go to this guy . . . they'd be setup right next to the scrapyards . . . and he'd buy your scrap off of you at half the price of the scrapyard. And then you know they'd just take it to the scrapyard on Monday." These after-hours scrapyards operate overnight too, taking advantage of the desperation of substance users or others in dire need of quick cash.

Grant had been scrapping longer than anyone else in my study. He reflected on how the scrapping landscape in Detroit has changed. He said about ten years ago

> there was metal everywhere. There were huge I-beams just lying in lots and I'd go cut them up and throw them in the back of the truck and take them to the scrapyard. I'd only get thirty bucks for a full ton of steel back then . . . As the prices went up you know all the crack heads came out. . . and started scrapping too . . . Yeah now the city's clean of all metal, you know there's nothing laying around. The buildings were full of cool tools and just old bridge part machines and stuff like that just laying around. Metal legs, twelve-foot metal legs you know. You can't find anything like that anymore.

This transition means that scrapping has become harder and more dangerous. Grant and other scrappers are now often forced to pull apart buildings in various ways to access the metals they seek—primarily copper, aluminum, and steel—opening up walls or dismantling structural components. It also means that heavily scrapped buildings have become more structurally precarious over time, which scrappers have to be careful of.

Scrappers sometimes navigate the changing nature of the practice by working together on a "good lick" (substantial scrapping job) and then divvying up the money, taking into consideration things like who found it, whose torch they used to cut it or whose truck they used to transport it to the scrapyard. Grant said this often leads to conflicts or even fights over the proceeds. Other times, Grant and other scrappers work to extract a "good lick" over time which can also lead to conflict if someone picks up on a job where another left off the day before. It's common for jobs to take multiple days, but Grant even pursued one "good lick" on and off for two years. He found six lines of copper (the most lucrative metal), each an inch thick, sticking out of the floor of an old industrial building, but he couldn't get them to budge free. He surmised that the lines had to come out of the ground somewhere else in the building. He finally found a metal box in the middle of an adjacent overgrown field. Inside the box was the end of the copper lines, which he unscrewed and was able to pull them through and all the way out.

But collaboration, patience, and perseverance have not protected Grant from suffering severe hardships because of the increased safety risks of scrapping. Grant, like other scrappers in my study, mainly worked during the day to have the necessary light to see. Working at night was more cumbersome because it required bringing bright headlamps or torches, which also could easily reveal scrappers' presence to anyone nearby who might happen to care about what was going on in a vacant building. However, one time the bright sunlight lead to Grant being severely injured. He recalled,

> It was in the middle of the day, but I was in the sunlight and it was bright, and I walked into the room next door just to stretch, 'cause I had been on a ladder. And walked into the next room and into a shadowed area and the light changed, I didn't, I couldn't see anything for a split second, I walked right into this hole. The next thing I know I'm falling you know and the next thing that went through my mind is "I'm falling a long ways."

Grant suffered severe injuries, including femur, pelvis, and skull fractures. Thankfully, he was working with a friend who called for an ambulance. Another time, Grant was cutting through an old pipe and did not realize it was supporting the weight of another large piece of machinery, which crushed his right hand as it collapsed. Not wanting to endure another hospital visit, which would likely entail going through heroin withdrawals, he avoided seeking treatment for several days, which caused permanent nerve damage in his dominant hand and rendered it largely unusable. This injury ended his scrapping career. For the five years prior to our interview, he had survived on disability, which afforded him just enough money to rent a small basement room in Detroit and fund his heroin habit.

In Detroit, more desperate scrappers than Grant are known to climb telephone poles to get the copper wires from the transformers, or to try to dismantle entire buildings to get steel I-beams, risking electrocution or being "pancaked," as local firefighters refer to the latter. The economically marginalized background of many scrappers means that they are desperate for income, but also cannot afford the tools or gear that would make their practices safer or easier.

BOND

Bond, a single Black man in his fifties, had spent the last several years scrapping metal and other saleable materials from across the city, selling his findings at scrapyards for money. Like many other scrappers in the city, Bond turned to scrapping when he couldn't find employment, and the money he earns is all that keeps him from being homeless.

We met at a fast food restaurant near his house for coffee. When I asked him why he was scrapping, Bond answered simply: "I ain't got no money. I'm broke, that's the thing." He elaborated, "I started after I lost my job (in) '07 and I was like okay I ain't got no income you know. Light bills starting to get shut off and then water bill coming in, gas bill and the gas bill got shut off . . . can't get a job . . ."

Desperate for money to pay his bills, some acquaintances invited him to help them pull the pipes out of an old house and haul them to the scrapyard. He recalled, "A couple guys was like 'I know where you can make a couple dollars,' you know. Took me around a couple places, a couple abandoned houses, couple abandoned buildings you know . . . You can take iron to the scrapyard and get money daily. You could make a living. You know somebody can make $300, $400 a week." They split that day's earnings and Bond was relieved to finally have some money in his pocket.

Bond lived in a house that was owned by his extended family, which provided a degree of security, but he was responsible for paying the utilities and taxes on the property. Scrapping was his only form of income and

thus, what kept him from being homeless. I asked how he felt about surviving on scrapping and Bond explained, "I don't know . . . Being homeless
is worser. Uh being homeless is worser. Trust me. Not being homeless, it
feel a lot better than being homeless. You can go buy you something to eat
when you leave the scrap yard." Scrapping fulfilled basic needs for Bond—
enabling him to obtain food and shelter.

Bond knew many other Detroiters—white and Black friends alike, he
emphasized—who were surviving in the same way as he. He said lots of
them were former auto workers who had capitalized on the trucks they
owned and turned to scrapping to support themselves and their families.
He explained,

> Most of these guys ain't got nothing to eat or pay their bills. They ain't going
> to starve and a lot of these guys doing it 'cause they don't want to rob nobody.
> You know what I'm saying? They don't want to go rob or hurt somebody . . .
> when [instead] you can go up and just take them swing sets loose that's
> been sitting there for the last ten years. That swing set, when are you all (the
> city) going to take it down? It's made out of aluminum. We take it loose and
> take it to the yard and get some money. You know we ain't hurting nobody.

Bond emphasized the level of desperation that is intertwined with scrapping: it is an alternative to securing money in ways that may involve
violence. At the same time, scrapping often causes hurt or harm for scrappers. Bond explained that while he generally feels safe while scrapping,
injury goes hand in hand with the job:

> I know how to scrap. I know what to knock loose so nothing won't fall on me
> 'cause we all got hurt. I've been to the hospital. Everybody who scrap done
> had to go to the hospital. A jack fell on my toe and broke it. This finger right
> here got broke. Don't forget we ain't got no insurance. I got poked in this
> eye—no, matter of fact I almost *lost* this eye. A crowbar slung back on me
> like a rubber band and hit me. Everybody I know, everybody I know done
> been to the doctor.

He added later, "If it fall you on your own. We ain't got no insurance and
it's almost like working on a demolition crew . . ."

While some scrappers (like Grant) already owned, or saved enough
money to buy, a torch for cutting metals, Bond explained that at the very
least for scrapping "you're going to need a sledgehammer, crowbar, hammer,

pliers, cutters 'cause you're going to run into everything, 'cause wires got to be cut. You got a sledgehammer that knock the bricks loose, knock some pipes loose this big." He held up his hands in front of him about a foot apart. Bond leaned back and took a sip of his coffee and added matter-of-factly, "The bigger it is the more money you get so yeah." Like Grant, Bond often coordinated with other scrappers for large jobs or to gain access to a truck; he didn't own one of his own.

Bond explained that "it's a dirty job you know. You look [like] a mechanic when you get through; like you're working in a construction job . . . but after you take all these [metals] out and load it up on the truck, take it to the scrapyard and splitting $150 everybody get a fifty a-piece. And that's only the first time you go. You can go maybe two or three times in a day."

I asked how Bond and his fellow scrappers found the buildings they scrapped from. How did they select them? What requirements did they have for assessing where they went that day? Bond explained that in Detroit "you ain't got to go find them, you got to be around, you could be walking 'cause abandoned houses are everywhere in Detroit you know. For the last decade houses, they've been burnt, they've been condemned. The city been talking about tearing them down, but they didn't." Bond added that he often focused his labor "mostly on the east side where the houses are already burned, tore down, buildings already condemned. You know it's steel in them buildings, pipes in them buildings, wires you know." While some scrappers like Grant focused on industrial buildings, Bond said that burnt houses are often the best for scrapping for two reasons: 1) because he said the police won't bother them if they are in a burnt house and 2) because burnt houses leave the metal more accessible. "They already burnt. No windows, no doors, roof already caved in . . . there's pipes still left there, there's wires still in them, there's pipes still in the basement you know. There's aluminum frames around the windows."

Bond also reiterated that he would never cross the boundary of the city to scrap "cause the laws is different." He laughed and added,

Outside [the city] you probably going to jail for real. Detroit laws is a little [more] lenient than the suburbs' laws. You know [the suburbs] ain't giving you no break. You go to Macomb County and Oakland County and try that . . . you . . . you sure enough gonna get hung . . . Detroit ain't going to hang you like them.

Despite the harsh working conditions, risks, and exhausting labor, Bond explained the mindset that first motivated him to keep scrapping:

> If you haul about three times in a day you might come out with $150 a day. You know I was making $200 a week, so now I'm making more than I was making before I lost my job. So it's addictive. I was addicted. Tomorrow morning we're going to do it again . . . 'cause now I can pay the light bill, the gas bill. I can give somebody some money.

The ability to get this much income depends on several fairly unreliable factors. The price of various metals goes up and down; a point that Grant mentioned when discussing why he started scrapping. For example, in January of 2004 the price of copper was $1.00/lb; in January of 2014, it was about $3.23/lb.[6] When the price of metal went up, it made scrapping more worth the time and effort it entails. The other key factor is how the supply of various metals available for appropriation in Detroit has changed over time. Bond reiterated what Grant had said—that the supply of easily accessible metals to scrap in Detroit has decreased substantially over the past decade, as more and more poor residents have turned to scrapping to secure income. Bond explained that it's gotten so bad that now "believe it or not, you got to have a real income . . . scrapping now is hard. You know that was um maybe two years ago. Now it's hard. You ain't going to get no $150 a day."

NAs get by from day to day by squatting or scrapping property in the city. Because NAs have few economic resources, they are only able to marginally invest in their practices, if at all. When they do make changes or improvements, they rely on social networks or their own time and labor. For some, like T.J., this is because he does not want to continue living in his run-down house and therefore doesn't want to expend much money or energy into improving it. Others, like DeAngelo or some of the mothers in my study who were squatting, would like the security that ownership can bring but don't have the resources to make changes that would dramatically improve their living conditions. Instead, in the city that used to be at the forefront of American industrialization and progress, men, women, and children are living without even basic utilities. They make do by siphoning water from nearby houses or warming bathwater on the stove.

They sleep amidst dozens of candles to get the temperature "up to fifty degrees" in the winter or heat the house with the oven. Even for squatters like Marsey who maintained semi-regular employment and most of the time could manage to pay her utility bills, procuring water required fabricating residency documentation.

For scrappers, gaining access to valuable metals has gotten riskier over time, and the nature of the work (like a demolition crew without the insurance, as Bond noted) is inherently dangerous. It is made even more dangerous by lacking the supplies or tools that might mitigate some of these dangers, such as proper safety gear or tools.

Interestingly (as I mentioned briefly in chapter 4), I did not come across any NAs during my research who were gardening or farming, even though this could be a productive means for procuring food for poor residents. I surmise this is because forms of agriculture require resources, time, and labor investment to get started, time to wait for the fruits of these investments to pay off, and perhaps the residential stability (frequent moves are very common among the poor) to know that one will be living proximal to their garden for the foreseeable future to make these investments worthwhile. There are a lot of resources from various nonprofits in Detroit to support gardening—classes, grants, supply and seed donations, etc. But accessing these resources often requires that you can prove you have permission to use a vacant lot, and/or the skills and time to navigate bureaucracy, grantwriting, or filling out applications. It is also very possible that other poor Detroiters use agriculture practices to meet needs, but likely these are going to be more stably housed residents who have reliable access to the space to grow their own food.

Also common in my research were stories from now more stable residents who recounted how they had squatted in drug houses during the height of the crack epidemic. These drug houses still exist—abandoned houses where substance users find shelter to use drugs, rest, or pass the time for a while. Sex workers often bring clients to abandoned houses also (or drug use and sex work may take place in the same spaces). Also, all too frequent in my research were instances where youth lived in squatted houses without their families. These were either queer youth (both now and in past decades) kicked out by family members or children who were left temporarily while their parents were on drug benders. In such instances, squatting was very transient and temporary. These examples may all fit the category of Necessity Appropriation in some way or another, but I did not receive IRB clearance to do interviews with underage residents and so only knew of these occurrences secondhand.

NAs often describe their practices as not a choice, something they are not proud of and wish they weren't doing or expressed that they would prefer *not* to endure the hardships that come along with appropriation. But NAs also deftly navigate the opportunities for shelter and income that informal appropriation provides, and thus put up with these hardships to continue avoiding the shelter, doubling up, or to procure meager income. In recognizing their skills and agency, it may be more apt to say that NAs lack *choices,* not choice: they choose appropriation from limited and all relatively undesirable options. The key features that define Necessity Appropriation are that 1) appropriators informally use property in order to navigate the difficulties of life at the bottom of the socio-economic ladder and 2) because appropriators have few resources, their day-to-day experiences can be risky, difficult, harsh, and often lacking even the most basic comforts we associate with modern life in cities of the Global North.

6 Lifestyle Appropriators

Lifestyle Appropriators (LAs) take over property as a means for fulfilling lifestyle goals. In their everyday lives, LAs report having struggled with unrewarding employment, lacking a sense of community, and insufficient time for creativity, leisure, and desired activities. They seek control over their time to focus on these priorities. For many, finding this time requires that they live frugally to avoid menial, formal work as much as possible and are willing to engage in informal practices. By homesteading, gardening/farming, and salvaging, LAs informally use property as a means for satisfying wants and desires. The vacancy and abandonment of Detroit present enticing opportunities for LAs, rather than burdensome conditions in which they must struggle to survive (as they are for NAs).

LAs are predominately newcomers to the city and more likely than other appropriators to engage in multiple forms of appropriation (homesteading, agriculture, and salvaging—see Table 3). Many LAs moved to Detroit specifically seeking the "wild open space" to homestead and live off the land—an orientation fulfilled by growing one's own food and gathering resources from the environment around them (i.e., abandoned properties). LAs are pulled by the enticing opportunities that lie ahead, rather than pushed by the urgency of survival. Informal property use tends to be more comfortable for LAs and less risky than it is for NAs because LAs have more resources they can deploy to improve these conditions. Also, because engaging in informal appropriation is a desirable choice, it is easy for LAs to cease their practices should conditions get too risky or uncomfortable.

The vignettes in this section are representative of the range of approaches by and practices of LAs in Detroit. They illustrate the following core components of this category: 1) LA's desire to be engaged in their practices—they choose them and as such want to continue them, and often ensure they can by purchasing the properties they occupy (discussed further in chapter 8), and 2) informal property use is more comfortable and enjoyable for LAs than similar modes of appropriation are for NAs.

OLIVER AND KEVIN

I spoke with homesteaders, gardeners, and salvagers Oliver and Kevin at a popular coffee shop in Detroit. They sat side-by-side across from me at the table. They were both white men in their twenties who were raised in the suburbs. They both had unkempt hair and well-worn clothing. Oliver carried a patched backpack. Both men had moved to Detroit from the surrounding suburbs to "find themselves" in one way or another. Their case illustrates a central unifying feature of the LAs in my study: their dissatisfaction with what they view as an unfulfilling, fruitless, nine-to-five daily grind that prevents them from realizing their own happiness. Moving to Detroit and engaging in property informality allowed them to challenge mainstream cultural ideals of "the good life" and create alternative lifestyles, where they spent their time in ways that brought pleasure and meaning to their lives.

Oliver graduated from college, but after searching for months could only find a job in the stockroom of a chain grocery store. Between his low wages and high bills, he couldn't even afford a place of his own. He reflected, "And yeah, I decided that uh, I needed to move out of my parent's house, nothing was really happening, like I just felt so useless. (short laugh) But um, I just like remember [visiting other squatters in Detroit] and just how great it felt, that just each day was just like a gift and you could go out and do whatever you wanted. And that freedom just attracted me back there."

Kevin dropped out of college and had been working an entry-level human services job, but he was very unhappy. He explained,

> And then for some reason in 2010, I had a major panic attack, the first panic attack I've ever had and all this energy came to me and was like: Why are you living like this? You're not doing what your passion is, you're not doing what you love doing, you need to do that. And I was freaking out for six hours and I had so much energy in me that the only thing I could do was go outside and pile snow.

In seeking to find that passion, he moved into the city and started squatting with Oliver and has been working on various artistic projects. On what motivates him to homestead in Detroit, Kevin responded,

> There is a lot of room for personal growth, personal expansion you know it's pretty free and open and it just like, I love creating things, I love art work and I love building and there's not a lot of authority to tell you like, "You can't do this," or "You need to fill out paperwork to do this before you do that." It's just like so much room to grow as a person and to grow as a contributor to the community.

Oliver added that in Detroit there is

> room, room to create your wildest dreams. They say that America is like this free country and you have so much freedom, but if you work a nine to five job and you pay bills and like you spend all your energy doing that and then you have maybe a few hours to work on like your projects, but here . . . it's like you have enough time and space to do that constantly and always, and you don't have to worry about like having to pay bills or having to pay utilities. I mean you do have to worry about gathering wood and chopping it, but I love that. That is so much fun, that is awesome.

Kevin and Oliver moved onto a block where several abandoned houses were already being occupied by other young, predominately white appropriators who had all moved to Detroit to homestead within the last few years. After visiting the appropriators on this block several times, the two young men moved into a large four-bedroom house that had already been taken over and cleaned up a bit by three other squatters. Kevin explained that when he and Oliver arrived, they "just saw a room that was not being utilized um, there's a lot of garbage and like tons of stuff in there, and so I just cleaned that out and pretty much like claimed it." They moved in and began sharing the space with the squatters who were already there.

Now, both Kevin and Oliver were formally unemployed. They worked odd jobs for occasional cash, dumpster dove and visited food banks in the winter and grew their own food during the summer. Oliver had recently obtained food stamps. Like many other LAs, they lived inexpensively and avoided monthly bills for utilities by procuring heat and water themselves—also an exciting but challenging component of this lifestyle. The ability to "rough it" by occupying a house without utilities and chopping wood to burn for heat, taking the time to salvage materials from nearby houses, or the labor of gardening in order to feed oneself are all precisely part of what LAs seek.

Kevin and Oliver's larger goal was to create a small commune of sorts, with the houses owned in common and open to housing whoever wanted to be part of their sustainable community. And while many LAs used appropriation as a stepping-stone to legal ownership, Kevin and Oliver were less sure about the prospects of legal ownership than many other LAs I talked with. Neither of them, nor any of the other people they were squatting with, had the money to purchase the properties at present. But Oliver explained that they'd like to own them to carry out their vision:

> The bottom line is we need to be able to own our property and be able to organize ourselves to effectively run, and still being like open and free to have just anybody get involved. But we just can't like have the liability of, we could get kicked out at some time . . . I think we can like come together, but it's just been this really slow process.

The area where Oliver, Kevin, and their friends were squatting is very blighted. Many lots are now vacant from past demolitions, but many empty, scrapped, or half-burnt houses still litter the area. To Oliver and Kevin, this was ideal. Kevin exclaimed, "You want to build a greenhouse like go and find the materials in all these abandoned houses! There is windows, gutters, two-by-fours like anything you can think of, it's all around here and you create like whatever you want."

I asked how they felt about taking materials from other houses nearby—were they contributing to the deterioration of what they claimed was "their community"? Kevin reflected and replied, "I feel like the houses are gonna be bulldozed anyway, and if we can take this material that's just gonna be garbage and create something sustainable and beautiful with it then that's our human right as earthlings, like we have a right to be happy. We have a right to create. It's gonna be garbage anyway." Further echoing aspects of the ethos of care, Oliver added,

> No I agree . . . it's like reclaiming material that's gonna be garbage anyways. I think of like how we go out and get wood. Right now we go through these abandoned neighborhoods and we like clear out downed trees that you know are just a mess all over the place and the same thing for fixing up these houses. Like a lot of, you'll see these houses with like spray paint like I think it's "W/O" and that means they're gonna get demolished so they've already reached that point and yeah, I think it depends on where you're getting it.

Oliver was referring to the letters "W/O" that are spray painted on houses to indicate that the water has been shut off, the first step in the demolition process. Kevin grinned and added, "One of my favorite things about living there is scavenging (salvaging). I love scavenging."[1]

ALLEN

Allen, a white male in his early thirties, was a homesteader and urban farmer who graduated from a prestigious university with a potentially lucrative degree. He grew up in a wealthy suburb and lived abroad for a few years after college. When he returned to metro Detroit, to his parents' dismay he decided to move to the city to farm on his quest for a pleasurable, meaningful life. Allen's case highlights how some LAs deploy various resources, like money and networks, to make their appropriation comfortable and eventually formalize their property relations by purchasing the property they use.

When Allen first moved to Detroit, he stayed with a friend in the city for several months, learning the craft of urban farming and searching for the right place to start his homestead. Now, several years in, Allen grew produce, had fruit trees, and raised and harvested chickens, all of which he sold for his sole source of income. He said he managed to earn about $8,000 a year.

Allen discussed what motivated him: "I wanted the freedom to not have the pressure of like going for a job . . . and not having the flexibility when you have a particular amount of financial obligations then . . . it's much harder to figure out what you want to do in life." The opportunity for "free land," as he put it, was enticing. Allen wanted the ability to figure out his path in life, and informal property use provided an opportunity to try something he wanted to do.

I asked if other appropriators he knew had similar motivations. He replied, "I think some of us are to some degree lost." He laughed and continued, "I don't want to say lost but like . . . we haven't found our calling in the so-called corporate world or wherever world that is, we want something different so we're just in the alternative lifestyles." Here, in this blighted neighborhood in Detroit, Allen seemed to have found his calling. He said, "I love farming . . . but I'm not good enough to do it on like a grand scale and I really like, I mean like it's a perfect size, it's perfect price . . . And I'm very intentional and I've built up that community and that's what I love too."

Allen carefully selected a house that was several years delinquent on its property taxes and might soon be available to purchase through the county property auction. The house had several vacant lots to one side and more across the street. Allen asked his new immediate neighbors if they minded him occupying the abandoned house before he began to rehabilitate it. Allen's house needed everything from plumbing and electricity to windows and drywall. He did not salvage many of the materials for his home like some other homesteaders.

Allen said when he first came across this house "the whole thing was boarded up and so I . . . kicked in the door and it was full of garbage . . . there was nothing left, no pipes, no electricity and when I say full of garbage—the garbage is taller than me." He held his hand up above his head. Allen moved into the house as soon as the garbage was cleared out. He put in a toilet, had a rain water collection jug rigged up, and put a futon in the living room: "I figured if I had a bathroom with water and a place to sleep, I could move in." He put a padlock with a bolt on the front door and proceeded to renovate the rest of the house room by room. Several "friends that are very talented" came over and helped Allen with the more complicated renovations, such as redoing the electrical, adding plumbing, and installing the bathroom. He had to put in all new windows.

He did things simply and frugally, investing several thousand hours of his time and labor he estimated, because "I wasn't about to invest in something that I didn't own,"—a funny statement for someone who remodeled an entire house that he had no legal right to.

As many other appropriators do, Allen looked up the house's property tax status online.[2] He found out that a company owned it, but they were behind on their taxes, so he guessed it would be up for auction in a year or two. Allen explained, "So that's important cause you don't want to look at a house and see someone's paying the taxes and maybe they do care about it." Tax delinquency on a vacant property is often used as an indicator that no one cares about owning the house because it will be foreclosed in three years if the delinquent taxes aren't paid.[3]

Allen was living in the house for well over a year before he was able to purchase it. He explained that during that time he couldn't get the water hooked up legally without proof of owning the house or proof of permission from the legal owner (such as in the form of a rental agreement), which he noted would be impossible. He told me, "So I mean we had hooked up the water, you know there's just a little thing outside . . . jimmy rigged that so we could hook it up. So we took care of that." Soon after he moved in, Allen and his friends put a shut off valve inside the house and illegally turned the water supply on from the street. He said he managed to sign up for power legally through DTE by providing documentation that he lived there (and fudging the legality of his occupation), but the connection was cut shortly after it was turned on.

That was the beginning of an arduous process for Allen. He found out the power had been shut off because his house was on the city's demolition list—the first step in the demolition process is getting all the utilities shut off properly. Allen noted in retrospect that he had seen a demolition notice on the front of the house when he was first cleaning it up, but he didn't pay much attention, figuring that the city was too backlogged to actually come to tear it down. Shortly after the power was turned off, the city came out to shut off his water. Allen flagged down a worker disconnecting water at several other lots nearby who explained that the only thing Allen could do was get his house off the demolition list. He said that the worker told him, "Listen, just park your car right where we're supposed to dig, just right there, we can't dig, but you have to take care of it cause we'll come back."

So Allen took photos of his house, showing all the improvements he had made to it, and went down to the Buildings, Safety, Engineering, and Environment Department (BSEED) for the city of Detroit to plead his case.[4] He talked to the person at the front desk: "You got to help me, I, what am I supposed to do, I can't purchase it yet 'cause I don't own it, etc., etc. and the guy says basically there's nothing I can do." I interrupted Allen and asked, "So you went to the city and said I'm living in a house that I don't own?" Allen grinned and explained that he figured the different departments weren't talking to each other—that BSEED was only concerned with the integrity of the structure, they weren't going to pick up the phone and call the police department. In a twist of luck, a familiar face walked past the counter in the BSEED office, and Allen realized the man lived down the block from his family in the suburbs. He called Allen into his office and Allen recalled him saying, "What are you doing? Does your dad know what you're doing? You're crazy! I can't believe you're doing this!" After lecturing for several minutes, Allen recalled he finally switched to providing advice and proceeded to explain to Allen who to contact and what to say to save his house. It worked, and instead of being demolished, the city funneled the house through to be sold at the county property auction a few months later. Allen recalled his house being listed at the auction for a starting bid of $10,800. He thought "It's not worth it, I'm not going to pay it," and rolled the dice, waiting until the second round in which all properties still unsold start at bids of $500. Luckily, no one bought the house, and it indeed moved in to the second round of the auction. To his surprise, someone else started bidding on his house, but he ended up winning the bidding war, paying $1,000. Later, he purchased one lot in the middle of his garden for one hundred dollars but other than that had not purchased the land he farmed.

Allen's social networks have not only helped him keep his house off the demolition list but have helped him expand his farm over the years. He began taking over lots across the street, and Allen was able to tap local resources for funding, seeds, soil, and, on occasion, volunteer labor. Some volunteers even helped him demolish a burnt-out house so that he could have more open space across the lots he was using. He added some farm animals and fruit trees over the years as well. He said through most of his expansion, he hasn't known where lot lines or alleyways were supposed to be. In a few instances, he culled back some weeds to expose the old sidewalk, but for the most part, the municipally defined boundaries were of little consequence for his practices.

JOHN AND ROB

John was a white male in his twenties from an exurb of Detroit. He graduated from college, moved abroad for work, and came back to be closer to family and for a new job opportunity in Detroit. He initially moved into an apartment in a rapidly gentrifying neighborhood near Downtown Detroit for about a year. Then he and his friend Rob, also a white male in his twenties from the suburbs, started squatting a vacant house in Detroit in a different neighborhood that John was familiar with because of his job. Like Allen, John and Rob invested significantly in a house they squatted and eventually were able to obtain legal title to it, though their foray into squatting was also characterized by a desire for fun and whimsy.

I sat at a small plastic table in John and Rob's dining room that looked like it used to sit on someone's back porch. It still had backyard dirt crusted in the flower pattern on top of the table and was littered with keys, pencils, dirty tea mugs and scraps of paper. John sat across from me. Rob sat in a low easy chair across the small room, eating sautéed vegetables from their garden out of a clay bowl with chopsticks. John recalled his decision process,

> You know it was time to move and first I was just kind of bored and wanted something more hands on and whatnot, and I was familiar with this community so there was a neighbor or two that I was talking to and telling them that I was looking for places and they said, "Okay, why don't you just occupy this one."

I pressed him to explain why he decided to squat, versus other legal alternatives for finding a house in this neighborhood that he liked. He thought for a moment and explained,

> I mean, I like to have projects and be active and go deeper with things, so you know [squatting] definitely seemed like an opportunity to do so and it was kind of like a right place, a right time too. Like my current roommates are moving away and . . . I've known the people here for a little while and was always interested in [the neighborhood].

John decided to squat, in part, because he was bored with the status quo and sought something different—a more engaged way of living—but also because he needed somewhere to live. Appropriating property was useful to him because it achieved both goals.

John explained that he briefly considered a few potential houses before deciding on this one because it "was in pretty good shape and has a really good foundation. The roof is good. You know it's near neighbors that can watch out for it." But he also reiterated that "it wasn't much of a thoroughly thought-out process to be honest. It was kind of like someone was suggesting it to me who I was close to—like a friend, a neighbor you know—and you know it was kind of like, okay this is a good house, this is a good thing to do." He laughed and said that in hindsight he should have given it all a bit more thought; the process was haphazard and a bit chaotic at first.

The house had been empty for a year or two before John took it over. He moved his stuff into the house one night in the early spring and spent the first week boarding and re-boarding up the door as he came and went but didn't stay there initially: "And for the first like two or maybe three weeks or a month even, I stayed at a neighbor's house. I had my stuff in here, and I might have stayed one night or something, but it was so gross. I mean like there was a lot of insulation, the walls that were knocked out and like wet and like I don't think it would have been very great to stay in here." Scrappers had decimated the house by pulling the copper pipes out of the walls and stealing the windows.

About a month later, John and Rob prepared the house to move in. Rob described the state of the house at that point,

> The first night here we were like "What the fuck are we doing?" Had candles, like there was nothing here, the walls were like a white, dirty with crayons and like, you could clearly see with the kids hand[prints] that they made like, it was the wallpaper, it just a border of dirty grime . . . There was like rubble on the ground and at that point there was just a toilet, I don't think there was a tub . . . Weren't too many bugs though, we were glad about that.

John and Rob filled dozens of trash bags with garbage from the inside of the house, boarded up the windows, and made a makeshift front door with a padlock on it. They slept in sleeping bags on the floor.

John gestured around the room as he described the process of cleaning up the house and making it livable. With the help of some of the neighbors and several *Idiot's Guide* books, John and Rob renovated the house. They had to put in windows, plumbing, drainage, electrical, and a chimney for the wood-burning stove. Their kitchen was cobbled together out of random salvaged materials. It was early spring when they first moved in, and they were without electricity through late the next fall and were contemplating how they could get DTE (the power company) to hook up the power. They both recalled DTE requiring proof of residency to get service (though my later research did not confirm this requirement), and John explained that "you can . . . easily forge that, although we didn't." When the winter weather was fast approaching, they considered getting an illegal hookup but John and Rob both reiterated, "We didn't fraudulently do anything." John pursed his lips and shook his head when I pressed for more information about how they finally got the power turned on.

One thing that drew John and Rob to their neighborhood was the sense of community they found there. Both emphasized the help they received from others they knew in the neighborhood who had done similar DIY renovations on properties (both informally occupied and legally owned properties). John explained, "You know I don't . . . *have* to rely on my neighbors, but I do somewhat intentionally rely on my neighbors and vice versa, and I don't think that's really the case in other places." He elaborated on an example of this:

> Like when I first came in here there is a neighbor who you know basically offered like all of his tools, more importantly all of his expertise. He's over here every day for a couple of weeks helping me with like the plumbing and the drainage and everything. If he knows I need something he'll . . . give a call and say, "Hey I know you're looking for a security door I've, you know, I got one for you," or things like that.

After squatting in the house for over six months, John ended up tracking down the legal owner. In John's words, the legal owner was "like some slime-ball foreclosure king." He had bought the property as part of a bundle of tax foreclosed properties and had never even seen the house, nor had he paid any of the taxes the last two years. John called him on the phone, saying he was a concerned neighbor of the "nuisance property" and tried to get the owner to give it to him. His hope was that the owner, want-ing to avoid any fines from the city for nuisance complaints, would unload the property to anyone interested. He didn't take the bait, unfortunately. Finally, after some back and forth, John offered to buy it. They settled on a sale price of $1,000 for the house. The owner did not know of John and Rob's significant repairs and investment in the property. John had to pay a few thousand dollars in back taxes to keep it from going through tax foreclosure again.

Both John and Rob loved their neighborhood and said they intended to stay for the foreseeable future. They speculated that perhaps squatting had been a way to figure that out. But of their time illegally occupying their house (before purchasing it), Rob commented, "It was like the ulti-mate like, don't give a fuck, just do it type of thing and I mean, it was just a lot of fun."

SARAH AND MATTHEW

Sarah and her partner Matthew were both white thirty-somethings from elsewhere in Michigan. They saw opportunity in Detroit and began their practices informally but eventually formalized them. Like many other LAs, they invested significantly prior to owning, but only in the land: they boarded up and "saved" a house to renovate once they were able to purchase it. At the time of this research, they had purchased one lot and were occupy-ing several others in Detroit and farming them. They rented a house nearby.

We sat under a tree in a corner of one of the lots they farmed, sur-rounded by neat rows of growing vegetables, fruit trees, and a large compost pile whose smell wafted our way every time the breeze picked up. Sarah and Matthew had gotten to know the area while doing a farming internship in the neighborhood. Sarah explained,

> We were going to try to go to [another Michigan city] because that's where my family is and start something like this there, but as we were coming here more we really liked it and just financially there's no way we could've gotten a house and space to do stuff for this price, like we would have had to get crappy jobs and you know it be just more of the same, like working in a restaurant.

The ability to informally access property in Detroit meant they could have the lifestyle they wanted. Trying to buy or rent this much property elsewhere would have required committing a lot of time to unfulfilling work, whereas in Detroit both were formally employed part-time in low-paying but enjoyable jobs. To Sarah and Matthew, property in Detroit was an opportunity of which to take advantage.

At the time of our interview, they had lived in Detroit for several years. Their friend Carrie had moved out of Detroit and offered them the lots. Carrie didn't own the lots either but had planted a small garden in one corner while renting the house across the street. Sarah recalled how the lots were informally passed on: "She moved and so she gave us permission really to take over her spot." That Sarah and Matthew felt they needed permission from Carrie demonstrates the significance of these informal rights to property.

Soon after Sarah and Matthew inherited the lots from Carrie, they were able to buy one of them. Sarah said, "We liked this space because there's a house that's in decent condition and it gets good sun and then there's all of those lots on the other side of the house." After taking over the garden, they began to investigate the small house situated in the middle of the lots. It was pretty clean inside, some of the plumbing was gone, but they assessed that there wouldn't be too much work to do (relatively speaking). They boarded the house back up to keep it secure and added lively paint to the outside to mark their care of the house, still living in their rental while they waited for the house to come·up for sale at the auction. Sarah and Matthew weren't comfortable renovating it without owning it, as that would make their monetary investments insecure.

I asked if their hesitations about working on the house before owning it was related to concerns of getting into legal trouble for any of their activities. Sarah shook her head and said, "I don't really think about it that much because I guess there's not much accountability around here, like people aren't going around saying, 'Should you be doing this?' I think because it feels like it's something good that, I mean otherwise it would just sit here and this house would probably be scrapped and end up like those and maybe burn down . . ." She gestured to the row of three decrepit-looking houses across the street.

Their farm was large and required a lot of work. Since they didn't own the house, they couldn't legally get any water hooked up for their farm, so they built an elaborate water-catchment system using half of the roof of the house. Sarah explained that they weren't so much worried about getting into any trouble, but

> we were more worried that people would come in and maybe wreck what we were trying to do. So in this neighborhood crime tends to go, come in waves so things will be so quiet like this, you know you feel like you're in the country and then maybe there's a couple of shootings or maybe there's, people go on a scrapping rampage. Um, so we were a little nervous that, especially with the rain collection, that was the big one . . . like maybe it would be vandalized or people would try to scrap whatever crap you could get off of it, (laughing) like the little valves. So we were a little nervous about that mostly because we live a few blocks away so we're not here all the time . . . but this street is pretty empty and the neighbors that we do know on this street have come into the garden and we've shared our food and we've shared seeds and they're really excited and I think that when they're around they probably kind of keep an eye on it.

But she added, "We would like to buy [the land] so we don't have to worry about it." Now, several years later, Sarah and Matthew own the house, have renovated it, and live in it. They also own several of the lots they farm but not all of them.

FERN AND RITA

Homeowners Fern and Rita, both white residents in their late thirties, farmed nearly an entire city block in a very blighted neighborhood. Their vignette demonstrates how informality can be desirable because oftentimes, in Detroit, it is more efficient than cumbersome, legal ways of doing things. Fern grew up in a suburb just beyond the Detroit border, and Rita was from elsewhere in the United States. They both had fulfilling but low-paying jobs in the city. Unlike many other LAs who had very recently moved to Detroit, Fern and Rita had lived in the city for nearly two decades. But they moved to their current neighborhood a few years prior to farm and appropriate property—they had long been interested in urban agriculture, but their former house did not have the space to do so.

My first glimpse of their property was in the middle of winter, and it was so dark out I could not see the garden, but I later got to know the space when I helped out there for several months during a summer. Inside, their house was cozy and eclectic, with mismatched cabinets, moldings, and doors taken from houses nearby. Fern offered me homemade kombucha while we sat in their warm kitchen, heated by a little wood stove they had built in the center of the small room.

About ten years ago, a friend offered Fern and Rita this very run-down house he owned that was situated in the middle of many vacant lots. They paid him a few thousand dollars for the house and immediately began renovating it and planting their garden. Without any formal permission, they demolished a very run-down, abandoned house adjacent to make more room for their garden. They even fenced in the alleyway and built it up with compost over the years to level off the space. They estimated that they grew nearly 200 pounds of food each year. But being able to save money at the grocery store while feeding their family was the least of the benefits, Fern said. What they found there, he said, was

> just the lifestyle of being able to have that much space to tend and like it's kind of overwhelming, but it's my life . . . like that benefit is just huge. I'm so in touch with the seasons and I'm so in touch with the soil and myself because I'm deciding what I'm eating and how, and plus like, I don't like people that much and I don't have neighbors . . . That sense of space is something that is valuable to me.

Rita nodded while her husband spoke, and added,

> It feels good to be able to look into the yard and just see prairie. I love that and to not have to also have the space limited so that every square inch of it is like completely used and tended. You know we will sit out there and just go, "Wow!" . . . You get to have a strip of wilderness . . . all the insects and the little animals in there. There's wilderness in the garden too and that's really, really cool, really good.

While working in their garden, I similarly relished the ability to look up and around and not see another built structure—just trees and plants. It was easy to forget you were in the city.

Fern and Rita spent several years renovating the house their friend had sold them before it was livable for them and their children. The house had no windows, no roof, significant fire damage, no plumbing or electrical, and was "full of crap" they said. They renovated the house using salvaged materials from nearby properties and some that were purchased from salvage businesses in the city. While explaining how they salvaged materials from houses nearby, Fern and Rita were very clear about their commitments to an ethos of care. They frequently boarded up houses nearby in the hopes of preserving them for future neighbors, even when they could have procured the sink or windows they needed for their own house. But in a neighborhood like theirs "there's tons of resources around here," Fern said. Rita compared Detroit to other cities, noting that other places may have re-stores,[5] but in Detroit "you might as well go to an abandoned factory or something . . . you know you might find those, but nobody will give them to you cleaned up or you know people might not have it organized for you, but they're out there, you just got to kind of find it and work for it." Fern and Rita estimated that well over half their house was salvaged and gestured around the room narrating where different elements of the kitchen had come from.

While Fern and Rita owned the house before they started renovating it, they had farmed the lots for many years without owning them all. Like most others I spoke with, Fern and Rita weren't at all worried about getting into trouble for their activities. In explaining why, Rita laughed and said that they "have great role models for getting away with stuff," as many of their neighbors had been squatting, farming, salvaging, or the like for many years. It wasn't just illegal appropriation that they got away with, but also informal construction (erecting or renovating structures in ways that don't conform to existing building codes or regulations). They didn't pull any permits to renovate their house, nor to build barns or storage sheds on their property, which Rita noted, "I don't think you could get away with that in too many places, you know." Rita said that these kinds of practices "all grew out of that attitude of just do it and then apologize later . . . with the lack of the oversight [from city authorities] comes also, there might not be anybody to tell you 'go ahead' you know . . . But once you do it and then people see that it's a good thing, then everybody's like, 'yeah, that's great.'" Fern nodded in agreement and added, "Yeah permission could take a long time."

Fern and Rita wanted to own the land in order to increase their control over the space. Before they began farming, the business one block over used a large lot adjacent to their house for overflow parking. Fern and Rita put up a fence to try to "claim" the lot, but this resulted in further disputes that didn't abate until they were able to purchase that particular lot. Like many other LAs, Fern and Rita's strategy had been to try to buy up the lots they used one by one over time, when they were able to afford them and when they could figure out how to buy them. But the process had been cumbersome and often frustrating. Rita explained,

> [One lot] just wasn't available, the city wasn't processing it in time you know or I mean that just wasn't available. And now a couple of these lots when I looked them up belonged to somebody, but then I couldn't find the person. You know like their address was the address [of the lot], but it hadn't been a house forever you know or you just couldn't figure out what. And there was a couple [of lots] where the city just said, "Well you know they're not for sale," or whatever. And one [was] owned by the state, so we bought [that one], because the state has pretty clear guideline of how to buy property and it's pretty straightforward. Those are the easy ones.

Over the years they have been able to purchase all but a few lots, which happen to be situated in the middle of their garden. Rita recalled one experience trying to track down the legal owner of the property. They looked up the owner on the city's tax records and then searched for him online. She called him up and said he was very friendly on the phone but said he didn't own the property anymore. "He couldn't really explain to me exactly what happened, but he said, 'You won't be able to get that, it's just kind of stuck in the system.'" Fern and Rita said that wasn't the first time they had encountered inaccurate city records or properties being "lost in the system" of sorts.

KNOX

Knox was a white male in his thirties from the southern United States. He had lived in Detroit for about three years when I interviewed him. He had purchased a house in Detroit because it was cheaper than renting, he explained. Knox liked to build, to tinker, and was a jack of all trades. Distinct from scrappers, salvaging was akin to a hobby for LAs like Knox;

he enjoyed the explorational process as well as the useful materials he found.

Knox walked me through the building where he took most of the materials he used for his attic renovation. The abandoned school's windows were broken or missing entirely, the doorways were wide open, letting rain, snow, and animals inside. Much of what was left of the inside of the building was covered with graffiti or splatters of paint from paintball guns. Gunshots had made peepholes through the heavy old wooden classroom doors. Knox gestured around the building, showing me where the walls, doors, and shelves of his renovation had come from. He had been through the building many times and narrated our exploration, telling me when this school had been shut down and pointing out the unique aspects of its architecture. I asked him why he started salvaging in the first place:

> I was just exploring abandoned property, and if you've ever been in some of the industrial buildings in the city of Detroit, there's usable shit all over the place. There's a lot of metal—some of it's easily accessible and some of it's not. The first time I went, I encountered a warehouse that was pretty full of lumber and I was thinking about what it is that I could do with all this material that was sitting there. And . . . you're in buildings or locations that are obviously, um, decaying and no one's been there for years other than graffiti artists or potentially other scrappers. So, I took a few . . . small things that I had picked up—usually metal—and then returned to that same place, because I had discovered a cache of useful material.

Knox described his initial response as a newcomer to Detroit: "When you see these structures in Detroit out of juvenile curiosity, and it's like, holy cow, I want go see what that place is." Later he added,

> It's just an interest. It's a big abandoned building, there's all kinds of shit in it. Maybe some of that shit is useful or valuable or maybe there's just the space. Like take a skateboard up to the fourth floor of an abandoned building and it's all concrete floors, there's nothing in there, and skate all day long inside one of these places. It's not so much the desire for adventure like I'm Indiana Jones, but there's also an anomaly—I've never encountered anything like that in my life. You see abandoned buildings in other places, but they're cordoned off and they're in the midst of being deconstructed. Or where I'm from they're so old and dangerous and made out of wood that there's not really any reason to go exploring, whereas these are categorically

different. I mean you have high-rise structures some fifteen stories tall that are completely abandoned. That's a lot of space, that's a lot of square footage to peruse.

Knox derided the white suburbanites who come through the city looking at "ruin pornography": photography of the city's decay to make new coffee-table books. I asked how his activities are different, and he responded self-critically, "Well, I mean, I take material, that's the only difference, otherwise it's not really." He added,

Half the time I'm not really prepared to take material, I just go and do kind of like a recon mission over the space. And look, ooh that looks cool, I want to take that! Or ooh, I could use that ladder or there's a ton of bricks here, you could load up all these bricks. And look at all this glass or that's a potentially useful window frame or this is a heavy door.

But what seems to differentiate Knox's practices from the suburbanite ruin-gazers he critiqued is that his practices enabled him to produce things on his own—"arts and crafts types of things." He defined salvaging as "reappropriating abandoned and disused material that can be constructively utilized or turned into cash." He primarily looked for metal, glass, or "something that actually has like a specifically useful design in it that I might be looking for—viable pieces of wood, thick things that can be used for frames or foundations of other structures." He used them in welding projects, home renovations, and what he generally referred to as "recycling."

While Knox said he didn't worry about getting into legal trouble for salvaging, he did act concertedly to minimize any potential disruptions to his practices. Referencing an industrial spot near the Detroit River where he had been salvaging, he explained:

If I get myself all ready to load my scrap material, then I can pull the truck up, load the scrap material and drive away. What I've seen people get caught for is parking the vehicle and slowly over-time scrapping material into their vehicle and then trying to drive away. And at some point the police or the port authority or the border patrol roll up on your car and then your car has got a bunch of scrap material sitting right next to an abandoned building, and then you can get cited or taken to jail, or the like. So what I do is, I get all of my material ready and then do the loading in one fell swoop and do it as quickly as possible. So it's not so much that you're scared, but there is a kind of nervousness such that you're moving quickly in order to do what it is that you need to do.

Knox said salvaging had benefitted him by enabling him to create useful things, and the problems it caused had been minimal:

> It's probably beat up my truck a little bit more than it would have without it. I've, you know, like injured myself a couple of times minimally, you know cuts and scrapes, shit like that, but I question, sometimes, breathing in the air in some of these places cause you're like in the bowels of industrial buildings sometimes and it's greasy and dank.

Knox acknowledged that for many people scrapping is "a tactic for getting by . . . for me it's not even a tactic for getting by, I don't need it to get by. It's a topping." I asked him to explain further and he added, "A topping because I can find gainful employment. I like scrapping. I like knowing that I can utilize my energy and activity in ways that can challenge the existing framework."

WILLIAM

William, a white man in his mid-forties, had moved to Detroit about a decade prior to be involved with the art scene. He had a somewhat menial job that almost covered his living expenses; he made up the rest with odd side-jobs every once in a while. William salvaged to help fuel his art, but as a lifestyle pursuit rather than one of necessity, he had the ability to distance himself when salvaging felt too risky.

Upon moving to Detroit, William started exploring vacant buildings and taking photos of them. After a while, he just started to pick up materials along the way to collect. He was initially interested in things he described as "sculptural material . . . things that were an interesting shape or color . . . some machine parts, just whatever the factory was making like a weird plastic hemisphere or something . . ." He added that now "I guess I scrap just for my art and my own desire you know? Just it's like treasure hunting. . . I guess part of it is art material and part of it is just kind of cultural gathering like find things that are interesting to me." William explained that he turned most of what he salvaged into art and stored the rest—every spare inch of his small rented apartment was crammed with these salvaged materials. He had either sold or given away most of the artwork he had made. Salvaging these materials made his passion—art—affordable for him. He explained, "I found some material that I've been able to turn into artwork and benefit economically from, and just other material I can use to make my artwork instead of having to buy stuff all the time."

He said he began salvaging more and more over the past seven to eight years, in part because his fear of who he might encounter in an abandoned building had gone down over time as he became more comfortable in the city. William explained, "Most of the people that're in the places, you just say like, 'What's up?' They're either scrapping or criminals or there for some other reason anyhow, so you know most of the time people there don't bother you." But, he said, if he ever got into legal trouble for salvaging, he would probably stop. Anytime William felt unsafe or like he may have crossed a line that could get him into legal trouble, he would just leave. He said to continue would not be worth it. The interactions he'd had with the police thus far had been benign. He recounted one instance:

> They took my ID, they ran my plate, you know I told them I was scrapping, but not for like metal, like weird junk and they said, "You need to get a junk license," and that it wasn't safe around where I was at. Other police encounters have just been brief interviews down [in the industrial area] by the river. Like, "What are you guys doing down here?" you know we tell them we're taking pictures, whatever, we're just kind of exploring. They're usually okay with that.

In another encounter, William was told by the police to leave the abandoned school he was in "cause you're going to get robbed," the officer told him. William's experience was that his salvaging activities were not the kind of illegal property use that were on the radar of police as something they should concern themselves with.

I asked William if salvaging had ever caused any problems for him. He half-laughed and said only one time, when a large nail pierced his foot, and he later detailed an encounter with another person while salvaging that scared him pretty good. But the materials William sought out didn't require that he dismantle structures nor put himself in significant danger.

And because he didn't rely on these materials for income, he could abandon his quest at any time without dire consequences for his well-being.

Property informality takes place much differently for LAs than NAs. LAs who occupy vacant houses spend substantial time and money fixing them up, and predominately try to purchase them or vacant lots if they are farming. Salvagers like Knox and William enjoy the process of exploring abandoned buildings as they search for reusable materials. LAs in my study have access to resources that significantly improve the conditions of their appropriation in comparison to NAs. These resources are not just monetary. LAs have the time to invest in their properties, often freed up by living frugally and reducing one's formal work (sometimes by quitting their jobs). While NAs tend to have expansive social networks (family, long-time neighbors, church members, etc.), LAs tend to be more embedded in networks of other appropriators—if not proximally then (or also) socially. These appropriators share knowledge about and assistance with building furnaces, rain collection systems, or renovating a property. And nearly all LAs in my study carry various other privileges that bolster their ability to navigate Detroit's obstacles, such as their whiteness, education levels, and connections with people in positions of authority.

In addition to having access to resources, the time and labor needed to improve the conditions of appropriation (such as searching for a salvageable door to fit one's squatted house) are part of the lifestyle LAs seek. And, LAs are more comfortable and willing to invest significant time and labor into their properties than NAs, because LAs expect to maintain these property relationships for the foreseeable future (most often by buying them). They may not have access to much disposable income, but LAs are more likely to be able to afford basic supplies necessary for DIY renovations and are interested in and willing to spend the time salvaging these supplies if need be. In Detroit, a home can be purchased via auction for as little as $500 and renovated for several thousand dollars. The conditions of appropriation are safer and more comfortable for LAs. And, because they choose them—they don't *have* to homestead, garden, or salvage to survive—they are not compelled to participate in ways that push the boundaries of safety or overall well-being in ways that many NAs do in order to secure the means for survival.

These vignettes cover only a few of the dozens of LAs I interacted with during my research. Many others differed from these examples in two important ways. First, while these examples here are of LAs whose everyday lives are very intertwined with and shaped by property informality, many other LAs are very casual about their participation in informal activities. Some work at squatted community gardens in their neighborhood, others occasionally salvage an appealing item from a vacant house when the mood strikes them (or when they happen to come across one). What continues to distinguish these informal property users as LAs is a combination of their relative newness to the city—often being drawn to Detroit in part by the possibility for these practices—and their orientation toward property informality—that it is something fun, interesting, and appealing to them. The ability for appropriation to be something fun and adventurous is in part shaped by their positionality as newcomers to the city.

Second, while all the LAs I referenced here are white, there are LAs who are people of color (I just did not come across many of them). Leroy, for example, was a nineteen-year-old Black male who moved to Detroit from a nearby state to be a part of the "rebirth" of the city. Subsequently, as a resident of Detroit, Leroy worked a low-wage job and spent much of his spare time participating in practices that informally used property—both on his own and in association with several nonprofits where he volunteered his time. He initiated tearing down properties that posed a threat to the community—as when a neighbor told him a man tried to drag her into a shack at the edge of an abandoned block and rape her. He created art on vacant buildings to beautify them. And he helped out at informal gardens in his neighborhood.

7 Routine Appropriators

Routine Appropriators (RAs) are Detroit residents who have grown frustrated with the lack of municipal response to social, economic, and property-related problems over the years. They gave up trying to do things "the right way" (i.e., formally) and have found their own methods for improving their blocks and achieving their goals. I call these informal practices "routine" because these appropriators tend to stumble into their practices in one way or another, and informal appropriation becomes part of their routine for ensuring individual and community well-being. They tend to become involved in very unplanned, spontaneous ways or via practices that start out small and incrementally grow and develop over time—often decades. RAs are longtime residents of Detroit—commonly homeowners—who are invested, in a multifaceted sense,[1] in the well-being of their homes, blocks, neighborhoods, and communities.

The RAs I met during my research appropriate property in a variety of different ways (see Table 2). Some remain in houses after foreclosure as holdover squatters, others take over vacant lots to blot ("squat the block") or garden. Others have scrapped to help make ends meet when their regular employment does not fully suffice, and others engage in informal demolition to help secure and improve their blocks. And still others have deployed art as a tactic for neighborhood improvement of one sort or another.

RAs "bridge" Lifestyle and Necessity categories because they have some overlaps with each but are still distinct in important ways. RAs tend to be longtime residents of the city (like NAs), but have more economic stability, if only marginally. But this marginal increase impacts their appropriation in important ways. RAs don't rely on appropriation to survive. And, their relative stability enables them to invest more of their time and resources into appropriation. Similar to LAs, there are ways in which some RAs come to appreciate or even enjoy appropriation because of positive "lifestyle" components these practices have brought (like an increased sense of safety or extra yard space), even if initially their practices were burdensome.

The vignettes here introduce various RAs and their practices, emphasizing two key points. First, these vignettes demonstrate the way that, for RAs, the entry into appropriation is neither an act of survival, like for NAs, nor a desirable foray like for LAs. Instead, whether it started abruptly or developed slowly over time, RAs appropriate to negotiate obstacles of living in Detroit and to make lemonade from the sour lemons grown from decline. Second, these vignettes demonstrate that the conditions of appropriation for RAs are characterized by cumbersome interactions or frustrations with the city's negligence, and, while the practices require time, labor, and some resources, RAs don't tend to experience as risky, precarious, or harsh conditions as NAs.

CHUCK

Chuck was a white, lifelong Detroiter in his fifties. He gestured animatedly while we talked, explaining to me how he first began boarding up and eventually demolishing vacant, blighted properties in his northeast Detroit neighborhood over the past fifteen years. Chuck's informal practices grew over time, as he and his wife stepped up to take care of their neighborhood when the city would not.

It all started with a vacant house nearby that turned into a rowdy drug house on the weekends. Over the course of a year and a half, Chuck and his wife documented making "hundreds of calls" to various city authorities to complain about the nuisance. He received no response. Finally, he says he got fed up and headed over to the hardware store for supplies to board up the property. He explained his frame of mind at that point,

> And after I called all the numbers and you know did everything I could do as a citizen, it really got to the point where I had a moral responsibility to protect my twins, my family, my home, my neighborhood. So, I really at that point wasn't concerned about, you know getting arrested for trespassing. I mean you can't even get arrested for selling crack, so you know I'll take my chances, right?

Chuck and his wife went over to the house and began boarding up the windows, painting the boards, cutting the grass, and trimming the bushes. After a few hours, a neighbor stopped by to ask what they were doing, and Chuck recalled his response,

> I said, well look, I don't know about you, I don't want my twins growing up in and around this, man. I said, you can help me board it up or get the hell out of my way. I'm boarding this up. I'm not listening to any more excuses or no more promises 'cause you know the city, they were gonna come out and the police said they were gonna come out . . . and I was just fed up with it and didn't want to have to deal with it anymore.

His neighbor began to pitch in, and together they spent eight hours that day cleaning up the nuisance property. The impact was significant for Chuck:

> And that evening three cars pulled up—all about the same time—right around dinnertime. It was in the evening—6:30, 7:00—and two of the guys got out of a little red car and they were walking up to the house and they looked at the house and they kind of looked at each other and they looked at their car: we had changed the frequency.

Like many other Detroiters frustrated with the lack of government response to the problems in the city, Chuck took it upon himself to improve the conditions of his neighborhood. Over the years, Chuck got bolder, and got more help from other neighbors who were similarly frustrated. The

boards they put up would only last so long, and since neighborhood conditions were still deteriorating, they found themselves surrounded by more
and more properties that sat vacant and blighted. They began demolishing the properties that were continuously problems. But demolition is no
small legal violation. Chuck explained what it was like to navigate the
legality of tearing down properties without permission,

> There was a number of city inspectors that had come out and threatened to
> arrest me, if, you know, I continued to clean out my neighborhood without
> pulling a permit. So all we would do, to be completely honest with you, is we
> would stop, wait for them to leave and we'd go back and finish up. I mean it's
> ridiculous. And you know clearly if he was doing his job as the Director of
> Building and Safety, that building shouldn't be in that condition. There's
> actually a law in the books that clearly indicates that no property owner, it
> doesn't matter if it's an individual or a corporation or an association, can
> maintain a damaged property in the city of Detroit for more than twelve
> months without either removing it or repairing it. So, there are ordinances
> on the books that clearly state that; so you are in violation of city ordinances.
> And the crazy thing is, the city owns most of these properties that have been
> vacant forever . . . so they're breaking their own rules. So, if you want to
> arrest me for cleaning up my neighborhood 'cause you're not doing your job,
> come on. Bring it on.

For decades, Detroiters like Chuck and his neighbors have been allocat-
ing their own money, labor, time, and other resources to try to stabilize
and improve their neighborhoods. When I asked Chuck how much of his
own money he had spent over the years, he shrugged and said, "I lost track
. . . lost track a long time ago." As I was leaving, Chuck was tossing around
guesses of how much money he and his wife had spent. He said he wished
he had started a business out of it like Blight Busters, referencing a nonprofit in Detroit that cleans up deteriorated, vacant property mainly in
Northwest Detroit. Many RAs in my study are relatively stably employed
homeowners in Detroit like Chuck. As such many have the ability to
devote some of their spare time and money to appropriation, and many
pursue practices like demolition or blotting as a way to try to improve
their blocks or neighborhoods. As property owners, they are concerned
with the social stability of their blocks, as well as their financial investments in their properties.

SCOTT

Scott, a single Black male in his fifties, was a lifelong Detroiter. He was divorced; his children were grown. Scott lived by himself in a home he had owned for three years, in the same neighborhood in the far North End of Detroit where he had lived for several decades. While Chuck began his informal practices after not getting any response from authorities, Scott had dabbled in various forms of informal deconstruction over the years to improve his neighborhood and his own financial stability.

At the time of our interview, Scott had been working a job in the service sector for nine years, but this formal work didn't always cover all his bills. He occasionally supplemented his income by scrapping but explained that he typically only brought in "forty or fifty bucks, no big deal." Scott said this kind of informal appropriation is one of the best opportunities in Detroit: "There's scrap, tons of it to be scrapped. That's opportunity," and then added, "Save it, put it in your yard. As it piles up and you get broke, take it in and turn it in." Sure enough, there were piles of scrapped materials neatly arranged next to the wood pile on the side of Scott's house, waiting to be taken to the scrapyard.

In a city where gainful employment is hard to find, scrapping fills in the gaps. For RAs like Scott, scrapping is not income that means the difference between being housed and being on the streets, or that keeps the power on (as it is for NAs like Bond). But neither is it a desired, enjoyable practice like salvaging is for LAs. Scrapping is a way to help navigate a city with few economic opportunities.

Scott's demolition practices started when he joined his neighbors to tackle some of the problems in their community. He recalled helping friends tear down houses in his neighborhood for twenty-two years. I asked him what initially motivated him to engage in demolition, and he replied, "It was these guys were doing something positive in the neighborhood—a neighborhood where I raised my kids. I raised my kids right around the corner there and the guys out here working and cleaning this place up. We'd get together on Saturdays and you know . . ." In neighborhoods in stable cities, neighbors get together to barbeque; in distressed neighborhoods in Detroit, they also get together to tear down blighted houses.

Scott explained how they went about it while also affirming an ethos of care: "We used to see something, a burned-out house, and we'd go ahead and we'd just take it apart and get rid of it. We know it's not gonna be rehabbed. It's gone . . . And yes, we have had city inspectors come by and issue tickets and say, 'You guys can't do this.'" Scott rolled his eyes and continued with irritation in his voice, "What do you mean, you can't do this? You guys are not doing it. Somebody's got to do it." I pressed further, asking if he was at all concerned about getting into trouble for de jure illegal demolition. Scott shrugged and replied matter-of-factly, "No, the city was corrupt. And they were busy."

MAXINE

Holdover squatting is a common practice among RAs in Detroit. Holdover squatters are occupants whose legal status has changed while still living in the same house: those who used to be legally housed but who are now technically squatting. Maxine, a Black lifelong Detroiter in her forties, found herself squatting the home she had been renting. She was single but shared the house with her mother, her mother's boyfriend, her sister, and her sister's son. Maxine's experience is one that would come to be very familiar among renters I spoke with.

Maxine worked as a housecleaner, went to school online, and spent a lot of time volunteering in her community. She had received food stamps and Medicaid since she was eighteen, which she credited with helping her to cover all her bills each month. Maxine paid half the monthly rent for her household—$300. Maxine explained that no one in her house had ever met the property owner, they only interacted with a man named Sam who came by to collect the rent each month. But recently a tax foreclosure notice was posted on the house. Maxine kept asking Sam if she could meet with the owner to talk about it but hadn't been successful. So Maxine and her household decided to stop paying the rent and eventually Sam stopped coming by. Her family's legal status in their rented house became unclear to them.

Many uncertainties accompany this transition to being holdover squatters. Maxine was worried about the utilities being shut off if the house was foreclosed. She was planning to move, and hoped to find a place in the suburbs, but said her mother and her mother's boyfriend would probably stay in the house as long as they could. I asked what was stopping her from staying put in the house. She explained,

> Oh nothing is not stopping me from staying, but I gotta look out for my 14-year-old nephew . . . He can't be out here like that. You know what I mean, because he going through stuff with the state that people come out and check over him, you know what I mean. So I can't have that right there . . . So that's who I'm looking out for. All the grown people they on they own. But I'm, I'm in interest of him right now.

Maxine planned to relocate with her nephew since they were no longer legally renting the house, and she was concerned this would be a problem for him adhering to the rules of his probation. But then she contradicted herself saying, "They had made squatters a right." I asked how she understood "squatter's rights" to work and she said, "I don't know how it work honestly . . ." and then referenced people living in a house prior to it going through foreclosure and to others who are living in a house in a way that's "decent." Whether or not some sort of tenuous legality vis-a-vis "squatter's rights" made Maxine's family feel comfortable remaining in the house was unclear. Hazy references to "squatter's rights" in Detroit were common in my interviews as a justification for illegal occupation, yet I didn't once come across anyone who had made a successful adverse possession claim (the legal term for what "squatter's rights" tends to refer to) to a property in Detroit.

OTHER HOLDOVER SQUATTERS

Holdover squatting is very much a response to local problems such as high tax rates, rampant over-assessments, widespread sub-prime mortgages, and an economically precarious population. It is an opportunity that only arises because of the lack of demand for property, such that after foreclosure no one purchases the property and subsequently evicts the occupants. And, it is an informal practice that these Detroit residents stumbled into as a way navigate obstacles in Detroit.

Depending on the appropriator's economic situation, holdover squatting may be classified as Necessity or Routine. Most of the situations in which I spoke with holdover squatters were informal conversations during tax fore-closure events in the city or while volunteering with local organizations to help people avoid foreclosure or resist eviction after foreclosure. Some of these conversations were with holdover squatters who were in very precarious financial situations and expressed concern that they would have to go to the homeless shelter or double up with family if they had to leave their squatted house. Other holdover squatters had at least a modicum of financial stability and had other plans for housing if they had to leave their home.[2] Some were former homeowners who were unable to stay abreast of their property tax payments, and their homes were foreclosed. Other holdover squatters were renters like Maxine, who, unbeknownst to them, were living in a house for which the owner stopped paying property taxes several years prior. This is one example of the practice of "milking" a property—wherein the owner extracts as much capital as possible out of the house while letting it deteriorate and eventually abandons it. Because property taxes in Detroit are high, landlords often buy properties, fail to pay the taxes, and let them go into foreclosure, abandoning them after just two to three years.[3]

Trying to stay abreast of property taxes in a city with high tax rates and rampant over-assessments can be impossible for low-income homeowners. Terrence, for example, was a Black man in his sixties who was struggling to gain legal title to his parents' former home. His aging widowed father did not stay on top of the tax payments, and Terrence did not know there was a problem until his father died and Terrence and his brother inherited the property—and its liabilities. They could not come up with the money for the back taxes quickly enough to avoid foreclosure. Nobody bought the property at the county property auction, so Terrence and his brother were taking turns living at the house to make sure no one broke in, tried to take it over, or scrapped the house. When I met Terrence, he was desperately looking for ways to buy back his parents' house, as he and his brother were sentimentally attached to it. It is also possible that Terrence's father didn't know the property was at risk of foreclosure. A June 2016 survey showed that 38 percent of the 1,789 occupants (including owners, renters, and informal occupants) contacted were not even aware that their house was going through tax foreclosure.[4]

One elderly Black woman, a lifelong Detroiter named Harriet, saw her property tax bill skyrocket when her homestead exemption was rescinded while she was living temporarily in Arkansas, taking care of her dying sister. At the time, she didn't realize this was something she could contest or change, so she continued to try to pay the increased tax bill on her limited social security income. Finally, the property was foreclosed and went up for sale at the county property auction. She didn't move out, hoping that no one would buy it. But it was a large house in an up-and-coming neighborhood and sold for over twenty thousand dollars. Harriet found herself technically living illegally in the home her father had bought when she was a child, that she had lived in nearly her entire life. For almost six months after the auction, nothing changed. Then one day, a young white woman came by with her father and notified Harriet that she had purchased the house at auction. Harriet was told to move out. Harriet said that the prospect of packing up a lifetime of personal items and family heirlooms was devastating. She pleaded with the new owner to let her stay; the woman threatened to evict her. The new owner finally agreed to let Harriet rent the house for $700 per month. When I met Harriet, she was at a meeting held by housing rights activists in the city and was trying to get help to stay in her house. She was struggling to afford the monthly rent and did not know where else to go.

Harriet's story is unfortunate insofar as someone bought her house and wanted her to move out. But many more homeowners and renters are able to stay in their property long after it is foreclosed. Data shows that nearly 75 percent of the 35,525 properties foreclosed for tax delinquency by May of the 2017 tax year were occupied.[5] In many of these houses, occupants choose to wait it out, hoping to continue living in their properties without interruption. A June 2016 survey found that 89 percent of occupants in tax foreclosed properties wanted to remain in their homes.[6]

For example, longtime residents Ted and Ashley bought their house at the county property auction nearly seven years prior to when I met them. They were both under-employed and had very irregular employment interspersed with periods of joblessness. Ted sold plasma and scrapped to make ends meet, while Ashley rotated paying their bills from month to month to avoid shutoffs. When they found out their property was indeed being foreclosed, nothing really changed for them. There was nothing they could do, and instability was a common feature of their lives. They figured no one else would want their house—a tiny, run-down property in a very distressed neighborhood. They were right; several years later now, and the house is still owned by the city (though, I don't know if Ted and Ashley are still living there).

Most of the holdover squatters I spoke with did not initially consider themselves to be squatters, and none expressed experiencing any opposition from neighbors for their presence (confirmed by some neighbors I spoke with). It's not necessarily evident to anyone else that these residents had transitioned from legal to de jure illegal occupants. Many (former) homeowners merely desire to continue living in their home either for sentimental reasons or because they owned the house outright and could not have afforded paying rent nor purchasing a new house. Some renters may move out when they find out their house has been foreclosed, in part because they do not want the legal uncertainty (like Maxine), while others may decide to lay low and live rent-free in the house as long as possible.

As they are no longer the legal owners or occupants of the property, holdover squatters face new obstacles and insecurities. Holdover squatters (like all squatters) live with the uncertainty that they will be forced to move out. They may be able to keep the utilities connected provided they stay abreast of payments. But if the utilities are disconnected, it may be hard to get them turned on again legally. Holdover squatters may experience better living conditions than other squatters because the property did not sit vacant prior to their taking it over and is likely livable (since they have been living in it). Holdover squatters worry about the legal repercussions of being found out, and of someone coming to announce they now own a house to which they may be very sentimentally attached.

DIDI

Blotting—squatting the block—is a common practice among RAs in Detroit. Didi, a white woman in her sixties, lived in a house she had owned in Detroit for over thirty-five years. Didi blotted several lots adjacent to her house and occasionally salvaged materials from abandoned houses nearby. Like many other residents, her routine appropriation began slowly and expanded over the course of about two decades.

Didi recalled wistfully how her neighborhood used to be: "There were a lot of houses, a lot of people, a lot of children playing on the sidewalks. I had a lot of neighbors . . . It was much different than today . . . And you know most of my neighbors were really nice. We had no problems. I knew most, a lot of the neighbors. Many of them are gone now." She said her neighborhood started to change drastically in the '80s and '90s. She recalled riding her bike down the street one day and suddenly noticing how shabby the houses were looking, that many homeowners had moved away and "left the houses to the renters . . . That's what happened. And I almost cried, I said 'oh this is horrible' you know." As conditions in the city worsened over time, even the renters left. The houses were left vacant and decayed or were burned. Didi noted, "I just remembered being really shocked and I felt really bad that I was kind of stuck here in Detroit and things were looking that bad." She was stuck because financially she couldn't afford to leave the city and live anywhere else. She had bought her home on a land contract, paying for it over the course of ten years. She worked many different jobs over the years, generally in the "caretaking" industry, but never made much money. After her husband died, she struggled to make ends meet most of the time. But she still owned her home in Detroit outright, and there was no way she could sell it and have enough money to buy a house anywhere else.

The six lots next door to her became empty starting about fifteen to twenty years ago, she guessed, after which she and her sons started cutting the grass and taking care of them. She added matter-of-factly, "a lot of people here in Detroit do that, they'll take the vacant lots next to them and they'll take care of them, even if they don't own them." She continued,

I didn't own the lot next to my house for a long time, but I grew flowers, I had a circle of flowers. I had a picnic table. I did whatever I wanted with it. I even think I had a driveway and like the people downtown told me, they says you know it's a thirty foot lot, nobody could build on it, what are they gonna do with it? So I just took it over and used it as if I owned it for many, many years.

This is a quintessential example of how many residents blot: they use vacant land in a manner consistent with how most residents use their lots—for yard space or parking.

Blotting is a form of appropriation that is very unlikely to raise eyebrows or invite any sort of adverse response by neighbors or authorities. Growing wildflowers, as Didi does, is not a very contentious mode of informal property use. But even so, Didi encountered some obstacles in appropriating the vacant lots. She explained that about a decade ago, the city still mowed some of the vacant lots throughout the city, including, sometimes, those she was blotting. A few times the city came by and mowed down all her wildflowers. In our interview, she laughed as she recalled what happened,

> But that was back when the city was being very aggressive with their lawn-mower and they came and they cut it down. I got really upset because I'd put a sign there saying wild flowers . . . I called the inspector and he came out and looked. Now I say, "Wow, they used to actually come out and you know care about our complaints!"

She continued to explain the encounter, "Well he just come out, I showed him what happened, that they had been cut down and that I was trying to grow wildflowers, you know and he said well he's sorry, and he would convey the message saying that they weren't allowed to do that." At the time of my research, due to lack of funds, the city had shifted to only mowing a strip along the front of a vacant lot (if at all).

When she first started using the lots, Didi didn't worry about getting into trouble because "it was a long time [ago] when the city just didn't care what anyone did. It was during Kilpatrick (mayoral administration), you know, nobody cared." Slowly over time, Didi had purchased three of the lots next to her house and eventually wanted to own all six of the lots she was using. Didi said initially she just wanted to grow wildflowers and that purchasing the lots was "an idea that came to me later on." In 2002 she paid fifty dollars apiece for two of the three lots she owns, and later in 2010 was able to purchase the one immediately adjacent to her house for one hundred dollars.[7]

Didi wanted to own the other three lots that she was using, in part because she wanted to plant some trees on them but didn't want to make that kind of investment unless she knew the trees would remain hers. She detailed her plans for the six lots:

I want to take a weed whacker and I want to make some paths going through all three lots and maybe circle the rose bush and a few things. And I want to walk my dog out there through the path and maybe a few kids will go out . . . I actually would like to put signs in certain wildflowers or trees giving them identification. And so I could walk a few children through there and say look, that's a certain type of flower or that's a certain type of tree. I want to put a sign up saying "Nature Preserve."

On her motivation for these future plans Didi said, "It's for the kids. I've always did things for kids. I love kids."

Didi also frequently salvaged usable materials from vacant homes nearby to use in the lots she was blotting. The fact that this practice is a legal violation seemed barely an afterthought for her. Of one such instance, a collapsed house down the block, she explained matter-of-factly, "I went and got bricks myself. I needed some bricks, I wanted to line my garden and I'd go get some bricks and stick them in my truck. It seems to me like they're all down there and nobody cares. You know, nobody cares." I asked if she was concerned about getting into trouble for taking materials like that, and she replied, "Well I don't know why not. I mean you're looking at a pile of empty brick. Who wants them you know?" She laughed.

For many blotters like Didi, appropriation started slowly, with defensive and/or caretaking strategies.[8] But as time went on, Didi went from merely mowing lots to taking them over, cultivating them, and imagining creative ways to repurpose them. Over time, the desire to own them arose as well, which Didi pursued to ensure that she could continue her practices.

JEROME

I introduced the book with snippets of Jerome's story, but it is worth diving into more fully here to illustrate one way that RAs stumble into their practices, and how these practices can change over time into something desirable and enjoyable. Jerome, a single Black man in his forties, was born and raised in Detroit. Several generations of his family lived on the same block in Detroit, a particularly run-down area of the city that was hard hit by the foreclosure crisis. Jerome had been living in Colorado when he lost his job and moved back home with his father and much younger siblings. Soon after returning to his childhood neighborhood, he began appropriating property "by accident," as he put it.

One chilly day in October, he walked me through the gardens that spread across several lots a block down from the house he shared with his family. He explained what happened his first winter back in the city:

> That February the snow started melting a little bit and I decided to go for a walk and when I came down to the end of the block here . . . it was a bunch of trash and stuff, it was so bad that the storm drains were covered up and the water was backing up in the street and stuff. And so I'm out there with a stick cleaning it up and I'm like, "Wow this needs to be cleaned up," because I had never seen anything like that before in our neighborhood. You know even when I was a kid we always had vacant lots you know . . . most of those lots there had been vacant for at least ten to twenty years. And so I decided that when it got warmer I was going to go out there and clean 'em up.

While he talked, Jerome gestured across the lots, describing the piles of garbage from illegal dumping that used to be littered about. Illegal dumping was a huge problem in most Detroit neighborhoods at the time of my research—furniture, trash bags, bed-bug infested mattresses (often spray painted with the word "bugs" so as to kindly notify anyone who might be considering taking the mattress), or construction materials (dumped to avoid paying disposal fees for toxic chemicals). So, come March, Jerome, who was still unemployed, started to clean up the lots. His dad sent his three younger brothers out to help, asking Jerome to put them to work. Over the spring break, several other neighborhood kids joined in. By summer, they were gardening:

> I tell people it was by mistake . . . (laughter) because now I'm a community activist, I'm into food justice and it was, I mean literally it was a mistake. All I wanted to do was clean up the vacant lots and I knew I needed to find a way to keep them from dumping again, you know you can't just clean it up and expect—you know that's like having a white wall that somebody put graffiti on and you know you paint it white again and you don't expect them to come do it again. (laughter) So I figured if I plant some grass, keep the grass cut, make it like a little park, plant some flowers, maybe a couple rows of vegetables you know.

Interestingly, when Jerome first started gardening on and tending these lots, he tried to do it legally. He looked up the ownership records for all the vacant lots in that area: "I checked as soon as we started working on them, who owned them because, you know, I didn't want to do something to somebody's lot [if] they were going to come and say . . . like dig all this stuff up." He found out they were owned by the city or various banks. For the city-owned lots, he initially got an Adopt-A-Lot permit, a now-defunct city program that granted residents permission to use and take care of vacant lots throughout the city.

Jerome groaned as he explained how cumbersome the process was to get an Adopt-A-Lot permit, echoing other RAs' frustrations with interactions with the city:

> That process was crazy. I was told to go to our neighborhood City Hall, and I went there and the lady didn't know what I was talking about. I'm like "Adopt-A-Lot permit you know," and she was like, "We don't have that." She was like, "Is it anything like Farm-A-Lot?" I said, "Yes, sort of like Farm-A-Lot." "Oh we don't do that anymore." I'm like, "I know you don't do Farm-A-Lot anymore . . . but it's Adopt-A-Lot, you know, so I can cut the grass and you know trim trees and whatever." And she was like, "I don't know what you're talking about baby." I'm like okay. I go out in the parking lot, I called down to the City-County building and the lady said, "Where are you at?" I said "My neighborhood city hall, I'm trying to get Adopt-A-Lot permits," and she was like, "Go back in there and tell that woman to look in drawer A . . ." And I was like okay and I go up there and the lady opened up the drawer and she was like, "Do you see anything in here?" I was like, "Nope, there is nothing here." [The lady on the phone] said, "Well tell her to stand by the fax machine, I'm going to fax it over and tell her to make copies of it and put it in the file." (laughing) I was like, "Ah, this is crazy!"

But Jerome quickly abandoned the legal route, in part because the regulations were too stringent: "[The rules] went from just don't put anything permanent on [the lot] to don't have a compost pile, um no permanent structures, don't remove any soil, don't add any soil, you know and I'm like 'They crazy!' you know." Navigating the bureaucracy wasn't worth it, in part because Jerome realized no one cared and in part because many of the lots he was now using weren't owned by the city and thus not eligible for the Adopt-A-Lot program anyway.

Jerome wanted to own the lots but recalled being given a quote of $19,900 (in 2010) to purchase seven of them from the city. In 2013, he said they dropped that quote to $3,400 for thirteen lots. Jerome said he would pay that if he had the money. Bank of America had been telling Jerome for three years that they would donate lots to him, but it hadn't happened. He gave up bothering them because it wasn't worth his time. While Jerome didn't worry about the city or Bank of America disturbing him for using the lots, he did worry that expanding some of his farming activities might bother the neighbors and that he may eventually face obstacles for illegally using the land. He wanted to expand his activities to include chickens and goats but was concerned the neighbors may be opposed to having farm animals in their neighborhood and could push back using his illegal occupation as a basis for complaints.

Jerome quickly reiterated that his neighbors appreciated the changes the garden had brought. But he recalled that some of his neighbors were initially skeptical. "We still had people being negative because people thought I was crazy for doing the garden, you know especially in the neighborhood, 'they're not going to do nothing but tear it up . . .' Well, it wasn't like negative towards what we were doing, more of like, 'Why? You know they don't deserve it.'" I pressed him to clarify—who didn't deserve the garden? Jerome explained,

> The neighborhood . . . like you know the kids are going to tear it up. You know 'cause we had some stuff going on in this neighborhood that I had never seen before, it was like people didn't care anymore about each other, wasn't speaking to each other, you know, um, it wasn't a community anymore, everybody was distant. So like we have an older guy, you know a senior citizen and he was like, "They're going to tear it up Jerome, you shouldn't do this you know," and I'm like, "Well I'm going to do it, if they tear it up I'll put it back."

Jerome smiled broadly and added, "But now, [my neighbor is] like 'I am so proud of you, this is amazing, it reminds me of where I grew up,' cause he grew up down south."

Gardening was something Jerome figured out along the way to continue protecting and cultivating the lots he and the neighborhood kids had cleaned up. He recalled that most of his initial knowledge came to him from years helping his grandmother in her backyard garden as a child. But after he began putting more time and effort into growing food on these lots, he reached out to local agriculture nonprofits for guidance. Other times, he learned through trial and error. He shook his head as he recounted: "Over the years I have made mistakes. I used to go pick up brew waste [from a local brewery] and dump them into the compost pile and not mix it up properly and then come back . . . like people walking through like, 'Oh God, oh my God you need to be in the country!' because the smell was so bad." Since Jerome started off without funding or resources for his garden, supplies were frequently salvaged from other run-down properties, and the water for the garden was often procured from the fire hydrants on the block.

Jerome's informal practices began as a burdensome activity aimed at making up for the city's failure to maintain vacant property nor hold legal owners, like Bank of America, responsible for doing so. But over time, it grew into something he enjoyed and wanted to sustain (somewhat akin to how LAs feel about their practices). This doesn't happen for all RAs, but it is useful to think about the potential for improving RAs experiences with informality.

ARTISTIC BLOTTERS

There are myriad ways in which artists have made use of Detroit's built environment: for supplies, for workspace, as a backdrop for installations, or even as canvas, from alleyway graffiti projects to painted butterflies on deteriorated buildings. Many of these projects can be understood as individual or community efforts to draw attention to the vacant and abandoned structures in their neighborhoods that are eyesores for neighbors, or even sites of crime and violence. And even residents who may not consider themselves artists per se, including some RAs, have used art as a way to combat problems in their neighborhoods. Several such residents I spoke with mentioned being inspired by The Heidelberg Project, a cluster of blocks on the East Side of Detroit where longtime resident and artist Tyree Guyton has repurposed found objects from vacant buildings around the properties to call attention to the vacancy and deterioration that was slowly overtaking his neighborhood.[9]

One such resident, Delilah, was a single Black woman in her fifties who had lived in Detroit all her life. Like many other Detroiters, she was frustrated with the increasing vacancy, arson, and dumping in her neighborhood. Mortgage foreclosures began ravaging her already distressed neighborhood in the mid-2000s. Vacant houses were quickly scrapped and/or burned. The empty house next door to her was often occupied by very transient people using drugs, and Delilah didn't feel safe with strangers going in and out of the spaces so near her home.

Years of telling drug users to scram, of asking "Who are you and what are you doing here?" got her nowhere. Calls to the city were futile. She considered burning the house down but was afraid the heat would damage her house (having seen this happen in other instances around her neighborhood). So, Delilah decided to take a cue from Tyree Guyton and clean up the exterior of the empty house next door to her and the vacant lot on the other side of the empty house. She affixed items she found in the vacant lot to the empty house—things like discarded toys and rusted bicycle parts. She explained,

> What choice did I have? There was nobody that really cared about the community. It was nobody that was doing anything, there was nobody that was making a difference in that community. There was no government funding coming into that community, so the hell with the permission. It's like I'm just going to start doing something and we'll see what happens.

This sentiment mirrors what a representative from The Heidelberg Project told me regarding others who have adopted Guyton's approach to creating art with and from abandonment and vacancy. She verbalized the organization's "official stance" being one that advocates following the law but expressed how frustrating that approach was for Guyton. She said,

> Well listen, I want to be very clear that we're not advocating for this whole guerilla method. We wanted to do things the right way, but no one was listening and then when people started listening it just wasn't happening . . .

Delilah didn't want to own the property next door, she just wanted people to leave it alone or the city to step in and do their job taking care of it. She said over time she added some whimsical paint to the front of the house and other found objects from around her neighborhood: she put up a fake Christmas tree on the front stoop during the holiday season and arranged broken chairs and a table on the lawn, taken from a pile of household wares discarded on the sidewalk after an eviction on the next block. She said the result of her interventions were positive. She believed the items adorning the vacant house next door stopped the drug users and other transient people going in and out, and that this was an example of how "people can transform their own surroundings and they don't have to wait for someone to step in and do it."

Other residents have worked collaboratively to use art to intervene in the problems in their neighborhoods. Wes, a white man in his late thirties who had lived in the city for about a decade, helped organize residents in his and nearby neighborhoods to decorate blighted houses. He recounted that this approach came as a response to residents saying, "What am I going to do with this burned house in our community? What are *we* going to do with this burned house in the community?" This is indicative of the fact that *residents* are taking on these problem properties, not the city or other authorities. Wes and other residents worked with some activists/ artists who helped guide discussions about what to do. They decided to first just try to call attention to the "middle ground" blight that is overlooked: the houses that aren't yet structurally dangerous enough to draw the attention of authorities, but that have deteriorated enough that they also don't draw the attention of investors. They began decorating the houses with all sorts of found objects—playful pieces one wouldn't expect to find on a house. Wes explained their surprise at the result:

> We actually didn't know that by bringing attention to them, we didn't necessarily think about it, [but] makes sense that this would happen, then the city came behind us and tore them down. So that was fine because did we really want a house covered in old CDs for very long? So it was fine . . . these needed to come down. So they just didn't tear down that house, they tore down all the houses nearby it so then the community began to see they do have the power to change their context by doing an action to it.

I asked if Wes thought that the city was intentionally targeting the houses they had decorated for demolition. He replied,

> I would say yes, and I don't mean that in a negative way. Like when we would be working on the houses, the police would come up to us and ask us

what we're doing. We'd tell them and they'd say, "That's cool," and they'd leave. They weren't like saying, "What are you doing?" (in a mean voice). Fire people came up and asked and we would tell them, the same reaction—"That's cool." They see that the community was doing positive acts in their neighborhood.

RAs informally use property as an everyday response to negative aspects of life in Detroit, often the result of failures at the institutional level. RAs' practices are aimed at improving stability, security, comfort, and the conditions of one's personal situation, block, or neighborhood. Demolishers like Chuck or residents like Delilah want to increase the safety of their immediate block. Blotters like Didi or gardeners like Jerome want to clean up and take care of vacant lots that the city has ignored. Some RAs experience economic instability, but they are not dependent on appropriation for survival (like NAs are). RAs like Scott scrap from time to time to help make ends meet in a city with few economic opportunities. Holdover squatters like Maxine's family try to save money on rent by remaining in a property after foreclosure. Or, like Terrence, they may try to retain control over a property they are attached to even if they lost legal right to it. RAs labor to make the best of the conditions in a city like Detroit.

Most RAs don't suffer under the same difficult condition of appropriation as NAs do. Holdover squatters' houses are at least already livable (though commonly still sub-standard) and often had utilities connected. Demolition isn't by any means a safe practice, but the RAs in my study had some tools, often worked collectively, and could disengage if the practice was too risky. Informal demolition predominately targeted houses, which may be less risky than trying to extract steel I-beams from industrial buildings like some NA scrappers do. RA blotters, gardeners, and artists didn't tend to engage in particularly risky or difficult practices. Furthermore, some RAs came to appreciate their practices over the years, and what was initially frustrating became enjoyable—a feature which some RAs shared with LAs. Didi, for example, initially was just caring for lots neglected by the city. But now she owns several and appreciates the opportunity to grow wildflowers. Over the years, Jerome has become an avid gardener. Another was able to turn her gardening activities into a nonprofit that provides her some income.

PART III

Informal Plans and
Formal Policies

8 Surviving the City or Settling the City?

The timing of this research bridged Detroit hitting rock bottom and its purported rebirth. Media headlines proclaimed that "Detroit is Cool Again,"[1] that it is "Better Than Any Other US City,"[2] and hailed "The Spirit and Promise of Detroit."[3] This shift has brought new attention to and concern with what these changes will look like: what kind of city will Detroit be in this new era? And whose imagined futures have weight? Conflicts over just this question abound in historical and contemporary examples of urban change. In studies of gentrification—urban spaces that are revitalizing while experiencing an influx of new residents—many of these conflicts reflect longtime residents' and newcomers' differing ideas about what a street or neighborhood should be like. These conflicts aren't just about competing visions for the future of one's city as laid out in planning documents, they are also embodied in the everyday practices with which residents continually shape and remake their city from the ground up. In my study, appropriators' informal practices reveal differing ideas about what the city is and how it ought to be, cleaving along the lines of longtime residents and newcomers.

Informal property use is one way in which Detroiters remake their city and shape it in accordance with their various wants and needs. When residents informally use property, they navigate around the legal/regulatory obstacles that may hinder their goals. But, as we saw in Part II of this book, the informal practices of property appropriators differ in important ways that cannot be fully understood simply by considering what laws or regulations are broken, avoided, or subverted. For example, Lifestyle Appropriators, Routine Appropriators, and Necessity Appropriators all trespass when they squat, but their practices are significantly different. How appropriators understand their practices to be responding to the city and shaping its future also differ. At this crux in Detroit's history, how does property informality influence, reflect, or dovetail with appropriators' different goals and varied visions for the future of their city?

In this chapter, I analyze appropriators' narratives to access these differing future visions. Narrative analysis—examining the way people construct and tell stories about themselves and their actions—enables us to consider these practices closer to the standpoint of appropriators, rather than with reference to an external rubric or measure like the law. I propose that using narrative analysis to uncover the latent "planning by doing" that appropriators embody with their practices demonstrates one way to begin to make sense of the broader significance of the variation across different modes of informality and informal practitioners.

This narrative analysis reveals that appropriators have very different understandings of the city, their informal practices, the law, and their futures. In her book *Cheating Welfare*, Kaaryn Gustafson analyzes rule-breaking among welfare recipients, demonstrating how differing backgrounds, resources, and knowledge shape how recipients "engage" with rule-breaking and their normative interpretations of their violations.[4] In Detroit, appropriators' spatial history with the city (how long they've lived in Detroit and why—i.e., by choice or by circumstance) intersects with their varying levels of privilege and poverty and results in very different views of the city as obstacle or opportunity. These differences significantly shape appropriators' informal practices and how they understand their practices to be not just meeting their own needs or wants but intervening in and reflective of the way they believe the city *ought* to be. As more privileged newcomers to the city who desire to be there, LAs understand the city to be a *terra nullius* opportunity and themselves to be new-age pioneers who come to Settle the City. Longtime residents (or impoverished newcomers who moved to the city as a last resort) understand the city to be, in part, a space of obstacles, and themselves and their practices to be directed toward Surviving the City. Understanding informality in the Global North requires attending to these variations among informal property users and how their practices are shaped by and aim to reshape the city.

USING NARRATIVE ANALYSIS TO UNDERSTAND INFORMALITY

The informal practices of middle-class residents are commonly privileged as a kind of urbanism from the ground up and given epistemic weight, as evidenced by the growing recognition of the value of community participation in urban planning.[5] Yet the informal strategies of the poor are not rigorously considered as having anything to offer urban planning or policy-making in the Global North.[6] Scholars concerned with informality in the Global South have long conceptualized informality as "a form of direct planning-by-doing undertaken by disadvantaged urban residents who may otherwise have little ability to communicate their needs to planners and policymakers,"[7] and a similar epistemic inclusion is needed in the United States as well, especially in cities wrestling with persistent social problems and widening inequalities.

Giving epistemic weight to the informal practices of LAs, RAs, and NAs requires trying to uncover the latent (or explicit) *planning-by-doing* that appropriators bring into being through their practices. To achieve this, I argue that scholars need to consider how informal actors understand their own practices as ontologically and epistemologically situated engagements in and with their city. That is, we need to draw out how informality grows from actors' different ways of *being in* and *knowing of* the city and how they understand their informal practices to be responding to, intervening in, and/or shaping the city in a way they believe it *ought* to be (a future-oriented normative claim). While Part II of this book described the motives and experiences of appropriators to illustrate the varied practices that are the focus of this study, this chapter uncovers how they understand their practices in relation to the city, the law, and their future visions for both.

Some legal scholars argue there is much to be learned from law-break-ing, even beyond examples of civil disobedience that are often viewed as exceptional and socially just.[8] In their book *Property Outlaws*, legal schol-ars Eduardo Peñalver and Sonia Katyal write that, similar to judges, lawbreakers engage in legal interpretation when they pursue their own normative visions through their actions in the world.[9] Because we live in a "nomos" (normative world), legal scholar Robert Cover writes, "law and narrative are inseparably related. Every prescription is insistent in its demand to be located in discourse—to be supplied with history and des-tiny, beginning and end, explanation and purpose. And every narrative is insistent in its demand for its prescriptive point, its moral."[10] Analyzing the narratives of appropriators helps to identify and understand these alternate interpretations of law. And, because these stories are constructed by the teller, sociologists Patricia Ewick and Susan Silbey argue that they also reveal "the social organization of power that sustains the world as it is experienced and known,"[11] to that person (their ontological and epistemo-logical situated-ness). That is, when appropriators tell their stories—of how they came to be in Detroit and why they started squatting, for example—they also articulate an understanding of the obstacles and opportunities the world (or, in this case, the city of Detroit) presents to them. Narratives articulate a storyteller's sense of self through the con-struction of stories that place her within broader social structures, space and time, networks of relationships, axes of power, existing norms, and opportunities for resistance.[12]

I first analyze the stories of LAs, who understand themselves to be akin to settlers—pioneers who venture into the wild, vacant city and tame it with their appropriation of urban property. Then I move on to assess the stories of NAs and RAs, who largely understand themselves as survivors of a failed city, whose practices are only necessary insofar as the city has failed its responsibilities and they are forced to negotiate and navigate these con-straining conditions. These worldviews exist in tension with each other in terms of their future orientations: their trajectories. Settling the City is a story of opportunity—taking over "the good land" to prosper and flourish. Surviving the City is a story of struggle and perseverance to make-do in a city that has all but collapsed, using methods that appropriators largely hope to move beyond; to improve past. Settling the City requires some of these conditions to persist (in some form or another) so they can continue desirable practices, while Surviving the City entails hope for moving beyond the current conditions and these often-burdensome survival practices. I conclude by discussing a few deviant cases of NAs and RAs, which offer insights that are informative for policy responses.

NEWCOMERS: SETTLING THE CITY

Colonial imagery has long been used to describe urban processes that entail the confrontation of newcomers and longtime residents. Gentrification, in particular, has been portrayed using colonial language, characterizing first-wave (and subsequent) gentrifiers, their practices, and their views of longtime residents/established neighborhoods. Early gentrifiers have been called (and call themselves) "pioneers,"[13] who tame the savage wilderness of the ghetto.[14] Many gentrifiers embrace what sociologist Daphne Spain calls the "frontier and salvation" mentality,[15] wherein newcomers understand themselves to be investing sweat equity into improving (and saving) their new homes and neighborhoods. To some gentrifiers, longtime residents are akin to "natives" whose presence poses obstacles to improving the neighborhoods they settle.[16]

At this time, it is unclear what role LAs will play in Detroit's revitalization. But, like early or "first-wave"[17] gentrifiers in other studies, they deploy colonial language and ideals as they narrate their informal practices, implicitly embracing what geographer Neil Smith refers to as the simultaneously dangerous and romantic ethos of the cowboy.[18] This ethos appeals to disaffected middle-class urbanites, who venture into the frontier (the urban "edge" of profitability, to Smith). Many LAs draw on the language and ideals of settler colonialism to frame what they are doing when they appropriate property and why it is just.

As one of many settler societies across the globe, settler colonialism in the United States has shaped many historical events, practices, and values that continue to undergird various aspects of contemporary society. Settler colonialism is a historical process of territorial seizure, native erasure, and population resettlement.[19] In other forms of colonialism, colonists set up avenues for resource extraction and labor exploitation and return to the metropole once these are solidified or exhausted. In contrast, settler colonists arrive with the intent to *stay*, to create a new society.[20] To do so, they must take control of land from native denizens to create space for their settlement. This land/territory is portrayed as vacant, empty, or disused—a *terra nullius* (no man's land)—to delegitimate native property relations. Through the lens of western liberalism, legitimate private property ownership requires "productive use" which is earned through settlement, cultivation, and investment. This ideology was used to justify settlers' appropriation of native land.[21] Research has noted the problematic orientation toward portraying declining/shrinking cities as "vacant," as this can be a rhetorical tool for promoting "revitalization" projects that perpetuate inequalities, like gentrification and displacement.[22]

In LA narratives, these settler colonial relations (to people and to land/property) are rearticulated as: Detroit is the frontier, LAs are pioneers, and they earn the right to be there by settling—intending to remain—and productively using the property they take over, thereby taming and improving the frontier.

Opportunity from Decline: Detroit as the Urban Frontier

When LAs discuss what the city is to them, they also reveal how they understand themselves in relation to the sociostructural conditions of Detroit. As (relatively) more privileged outsiders, they have not been burdened by the obstacles of life in Detroit for decades and instead see the city as an enticing opportunity for (re)settling the wild, wild (mid) west and playing out fantasies of themselves as new-age pioneers.

LAs in Detroit appreciate many of the conditions that decline has created—to outsiders, these are opportunities. While longtime resident appropriators reference the distressed conditions of the city as constraining obstacles, LAs reference many of these same conditions positively. Salvager Knox explained,

> I like the fact that the city is relatively unpopulated, given its size. I like the fact that half the stoplights don't work (short laugh) so you can proceed down the roadways at your own discretion. Um, I like the history and the current makeup of the city. I like being able to move through urban space at my own discretion without as many borders or boundaries that you would

encounter in more densely populated cities . . . I like the environment that has been created by the fallout of Fordist Production.

To newcomers, Detroit offers sociospatial conditions that may be starkly different from what they experienced in other places—but that they appreciate. They like the space, the vacancy, the lax municipal regulations, and what they see as opportunity to create something new. Former squatter (now homeowner) John countered Detroit with the typical suburban place where he grew up, complaining of its strict rules about manicured lawns and the like. He said that one of the things that drew him to the city was "the kind of downfall of this city and the kind of new ways people are trying to make it work in maybe something a little different than you would have in your other large cities that are more established and, kind of, have this very set order, I guess."

To John and many other LAs, the conditions of Detroit open up possibilities—socially and spatially. The vacancy that characterizes many of Detroit's neighborhoods creates the space wherein to remake the world in line with individual and collective visions. But, because Detroit is not actually *empty*, this orientation conceptually erases the presence and value of longtime residents. Homesteader and salvager Oliver, for example, told me, "I decided to live [in Detroit] because I want a space to start creating what I consider like my own vision for the world . . . There is just so much potential in this neighborhood [which] is essentially a completely—not completely but *largely*—abandoned neighborhood . . . You can just see and feel by being there, a potential." Oliver stopped short of verbally erasing his neighbors; it is true that his block had a high vacancy rate.

Sociologist Derek Hyra argues that the rebranding of Black "ghetto neighborhoods" has incited more white residents to move to them, seeking to be part of neighborhoods with "authentic" Black culture.[23] But in Detroit, newcomer appropriators tend to portray Detroit as appealing not *because* of its legacy as Motown, for example, but for its "emptiness." I find that the only aspect of a "ghetto neighborhood" these newcomer appropriators are really drawn to is the deteriorated built environment and high vacancy rates. In addition to reproducing problematic stereotypes of Black neighborhoods (as Hyra finds), some newcomer appropriators in my study engage in ideological erasure of longtime Detroiters.

In this *terra nullius,* LAs understand themselves to be remaking sociospatial relationships and creating new ways of being in/with the world and each other. Sarah, the farmer, offered her take on Detroit saying, "It's a city in an interesting time. Like industry is dying and failing and it's probably a model for a bunch of other cities. So, it's like what, what next, what do we do? Like the local government is, you know," she shrugged and laughed, reflecting her expressed view that Detroit's government is inept. She continued,

> So what do you do as a group of people? How can you do things on your own? Because I think that's what it's going to come down to, like these other systems aren't sustainable and they're not going to last forever. So I think now, before that collapse happens, relearning all these skills that we used to know that we're so removed from. Like reestablishing a relationship with your land base, reestablishing your relationship with your community. I see that more here than I do in cities maybe that are functioning more ... because you kind of have to, it's more of a DIY culture.

Sarah identifies a do-it-yourself culture in Detroit—an approach that, in the urban context, frequently grows from situations where government and institutions are failing to provide.[24] But she added that "getting your neighbors to help you . . . find an alternative way to heat your home . . . and doing it because you need to survive. Like that is fun, first of all." Viewing DIY utility/food procurement methods as "fun" rather than burdensome is a key difference from longtime resident appropriators. Championing DIY practices can implicitly support neoliberal abdication of social responsibilities by government, which disproportionately harms the least well-off, who may lack the resources to procure these services or necessities on their own.[25]

Detroit is imagined as a place where one's rough-it, self-reliant, live-off-the-land pioneering aspirations can be realized. But many LAs go a step further to imagine their informal practices as integral to helping "fix" Detroit, as a possible way up from the depths of decline. This savior-esque mentality is also reminiscent of colonialism, where settlers "bring" civilization to natives, who are implicitly (or explicitly) perceived as "backwards." Oliver explained,

> You see Detroit and it does look like a war zone and I feel that's exactly what it is and the people that have been here for so long are like, they're like the warriors after a long hard battle, they got post-traumatic stress disorder and

they tell us about all these experiences that happened, going through this. But once we talk to them more and more and like express our visions and our dreams and they get really excited and like wide-eyed and they're all about it, they're all about the like beautiful energy that's coming to them.

Oliver discussed bringing a new vision and "beautiful energy" to the bedraggled residents, asserting his vision for the city as the way forward and added, "It's time to create, you know, a new world." Oliver's orientation toward the city reflects the values shared by the LAs in my study. Detroit is a blank slate opportunity to create something new, and LAs promote progress in the city by enacting a new way of being in the world— one based in pioneering principles like self-reliance, doing things off-the-grid or in unconventional ways, and making good with the resources one has around them (the "resources" left by the city's decay). Furthermore, and perhaps most problematically, some LAs understand themselves to be "bringing" this change or vision to the prior inhabitants of Detroit to save them. The way LAs explain what the city is to them reveals their relative privilege, occupying a structural position outside of and unconstrained by the conditions of the city.

Settlers Remaking the City in Their Vision

LAs understand their pioneering/settler practices to be positively shaping this wild, *terra nullius* through their appropriation; they believe these practices to be good for the city and something that *ought* to continue and expand. *Ought* is a temporal (futural) and normative claim, revealed in the ways that LAs legitimate their informal appropriation via narratives of productive use and plans to *settle*—to continue these practices in the future. Their practices are evidence of a particular vision of the way forward for Detroit: what the city needs is sweat-equity and investment, long-term commitments to productive use of property, and a do-it-yourself ethos which doesn't rely on dominant, mainstream ways of being or doing.

Reflecting and promoting the idea of the right to property being rooted in settlement, investment, and productive use, the Homestead Act of 1862 aimed to stimulate the development of the western United States.

"Homesteaders" could gain legal title of up to 160 acres of land provided they built a house, farmed at least ten acres, and lived on the land for five years.[26] In helping bring about the Homestead Act, settlers argued that "the claims of those who actually work the land should take precedence over the fungible interests of absentee land speculators."[27] LAs reiterate similar understandings of what legitimates their informal claims to property (over and above the city or absentee owners), but they expand their notions of "investment" in a multifaceted way to include labor, resources, time, money and emotional investment.[28] Salvager Knox even referenced Locke as he reflected on his practices:

> [Salvaging] is more of a mindset in relation to finding material that's out in a state of disuse, recognizing that you can put it back into use, by mixing your labor with it to use a formulation from Locke ... Taking something that has unquestionably fallen to such a state of disuse, that it's like fruit that's rotting on the ground. And the existing norms and laws and rules say it's illegal to do that.

Knox explained that he felt right salvaging materials from abandoned buildings because he believed they were literally being wasted. He viewed his practice as having rescued a valuable resource, putting it to good use in his own property as he invested in it. For LAs like Knox, salvaging is a practice that treats the ruins of the city as a kind of urban resource to accumulate and reinvest. Salvagers invest by mixing their labor with the appropriated property to create something of value. For Knox, the objects of value were his home-remodeling projects, which increased the use and exchange values of his home, and for artists like William it was creating works of art.

Seeing opportunity in Detroit's environment, homeowners and farmers Fern and Rita reflected upon how they felt about the fact that squatting vacant lots to farm them violated property laws. Fern said, "It's just sitting there empty, why not plant some fruit trees or something? It's only a good thing." LAs subvert the normativity of the law to rearticulate their informal property claims as moral.

John had purchased the house he homesteaded from an investor who had bought the house as part of a bundle of fifteen houses at the county property auction. Only wanting a few of those properties, the investor never even visited the house John and his friend Rob were occupying, leaving it vacant and unprotected to deteriorate. John explained how he felt about the fact that he had been illegally occupying his house. He said, "I think in this situation it's totally good. I mean, the person who owned it, you know, he legally owned it—he didn't morally have a correct stance." John believed his practices to be moral even though illegal. Like most LAs, John did not fault the institution of private property per se, but instead problematized that the law protects the rights of owners who are not caring for or productively using their properties. Homesteader Allen reiterated this idea when discussing his house:

> It was abandoned for years. And at some point you've lost your rights to it. Legally I don't know, it was technically not legal, but I feel no harm taking these lots and doing something great with them. You've lost your rights. Sorry, but you know if you're not going to take care of your property, it's not yours anymore.

Allen knew that he technically did not have the law on his side, but he rearticulated what the right to property *should* entail.

The temporality with which LAs envision and carry out their practices is central to their claims to property. Colonial settlers—pioneers of the American West—didn't earn the right to property by just using it and tossing it aside. They did so by cultivating it over time, protecting it, and "improving" it for the future. LAs are oriented toward establishing a long-term, future relationship with the properties they take over, which they believed to be the morally just way to engage in these practices. When LAs informally use property, they do so in part to create what they imagine to be "the good life." This means that LAs choose this option among other ways of living and want to maintain the lifestyle they've created.

In her study of similar neighborhoods in Philadelphia, Debbie Becher finds that citizens and officials imagine property as a vessel for investment of value over time.[29] As explained in chapter 6, LAs tend to invest significant time and resources into the property they appropriate, such as by completely remodeling a house to live in or cultivating large gardens/farms or even in the careful salvaging of materials for creative projects. Investing in their properties entails at least some imagined future with the property, such that the investment would "pay out" either in use-value or exchange-value. Beyond that, LAs describe their practices as ones that, because they enjoy them, they want to be able to continue. They want to establish a kind of rootedness in Detroit, which also helps to justify informally appropriating property—its good because it's for the future, not just for right now. For example, farmer Rita discussed the lots she and her husband took over:

> Our intentions were to have them and to have them forever. So it was fine. And we always had the intention of making it home, you know like this is our home and this is where we want to feed ourselves and feed our children and so it seems like that's such an honest and legitimate reason to, to take a space. You know if we had been like, "Oh let's build a condo and then turn it over," you know like if it was just for the sake of money or exploiting something I think it would be different, but we always just felt completely honest about it all and so that made it not even a question in my mind if it was right.

Rita and her husband felt their practices were right in part because they intended to productively use the properties they took over for the long term—rather than using them temporarily in an extractive manner (i.e., the reference to flipping a condo). Urban agriculture in and of itself is indicative of a future commitment because it takes time to prepare the land, plant the seeds, and to reap the benefits of one's time and labor. Invoking their children as part of this justificatory framework further reiterates the settler mentality—with children, one settles down and stays put for a while.

Homesteader Allen reiterated this idea that long-term investments legitimate informal property claims, interrupting me after I used the term "squatting":

> So I still take issue with that term squatting because I think, I really do think there's two classifications . . . cause I've seen squatters, they just come into a house, they destroy it, whatever, they don't care. But this (he gestured around his kitchen where we sat) is like settling down and you may or may not be there forever but you're going to leave the place better. So I, I hate the term squatting. I mean I think there's a legitimate squat. If you're going into a place and you're just using it and you're destroying it or you're just using it with no intention of making it better—of claiming it eventually—then yes that's squatting.

Allen specified that homesteading entails "settling down," "making it better," and "claiming it eventually"—all involving improvement and a futural relationship. To Allen, these components made illegal appropriation moral. This is also an example of the discord that may arise across various kinds of property informality: Allen denigrated squatters who don't strive to claim their properties.

The idea of ownership is intertwined with how LAs envision their future relationships to the properties they appropriate. Ownership is a common goal among LAs who occupy land or buildings. Nearly all occupier LAs in my study specifically sought out properties that they expected would be coming up for sale soon at the county property auction so they could try to purchase them. NAs also often sought out properties that were tax delinquent. But, as the next section will discuss, rather than expecting to be able to purchase them at the auction, they often did so hoping they would have several years to occupy a house before it was possibly going to be purchased by someone else at the auction.

LAs who are illegally occupying property purchase the land or houses to be able to continue their practices. This is a simple point but one that is very important: because LAs *enjoy* and *desire* what informal appropriation allows them to do, they want to continue these practices for the future—even in the face of other opportunities (like buying a house in the suburbs or renting an apartment downtown). The urban pioneering/settler lifestyle does not depend on the ability to do these practices informally or illegally. For some, the illegal nature was fun and exciting, but it was not why they squatted or started gardening in the first place. Rather, informally appropriating property enabled them to move ahead with their desired practices without being encumbered by institutional hurdles and slow bureaucracy.

As new-age settlers or pioneers, LAs deploy informal property appropriation as a means for fulfilling their dreams/goals and for carrying out their visions for the city. For them, the city is a blank slate, an opportunity, a space where they can create a new world as they see fit, unencumbered by the obstacles of expensive property, homeowners' association rules, and mainstream lifestyles/values. The ability to experience Detroit's conditions as an opportunity is reflective of their sociostructural positions of

relative privilege which affords them the choice to engage with these conditions, and wherein these conditions—of economic hardship and few job
opportunities, institutional racism and disinvestment, violence and a
deteriorated, unsafe environment, etc.—have not circumscribed their
lives. Property becomes a resource that they take over to create homes,
fuel their art and home renovation projects, or feed and support themselves. Illegality is not a necessary component of their practices, but rather
negotiating around property laws enables them to realize their goals more
efficiently. They pick and choose when to participate in formal, legal property relations and when to transgress them. LAs understand their practices as a way to achieve their personal dreams and desires, but also as a
way to help tame some of the problems in the city by improving property.
To acquire property in a moral way requires investment: labor, resources,
time, and a future commitment.[30] Settling Detroit is the way forward.
LAs do not shy away from property ownership, instead it is more accurate
to describe informal appropriation as an avenue toward solidifying ownership—a practice which aligns with their commitments to future productive use and investment.

LONGTIME RESIDENTS: SURVIVING THE CITY

For longtime residents of Detroit, the obstacles of the city have influenced
their lives in a much more salient way in comparison to newcomers who
grew up or lived for a long time in less disadvantaged spaces. Racism,
suburbanization, and the deindustrialization of cities like Detroit came to
a peak around the 1950s, spawning a process wherein whites and those
with capital left the city for the suburbs, leaving behind what William
Julius Wilson calls the "jobless ghetto."[31] According to Wilson, prior to the
1960s, "institutional ghettos" were pockets of poverty within the urban
landscape which contained all the institutional elements of thriving
neighborhoods, just in worse condition: schools, libraries, grocery stores,
and even employed residents. Post white/capital-flight and concerted disinvestment,[32] urban areas like Detroit were left with jobless ghettos, more
extreme in condition and harmful in effect than institutional ghettos
because the institutional elements of daily life were no longer present

(libraries closed, grocery stores were replaced by quickie marts and liquor stores, check n' cashes replaced banks), and daily life was no longer structured by the rhythm of nine-to-five employment (even very low-wage employment).

The result is that Detroit is a quintessential example of a city with many neighborhoods suffering from what scholars call concentrated disadvantage.[33] Concentrated disadvantage is an indicator of the level of deprivation of a geographic area, measured along dimensions such as poverty, joblessness, educational opportunities, crime, and health. The concentration of these disadvantages exposes residents to negative social conditions more extreme than the "sum of their parts" because the social ties that often help residents manage disadvantages diminish as well.[34] Longtime residents of Detroit have had their lives shaped by these various intersecting, accumulating disadvantages.

Studies of life in disadvantaged neighborhoods show that residents deploy many strategies to aid their survival and well-being;[35] in Detroit, informal appropriation is but one of these strategies. In Necessity and Routine Appropriators' narratives (as predominately longtime Detroiters, which I shorten to "longtimers"), their law-breaking is moral by right of need and immediate context: the malfunctioning of Detroit's government, corrupt authorities, and few formal opportunities for cultivating and improving individual and community well-being. Research finds that actors often justify rule-breaking by deference to need; and indeed, there is legal basis for such an argument.[36] But struggling to meet needs and navigate a difficult sociospatial environment means that Surviving the City is also a story that these longtime residents hope will soon come to an end.

Responding to Decline: How to Survive Detroit

When asked how they felt about Detroit, many longtime residents—even very poor residents—expressed feelings of warmth and love for the city. It was their home, their extended family lived close by, etc. Many had even experienced or grew up hearing stories of Detroit's vibrance in the mid-twentieth century. Some felt optimistic about Detroit's future. But all noted the many obstacles and hardships the city had presented them with and had done so for decades. When I asked Routine Appropriator Ted what opportunities Detroit had to offer, he responded by shaking his head and replying, "Nothing. I mean I done looked everywhere for opportunity and opportunity just looked over me so I'm just here like passing time and all, but eventually . . ." Rather than cite the conditions of decline and deindustrialization as an opportunity for her to create art as LAs do, RA Delilah explained the conditions of her neighborhood this way:

> It's the flight, it's the flight. People call it white flight, but it's quite frankly anybody who's able to leave because you can't exist in a neighborhood where there once stood sixty houses and now there's four. There's not city services and so people walk away and then that land reverts back to the city for nonpayment of taxes.

To RAs like Delilah, their practices respond to what they view as very undesirable conditions, not enticing opportunities. This is very different from LAs, reflective of how different categories of appropriators emplace themselves in social structures when they narrate their informal practices. NAs and RAs express feeling constrained by the conditions of Detroit: it can be a difficult place to live, a city with few opportunities and many hardships.

It is illuminating, then, the way that newcomer and longtimer appropriators create different connections in their stories between the morality of their practices and the conditions of the city. LAs spoke of the city's conditions as a blank slate, and in this *terra nullius* their practices are moral because they make future commitments to and investments in property. But in NAs and RAs stories, they link the conditions of the city so tightly with the normativity of their de jure illegal practices that I could not disentangle these ideas in their stories: appropriation is moral because they are responding to the conditions of the city, not because they are creating a new future alternative. Scrapper Bond explained his views on his practices:

> People shouldn't blame the scrappers that the city look bad. They should blame the city-county government.[37] That's what I say. Scrappers didn't do it. City-county done did it—stole all that money, made all the people leave they houses and all them homes just sitting there. That's how it started . . . That's how people wind up leaving—forced to leave because they ain't paid their taxes. Now the houses are sitting there. Who own it—the bank or the

city in Michigan owns it? Now the guys sitting around here looking at that house [thinking], "Ain't nobody staying here, we're going to scrap it." That's how it started. It would've never started if [the government] wouldn't been taking all that money. If they had been doing the right thing with that money . . . when Washington sent them millions to here years ago.[38] That was supposed to been for the potholes and the demolition. They supposed to demolition all these homes that was standing there 'cause people started dumping bodies in them. They supposed to tore them down but they kept stealing the money.

Bond blamed institutions and authorities for the local conditions that have enabled scrapping, referencing factors such as city authorities and banks that foreclose properties and kick people out of their houses, exacerbating vacancy. He blamed a legacy of corrupt government for the conditions within which he and others have to survive.

When NA Marsey talked about the illegality of squatting, she subverted its pejorative, criminal association by calling into question other harmful aspects of the city that persist under existing conditions. She declared passionately,

The city don't care. The banks don't care. Nobody cares. Where do it become illegal? Really? But yet it's legal for drug dealers to go in there . . . It's legal for it to be an eyesore to the community. That's the illegal shit allowing it to be legal.

Marsey delegitimated powerful city authorities and institutions, positioning squatting as a legitimate response to their failures and ineptitude. Other NAs and RAs specifically referenced the morality of illegal property use. When former squatter Lisa discussed her views on squatting, she juxtaposed other local problems with the morality of fulfilling one's duties and responsibilities. She explained,

It matters [that squatting is illegal], but certain situations force a person to do what they have to do, because it was illegal for the balloon [mortgage] payments that they played on people. It was illegal for [government] funds to be misplaced that supposed to came here to help community. It's illegal for when Obama sent 90 million dollars here to help people that foreclosed on their houses and they just sat on the money.[39] That was immoral you know. It's immoral for us to be an Emergency Manager State and all the money [go] back. Why does the money keep going back if we're so broke you know? So morally you do what you got to do. You know, but legally who's doing something illegally now? You know what I'm saying?

In the same breath, Lisa switched from commenting on what she viewed as illegal practices of local government, to their immorality, to the morality of the practices residents use to navigate these conditions.

Despite their feelings of moral legitimacy, and partially faulting institutional actors, appropriators aren't protected from, at times, being subject to regulatory enforcement that brings glaring contradictions to light. Marsey is one of the squatters in my study who recounted several run-ins with the police. In one instance, a police officer over-stepped and arrested her (charges were dropped). She explained that, in a context wherein these other "real" problems are prevalent, her actions are a solution to the problems facing city residents:

> You know, where's the crime? It's a crime cause I'm trying to survive. I'm trying to live. We gonna make it a crime—really? . . . And people need to get over it. People need to understand that for every situation, there's a solution. But if you do nothing about it, nothing changes. And at some point when a person leap out on faith to make a change, some support should be given.

RA Delilah made a similar connection in how she narrated the conditions of the city within which her appropriation practices arose: she argued that informal property use is a rational response to the conditions of Detroit. Delilah passionately explained,

> When you're able as a lawmaker to get back up on your own damn feet, then you can start, you know, administering or enforcing a law that helps people continue to be civil because this is not—what the lawmakers are doing now—it's not civilized. It's not civilized to have thirty thousand abandoned houses over here, and thirty thousand people on the street and you're saying that you can't go here and do something with this [i.e. squat a house]? That is senseless. I mean it is, if you just really stop and think about it, it's the dumbest thing.

Echoing points made by many other longtime resident appropriators, Delilah explained that within this context, the legitimacy of the laws, policies, and ways of life that are regulated by those systems of authority have-broken down. Squatting may not be the ideal scenario, but in the context of Detroit's decline, it is rational. Former squatter Leslie said simply, "I say squatting is the key to homelessness, that's what I say." Longtimer appropriators articulate what many urbanists in the Global South have long noted: that informality based in need demonstrates rational responses to local conditions (and, as I discuss in this book's Conclusion, planners and policy-makers can learn from these practices in order to schematize a more just and equitable city).

Both newcomer and longtimer appropriators understand their practices as moral despite their different understandings of and experiences with the city of Detroit. For LAs, Detroit is a space where their desired lifestyle is possible, where they can roll out their new vision for alternative ways of living. Conversely, NAs and RAs tend to view their practices as *responses to* the city's conditions, rooted in past difficulties and an understanding of how to navigate the constraints imposed upon them.

Moving beyond Appropriation

Longtime resident appropriators frequently referenced a lack of choice regarding their informal practices, which relates to their understanding of appropriation as a response to undesirable urban conditions. This influences the *temporality* with which appropriators view their future relationships to the property they appropriate: most longtimer appropriators wished they had viable alternate choices so they could cease appropriation. (Some RAs who came to enjoy their practices were an exception, which demonstrates some potentially promising ways in which appropriation practices could become more desirable.)

For NAs, this reported lack of choice was often related to their need to secure the requirements for their survival. T.J. for example, argued that squatting should be formally legal "because you got too many people homeless that's out here in the street . . . it's not by choice for a lot of them. It was the economy, you know. When the plants shut down, it killed a lot of people. It virtually like, took the life out of them." Later in our conversation, he discussed scrapping and the fact that even scrapping that *doesn't* adhere to an ethos of care is at least understandable because it might be their only option for making money. He explained, "And I think, you know, this is, is, is, bad what they doing, you know, how it's making the city, but you also got to realize the people that's doing it, the situation they're in, that might be the only way they can get a meal that day." Squatter Jackie who had moved with her grown sons to a vacant house in Detroit because they couldn't afford the suburbs, expressed this lack of choice saying, "You know personally I'd rather be out there where I was raised, you know what I mean."

Even RAs—who weren't relying on informal property use to meet urgent needs like shelter—discussed a lack of choice with regard to their practices. RA Chuck—who demolishes blighted houses in his neighborhood—explained,

> So, you know I'm really very conservative if you looked at it. I mean all I want is a white picket fence around my garden and I want the neighborhood to be clean. That's very conservative. But when you have to, you know, hand-wreck a block of housing 'cause the city's not doing their job, some people consider that radical. I consider it you've given me no choice. You know it's really a catch-22. I don't want to live around trash, and I don't want to move. So I got to clean it up, unless you got a better idea.

Chuck's demolition practices arose as a direct response to the growing blight in his neighborhood over time. Both options are burdensome: increasing blight in his neighborhood and taking on the government's responsibilities to clean up unsightly and potentially dangerous spaces. As such, he did not wish to continue his practices—he wished they were unnecessary.

Feeling like they have little or no choice about participating in property informality shapes the temporal dynamic of longtimers' appropriation practices. LAs narrate their informal practices as "right" in part *because* of their long-term/future commitments to productively use these properties. But for longtimers, property informality is often *urgent* and/or viewed as a *temporary* practice. Scrapper Bond expressed this kind of urgency while searching for work after losing his job in 2007: "If you do put out for a job, it might take a year before they call you. You know, light company ain't going to wait on you . . . you can take iron to the scrapyard and get money daily." Most scrappers need income, and so taking materials from abandoned properties is not so they can keep them to use in

future home renovation or art projects like salvagers (wherein appropriators *invest* in or with these materials), but because they exchange the
materials for cash as quickly as possible. Sometimes this need is so urgent
that scrappers sell their materials at informal overnight scrapyards—
someone sets up shop outside the scrapyard while it is closed and pays
reduced rates for scrap material to those who can't wait for normal business hours.[40]

Like many studies of poverty demonstrate, the extent to which poor
people are able to plan for the future is deeply compromised by the obstacles and work of procuring the means for survival in the present.[41] This is
the case for many NAs who use property informality to get by day to day.
As Bond indicated, he doesn't have the luxury of time to wait to hear about
a job that may not materialize.

But experiencing a lack of choice about their practices and the urgency
of securing daily needs doesn't preclude longtimer appropriators from
viewing their practices as long-term solutions to the conditions of the city
or their own personal obstacles (like LAs view appropriation). Instead
what became clear is that most NAs and some RAs also just don't *want* to
continue their appropriation practices.[42] They instead discuss their
practices as temporary getting-by strategies that they hope to move
beyond.

T.J. expressed the temporariness with which he viewed his informal
practice (squatting), saying, "I don't want the house . . . I'm trying to get
with somebody so I can get some subsidized housing, Section 8 or something. I'm getting out! Oh yeah." Then he added,

> And you know, it might be up in the air, but you know I want to just get me
> a stable place. I would like a nice upstairs place you know and everything,
> like these ones that's right here off of Vernor—I got a friend that stay over
> there and he paying ninety five dollar a month and he got two bedrooms.
> One of the bedrooms is a master bedroom with a walk-in closet. He got a
> nice-ass kitchen with a refrigerator, stove, and dishwasher and brand new,
> plus a washer and dryer in his unit.

T.J.'s goals for the future were simple and quite conventional: he wanted a
stable, comfortable apartment. But he had an urgent need for housing.
He did not invest significant time or money into renovations in part

because he did not have the latter, but because he was always ready—and wanting—to leave.

For NAs and RAs, squatting is one among many forms of unstable housing that low-income residents rely on. Like most homeless persons, NA squatters in my study cycled in and out of outright homelessness and other insecure housing situations.[43] This broader housing instability is evident in Leslie's explanation of why she moved out of the last house she squatted:

> I had got into another program that they moved me into Midtown, into a beautiful apartment and they said they would pay my rent for a year. And I figured, okay if they pay my rent for a year, I can find a new job by then and blah, blah, blah. So I moved into this beautiful three-bedroom townhouse in Midtown and they informed me that we could only pay your rent for six months . . . So I was thinking about moving back in that house (her squatted house) but someone bought it.

Leslie preferred a townhouse in Midtown over squatting; but then had to move again after only six months and couldn't move back into the squatted house so she ended up doubled-up with her mother. For many longtimer appropriators, informal appropriation becomes a stepping-stone to get by in between other more stable forms of housing or employment. Lamenting his reliance on both squatting and scrapping, DeAngelo commented, "Yeah that's about the biggest [problem] not having no job. I would just get me *another* place you know, and I have my light and gas and everything on." Even though he had lived in his same squatted house for several years, it was still impermanent for him. Similarly, many RAs just wanted their neighborhoods to be places where informal demolition or blotting wasn't necessary to keep order. For these longtimer appropriators, having few resources and not really wanting to have to appropriate property to meet their needs means they view property informality as a temporary practice.

Interviews with informal occupants often segued into discussions of property ownership. NAs didn't tend to pursue ownership like LAs. RAs were more diverse, as some were former owners who wanted to but often couldn't regain ownership of their houses.[44] Most of the NAs in my study who were squatting had complicated orientations toward the idea of owning the properties they occupied. DeAngelo, for example, asked, "You think if I go downtown they give me the deeds to this place?" I explained the fifteen-year requirement for adverse possession in Michigan and then asked if he ever tried to find out if his house was for sale at the county property auction. He shook his head and lamented, "Where am I gonna get five hundred dollars?" While in most parts of the United States it is impossible to purchase a house for as little as five hundred dollars, even this poses a significant hurdle to many squatters.

But the initial cost of purchasing property was not the only hindrance for NAs and RAs. Several squatters in my study were former homeowners who had previous experience navigating entry into and responsibilities of homeownership. Jackie, for example, had owned a home with her late husband in a far suburb of Detroit. Given Jackie's history as a homeowner, I pressed her to consider if being able to own the property she and her sons squatted would change her feelings about or experience living in an abandoned house in Detroit. She replied, "It needs a lot of work you know. I mean there is no kitchen, there is no bathroom. It needs all new wiring. I mean that stuff costs a lot of money you know . . . I don't have that kind of money, you know what I mean? But, um, yeah I suppose." Jackie shrugged, as if conceding to the possible merits of property ownership. But without the ability to invest in her property, ownership alone could not improve her daily experiences. Squatter Leslie even bought a home for five hundred dollars from the county property auction one year. But after visiting the home after she purchased it (they are not formally open for viewing ahead of time), she realized how much work it needed and resold it as quickly as she was able.

In popular imagination—and within the context of many growing urban environments for people with economic resources—property ownership brings stability and promotes economic prosperity. But for poor squatters in run-down, dilapidated properties, ownership would bring liabilities without significantly changing their lived experiences from day to day. Taking on a run-down property and fixing it up to make it more comfortable requires affirming a kind of lifestyle that most of the NAs in my study simply weren't interested in. In order for ownership to be more desirable than squatting, squatters would need to be willing to engage in the urban pioneering lifestyle: to spend their time salvaging materials

from other abandoned buildings to remodel their homes, to invest significant time and other resources (which they may not have) into improving
the property so that their living conditions could improve. Only then does
ownership make sense—as a means to secure these investments and enable such a lifestyle to continue.

For most longtimer appropriators, informal property use is something
they rely on to survive the city—to get by, meet needs, and stay afloat until
something better is available or conditions change (hopefully for the better). And these are *not* practices they feel they have had much choice about
participating in in the first place. These are practices they don't want to
continue in the future; they are viewed as temporary. Squatter T.J.
summed up these various facets when he explained, "I'm surviving right
now. I'm living. As long as the good Lord waking me every morning and I
can [get] out that house, then I'm fine, really, for right now until I can get
better on my feet. Then once I'm on my feet, hey, you know I can look back
and say, well this is something I experienced, you know."

As longtime residents of the city, NAs and RAs root the legitimacy of
informal appropriation in the conditions of the city, situating illegal practices as justifiable responses given the seeming collapse of local government, institutions, and authorities' ethics. This also means that, should
these structural conditions in the city change, so must their practices
because they are not a priori ethical—their legitimacy is relative and situ-
ational. Another way to think about this is that NAs and RAs understand
themselves to be responding to the accumulated conditions of the past
that persist today; whereas LAs understand themselves to be starting
fresh to create a new future.

The NAs and RAs in my study expressed disinterest in the urban pioneering lifestyle that LAs have embraced (even though some RAs, especially gardeners/farmers, come to enjoy their practices). Many NAs and
RAs were baffled by the influx of LAs in the city, struggling to imagine
privileged young white folks wanting to engage in property informality.
Perhaps, linking back to having to survive in a city of concentrated disadvantage for decades and all the obstacles that brings, longtimer appropriators just want a measure of comfort in their lives, especially those who are
aging or who have children. For NAs and RAs who are parents or respon-

sible for the care of others, the risks of informal appropriation (occupation in particular) are delicately balanced with its rewards—and if an alternative way to secure their needs was possible, they took it.

Necessity Appropriator Rhiannon was the outlier with respect to property ownership. A younger, politically active white woman, Rhiannon squatted out of necessity, but was able to deploy her resources as an activist into various forms of support that she needed to make her squat a comfortable home for herself and her children. With the help of the networks she was embedded in, she resisted eviction, raised money to fund repairs in the house, and eventually joined a Detroit program that enabled her to gain ownership of her home. As deviant cases often are, this one is particularly revealing about ways to potentially support NAs and RAs to decrease the burdens of their practices (like supportive networks, access to resources, and minimal funding).

CONFLICTING URBAN IDEALS

In her oral history research with former squatters who occupied abandoned buildings in Lower East Side Manhattan, Amy Starecheski uncovers tensions that arose among squatters as they negotiated collective responsibilities over the spaces of the buildings they occupied, and balanced differing needs and goals among occupants.[45] In my research, overt interpersonal conflicts between different kinds of appropriators did not emerge as a significant theme. This is likely in large part because these practices are spread out across blocks and neighborhoods throughout the city of Detroit. There is little need at this point in Detroit's history for these appropriators to step on each other's toes or compete for space.

But while interpersonal conflicts were not significant, differing ideological orientations toward appropriation, rooted in these newcomer/longtimer categories, were apparent in the narratives they construct *and* how appropriators discussed each other. Longtimer appropriators were often bewildered by LAs who willingly moved to the city to do what they largely disliked doing—i.e., squatting or forms of deconstruction. Recall squatter Marsey who, at the beginning of chapter 4, said, ". . . but every person who ever squatted, it had to be because that was the choice that was available . . ." The idea of squatting when an alternative way to meet needs was possible seemed ridiculous to many longtime residents in my study. RA Delilah was more direct, saying, "The other thing that really just, just pisses me off is like suburban, Caucasian children, young people who see the city as a playground. And then when it's time for you to stop playing, then you go back to your comfort life. I hate that, can't stand it, and because it's a privilege. Now this is not about race, it's just about privilege basically and who's doing that." At the same time, some NAs and RAs (particularly squatters and gardeners) appreciated the strength in numbers and the legitimation of their practices that can come from more privileged residents (like white newcomers) partaking in them.

Race is a salient difference between newcomers and longtime residents in Detroit due to the city's legacy of segregation. Many appropriators were aware that racial differences intersected with appropriation—who participates, in what ways, how, or why. Farmer and former homesteader Allen commented that the participants in pioneering lifestyles were disproportionately white, relative to the demographics of his neighborhood overall:

> I mean honestly the active participants I would say doesn't necessarily represent the demographic in the neighborhood. I mean it has to do with a lot of us transplants, like I didn't grow up in this neighborhood, [neither did] my friends down the street. The people who have transplanted into the neighborhood are overwhelmingly white, I'm trying to think if there's anyone, there's, uhhhh yeah there's a handful, there's a handful [of Black residents], but most of the people who come to this neighborhood of this newer wave are, are, yeah they're white.

Further, many LAs were cognizant of the way they—as younger, white newcomers—and their practices might be viewed by longtime residents (who are predominately Black). Sarah, the farmer, said,

> Like to be totally honest, we were a little worried that we were like these two young ambitious white kids coming in and like we have a lot of time and we have a lot of ideas so we just started doing stuff right away, like as soon as we moved over here. I guess we both weren't really sure how that would be received. I didn't want people to think that we were just being opportunistic and taking advantage of the space because we were so new. But as we slowly got to know people, I think that sharing and bringing them into this space (their garden) and you know letting them know that . . . that we *want* to live

here that we're *trying* to live here, I think really helped. But yeah, I mean you still get like weird looks sometimes from people but . . .

While her partner Matthew nodded in agreement, Sarah expressed a theme that was common in my interviews: the issue of whether or not newcomers' informal practices were understood or welcome by longtime residents.

In seeking to understand longtimer/newcomer appropriation and visions for the city, race and history are salient. Race intersects with varying visions for the city in part due to the history of Detroit's decline, interpersonal and institutionalized racism, and resulting segregation.[46] But abhorrent legacies of slavery and sharecropping also influence how some residents interpret agriculture practices and who participates. Some of the tensions here really center on what kind of practices are considered appropriate for a city. LA Fern discussed this more explicitly, while tiptoeing around the racial differences he saw:

> Like the prevailing attitude among the, I don't want to say, um, probably non-white neighbors and—I would almost generalize across the city—is that, that mowed grass is better and it shows that stuff is cared for. But all the like hippie, hipster white kids are like, "Let it grow, we like pheasants, like it's natural, it's less chemical, it's less noise." So, there's that attitude and they really, they don't jive . . . because people who've lived in Detroit for a long time feel like that, that tall grass is a symbol of neglect you know.

Fern awkwardly reflected on his sense that longtime residents didn't always support the "naturalizing" of Detroit's land, which, in contrast, Fern believed was often embraced by "white hipster kids." He was pointing out this tension over what a city ought to be like. As Fern aptly noted, tall grass is a symbol of neglect from the standpoint of longtime residents, whereas newer residents don't have the same history with the city such that these conditions are experienced differently.

RA Jerome expanded on this tension saying, "The whole concept of gardening in the city of Detroit . . . Honestly, it's a lot of people that still don't like the idea." I asked what he felt they disliked. He replied, "Well I mean they want it to be a city, which I understand." Jerome paused, then recalled, "Like when I was out there and working in the garden and stuff and people would come up to me, they were like, 'Well don't you think it's like um sharecropping and slavery?'" He scoffed and continued, "You know I've heard [it all], from creating rats to the sharecropping slavery thing, to reverting back to our past is not necessarily the best way to go, to you know you're turning the city into a farm, and I'm like no I'm not!"

Helena, a Black longtime resident and city authority identified another important way in which these newcomer–longtimer racial tensions are significant. She explained how the presence and orientations of these newcomer appropriators can reproduce negative stereotypes about long-time residents:

> I think it depends on how people come in and how they engage. And if you're coming into Detroit with the idea that Detroit is a blank slate, that's a problem, because it's not. There's people here that have been here that are doing things, that are creative, that are invisible—whether that's the fault of the people that are coming here or the fault of the media or a combination, I don't know . . . Some people don't understand the push-back and the resentment (from Black residents). But you know when you're a person of color and you've been here and you've struggled and it's very difficult for you to get things done and get access to resources, and you see young whites who come in *choose* poverty, who choose to live a certain way but have access to be able to live a certain way but on their own terms, then there is, it, on the negative way it helps to fuel the perception that, "Well look what we're doing and you're not doing anything so therefore you must be lazy."

Helena articulated how some of the tension is due to the positive light with which new, white appropriators' practices are portrayed and the support they receive for their efforts in the city. She explained that longtime residents of color who are engaged in similar practices have struggled to garner the same attention, resources, or supports. As a result they and their practices often go unrecognized and/or are potentially denigrated in comparison. For example, I've shown that new white appropriators often squat houses, fix them up, and eventually buy them. But many longtime Black residents don't want to and/or don't have the resources to do the same with their squatted houses. Failing to recognize the privileges that are required to be able to do what LA squatters do perpetuates negative stereotypes about these Black residents.

Whether or not many Detroiters explicitly associate agricultural practices with abhorrent histories of slavery and sharecropping, the tension that

Jerome and Helena pointed out was prevalent across my research: What ways of engaging with Detroit's property ought to be cultivated and encouraged, and what practices are better left in the past? Are squatting and increased "natural" or green space features that ought to be bolstered or emblems of problematic conditions that the city should "improve beyond"? That these differing perspectives may map onto different racial identities is due to the legacy of segregation and ghettoization in Detroit, and correlated experiences enduring the hardships of life in Detroit over time.

NARRATING AND NAVIGATING DETROIT

Since I focused this chapter on how longtimers and newcomers view the city—what the city *is* to them—I'll close with a brief discussion of what their practices suggest about what the city *ought* to be. Informal practices reshape the city in ways that reflect different appropriators' desires, needs, goals, and imagined futures. What is the future of Detroit as narrated by informal property users? What kind of vision is revealed through their planning-by-doing?

While LAs narrated themselves as urban pioneers venturing into the wild city, NAs and RAs narrated themselves as survivors of a failed city. The latter justified their practices with reference to the collapse, corruption, and dysfunction of local government, authorities, and institutions. They also narratively situated themselves in very constrained positions within existing social structures: they discussed limited options and oppressive social forces. LAs set themselves outside the problems of the city and openly challenged and rearticulated the moral basis of property laws. These newcomers viewed themselves as improving their own situations and the city through appropriation.

LAs bring various forms of privilege and capital to the city that can't be reduced to income or wealth (some had relatively few economic resources). But they bring their whiteness to a city that is close to 85 percent Black. They are young, often college educated, and have social networks, knowledge, and forms of cultural capital that go a long way in paving their pathways in the city. In many respects, Lifestyle Appropriators may be looked upon as first-wave gentrifiers for Detroit's outlying neighborhoods. But thirty-somethings with University of Michigan degrees and comfortable suburban upbringings settling down in little colony-like configurations amidst the weed trees and burnt out houses in some of Detroit's hardest-hit neighborhoods purports to change community and neighborhood dynamics in ways we ought seriously consider. This is imperative if some of them arrive with a savior-esque mentality, as though longtime residents of Detroit need these newcomers to "bring" them solutions to persistent problems in their city.

NAs and RAs narratives suggest a future in which they are able to move past appropriation as a tool for personal survival and/or neighborhood stabilization. This future city is one wherein local government functions well; formal employment opportunities are robust; city services are up and running; police and other authoritative bodies are reliable, responsive, and non-discriminatory; and deterioration and vacancy don't circumscribe the sociospatial environment. Such aspirations are similar to those of longtime residents in other research on distressed neighborhoods.[47] NAs and RAs narratives and practices largely suggest a desire for a modern city with basic comforts and amenities one can (seemingly) expect from a city in the Global North.

But many of the features of declining, shrinking cities are precisely what enable LAs' practices to continue. Similar to the gentrifiers in Japonica Brown-Saracino's book whom she calls "social homesteaders," LAs seek to preserve certain aspects of the spatial/built environment, with less explicit concern for the preservation of longtime residents or authentic culture.[48] For example, LAs Fern and Rita discussed the future of Detroit and speculations of gentrification in the city. Rita said,

> What if things do get built up and then all of a sudden we can't afford to live here anymore, you know like what happens then. So that's always an interesting question. And just, you know, just hoping that the things that we love about Detroit will still be here. Like who knows how long space will be available, who knows how long the pheasants will be around. Who knows how long you will be able to get away with, you know, all this stuff that we're getting away with?

She and Fern laughed, and Fern added, "Putting an addition on your house you know on the weekends, yeah," referring to the lack of oversight that has allowed them great latitude with regard to renovating their home.

LAs narratives and practices suggest a future city in which they can still have access to low-cost/free housing and land; continue to build in ways that currently violate codes, like using DIY water catchment systems; and where they can still access salvaged materials and farm urban land. Continuing these practices does not mean they must be done illegally; but the sociospatial/political conditions must allow the practices to persist. They might persist because laws are selectively enforced for budgetary and/or political reasons. Or, these practices might persist because they have been formalized in some way.

Analyzing the stories my participants tell about appropriation reveals that 1) these informal practices respond to and grow from very different standpoints and understandings of what the city is and how to navigate it and 2) they are oriented toward very different ways of being in the city and shaping the city in the future. The question is, whose vision for the future of Detroit will be supported and promoted? Will both longtimer and new-comer appropriators' practices be made impossible? Or will both be embraced? Detroit has a large footprint, so spatially we can imagine a city that offers both modern comforts while also creating avenues for urban pioneering types to continue their practices.

Even when longtimer and newcomer's practices moreso align, as with some urban agriculture, there can be tensions. Longtime resident and city authority Helena said that failing to recognize differing orientations toward appropriation "helps to fuel that resentment of the people that are there, when these new folks come in and it feels like they take over. But in other instances when people come right and they connect with the community, you know it's been a beautiful thing. But we'll see what happens in moving forward." Bolstering newcomers' understandings of how to "come right" and "connect with the community" may promote more mutually beneficial informal practices.

In cities of the Global South, informality is increasingly understood as a mode of urban planning, wherein some authorities and planners recognize the way that need-driven informality can be read as a kind of "planning-by-doing" that reveals existing, vernacular ways of navigating local conditions: a true planning from the ground up kind of approach. In the Global North, this kind of epistemic weight is often only given to more privileged residents who engage in DIY/insurgent/guerilla urbanism, etc.—understood to be deliberate urban interventions rather than (what is often viewed as) reactionary survival tactics by the poor. But giving epistemological credence only to more privileged informal urban actors lends to a very limited view of what the city is and how we might reshape it. The transformative potentials of informality based in need are denigrated when characterized as merely reactionary survival tactics. These informal practices could be read as a rearticulation of how to structure access to the city in ways that are more socially just and provide more equitable access to the city's resources.

Urban scholar Ryan Devlin argues that planners need the tools to parse out the differences in need versus desire-based informality.[49] These differences may not be immediately apparent to outsiders or authorities, especially when they violate the same laws, and thereby through the lens of legality they are the same. Squatters and homesteaders take over property; salvagers and scrappers take from property. But analyzing the narratives of informal actors reveals how they view their practices in relation to larger social structures like the city and the liberal private property regime; reveals how they understand the normative grounds for their de jure illegal practices; and temporally situates their practices with regard to the future. We see that along all these axes, informality based in need and desire are very distinctive programmatic interventions. When authorities respond to informality (if they do), there are different issues at stake, and they cannot be lumped together without risking harm to one group or another. What policy responses "work" for Lifestyle Appropriators may be detrimental to Necessity or Routine Appropriators.

9 Regulating Informality, Reproducing Inequality

Recent changes in Detroit seem to have reversed the decline of select areas in Downtown and Midtown, where signs of gentrification glimmer. Whole Foods arrived in 2013, along with a hot yoga studio and pour-over coffee bars. But the future of Detroit's revitalization is as yet unwritten. Toward the tail end of my time in Detroit, there was still widespread anecdotal consensus that, while Detroit had hit rock bottom and thus conditions could only improve, the majority of neighborhoods had seen little meaningful change. But as Detroit continues to change, what is the future of property informality and how will appropriators be impacted?

This chapter examines the way that new regulations, designed to promote revitalization in Detroit, are positioned to impact the appropriators in my study and their informal practices. Decline is a significant part of why property informality is able to proliferate. Stabilizing the city or reversing decline could undermine some of the conditions that enable informality. There is also hope that stimulating growth in the city would alleviate some of the problems of poverty and instability that motivate some property informality, but history tells us that revitalization efforts typically serve better-off urban residents and that poorer residents are often excluded from such improvements. As the city anticipates and promotes revitalization, what happens to the informal practices and the people who rely on them to meet needs and desires? In some sense, only time will tell. But—in part because of the hidden nature of informality—unless researchers are paying attention to how local changes are impacting informality, we won't capture these nuances. My aim is for this analysis to inform property-related policies that will help to create a future Detroit that is accessible rather than exclusionary.

This chapter analyzes six revitalization-oriented "regulations" (including laws, policies, ordinances, and programs) rolled out in Detroit during the time of my research. These new regulations all variously address the "property problems" of declining cities (abundance, poor condition, abandonment, etc.). Reinstantiating control over real property in Detroit is a central task for promoting market-logic revitalization. That is, in order to entice new residents and new capital investment, newcomers must be assured that real estate (property) is indeed a safe investment and government must try to create the conditions in which there *is* a market for property.[1] Toward that end, signs of neighborhood "disorder" that might deter newcomers must be curtailed and cleaned up, and property rights must be demonstrably upheld and protected.[2]

Urban scholars lament the ardent focus on growth models for improving conditions in declining cities.[3] But only some of Detroit's property-related revitalization efforts call on the growth machine to save the city. Viewed charitably (and optimistically), other approaches in Detroit embrace somewhat creative avenues for improving local conditions. Many plans for and visions of the city challenge traditional ways of using urban land and property, repurposing "vacancy" from a blighted liability into "green space" as an asset for the city. In Detroit, neoliberal efforts to bolster government's role in protecting property rights and creating the conditions in which markets can flourish dovetail with more alternative approaches to reinvigorating the city via urban greening projects.[4]

The regulations I analyze in this chapter impact residents' access to and control over property in the city in various ways, and thus all have important implications for property informality, even though "formalizing informality" is not the explicit goal of these regulations. My aim is to disentangle the ways that these new regulations are likely to impact the categories of appropriators in Detroit differently: some stand to be harmed, others will benefit.

Research has variously demonstrated that regulating informal practices can be at best ineffective and at worst detrimental to informal actors'
well-being because there is often a cost to complying with the law.[5]
Informality scholarship has uncovered some of these impacts in both the
Global South and the United States.[6] In Detroit, the costs of compliance
are not the only barriers or obstacles to formalization. Detroit's new regulatory schema also promotes and formalizes the urban settler lifestyle that
Lifestyle Appropriators are so drawn to, enabling them to continue their
practices more easily through expanded avenues for property ownership.
But at the same time, new regulations criminalize and/or erase (meaning,
remove the possibility for them to take place) the informal practices of
Necessity Appropriators and some Routine Appropriators.[7]

As such, these approaches to improving conditions in Detroit that aim
(or profess) to be creative, alternative, and locally responsive, stand to
reproduce longstanding urban inequalities like race and class by privileging newcomer appropriators' (like LAs) "right" to the city over longtime
resident appropriators (like NAs and RAs). Because real property ownership is the most significant source of wealth for most Americans and is a
key mechanism for the intergenerational transmission of wealth,[8] these
formalization policies may increase the wealth of LAs while keeping more
marginalized appropriators outside of the domain of property ownership.

FORMALIZING INFORMALITY

The expansive literature on informality in the Global South demonstrates
that responding to informality is a complex issue (to say the least).[9] The
obstacles of responding to informality are complicated in the United
States by a legal culture that privileges the liberal ideal of equality before
the law: individuals are not excused from compliance with nor denied
protection of the law. Critical race and feminist theorists, for example,
have long reiterated that states are not permitted to deny rights to individuals based on race or gender.[10] Informality is an abuse of law. To allow
informality to persist undermines the law by allowing noncompliance.
Permitting informal practices also sends a message of toleration for forms
of exploitation and inequality, like, for example, allowing people to live in

substandard housing conditions (which are characteristic of squatted houses). But, expecting compliance with the law without addressing underlying economic inequality can be unfruitful at best or exacerbate problems. For example, the city of Detroit is not allowed to only enforce building code compliance for residents who can afford the cost of repairs to bring their houses up to code. But citing homeowners for not complying with building codes can exacerbate problems by adding another economic burden to poor households, which could further compromise their housing stability.[11] At the same time, ignoring legal violations like noncompliant housing in poor neighborhoods (or other informal practices) risks undermining the law and sending the message that lower standards are acceptable for more marginalized populations.[12]

When scholars talk about formalization, we are referring to the processes by which practices that persist in violation of the law or that aren't yet regulated by existing laws come to be explicitly regulated by the state, either through the creation of new laws or regulations, or via the enforcement of existing ones. But, as I have shown, the problems that lead individuals to seek informal solutions are varied, and it is possible that the positive impacts of informal practices may be stymied by formalization. In other case studies, states/authorities have responded to informal practices in a variety of ways.

Perhaps the most studied type of informality in both the Global South and the scant literature in the United States is informal housing—such as squatting in rapidly urbanizing Global South cities,[13] illegal apartments created by subdividing housing in Los Angeles,[14] or self-built housing on illegally subdivided land in rural Texas.[15] The latter example—called colonias—serves as an important source of low-income housing in Texas. These housing developments often lack access to services such as sanitation, water, and electricity. In 1995, regulations to address colonia conditions and proliferation were implemented that required conformity to building codes. Instead of creating improved housing conditions for colonia residents, these developments became unprofitable to developers and thus few new colonias have been developed, removing a key source of affordable housing for poor Texans.[16] This case is emblematic of the way in which equal enforcement of the law amidst conditions of economic inequality can exacerbate these inequalities and worsen conditions for the poor. In the United States, informality is interspersed throughout and interwoven with spaces where legal and formal regulations are comprehensive and reliably/effectively enforced. For many instances of informality, existing laws just must be enforced to curtail informal practices. In contrast, in mega-cities of the Global South, Ananya Roy conceptualizes informality as a mode of urban planning because these informal practices shape new laws and forms of regulation that are designed to accommodate them.[17]

In Detroit, I argue that formalization is occurring through two different avenues: co-optative formalization and suppressive formalization. Co-optative formalization is occurring through the expansion of legal avenues and opportunities that LAs, who relate to property with this pioneering/settler mentality, are situated to take advantage of (along with some RAs, like the few in my study who want to continue their informal practices). But similar opportunities are not being created for those who want or need to temporarily use or immediately extract income from property (like NAs and some RAs). Instead, their informal practices are subject to suppressive formalization and are being increasingly criminalized or erased. The case of Detroit allows us to explore the potential implications of regulations that formalize informality in a US context and, more specifically, to consider how formalization has different impacts for the three categories of appropriators in my study. This is particularly important at this time when revitalization efforts are underway in the city.

MUNICIPAL CONTEXT

While Detroit has been planned and re-planned throughout the decades of its decline and with the turnover in mayoral administrations, there were a host of significant changes that occurred fortuitously just prior or during the course of my research (from late 2011—mid 2016). For example, in 2010, Quicken Loans founder Dan Gilbert moved his company's headquarters to Detroit and began the process of buying up properties in the core of Downtown/Midtown, where his real estate company Bedrock now owns around one hundred properties.[18] In 2013, the city was put under control of Emergency Manager Kevyn Orr (appointed by Michigan Governor Rick Snyder) and subsequently filed for bankruptcy. Later that year, Mayor Mike Duggan was elected—the first white mayor since the early 1970s. Bankruptcy was, to many, the key indicator that Detroit had hit rock bottom—things could only improve from there. Many other changes were instituted during my research, but there are three facets of the broader municipal context at that time that are significant for understanding how property is being re-regulated in the city and for understanding how these regulations are situated to impact residents' informal practices: the Detroit Strategic Framework Plan, the Blight Removal Task Force, and the Detroit Land Bank Authority. These three facets of the municipal context all directly respond to and shape the future of real property in the city. I first introduce each of these to lay the background for my examination of the new property regulations that are the focus of this chapter.

Detroit Strategic Framework Plan

Detroit Future City (DFC) is a nonprofit charged with implementing the Detroit Strategic Framework Plan—a fifty-year plan for improving Detroit (hereafter referred to as "Strategic Framework"). The organization was set up by local government in 2010 and is largely funded through various local foundations. The Strategic Framework, published in 2012, details plans and recommendations to guide Detroit's recovery and promote neighborhood revitalization.[19] It outlines a vision for repurposing Detroit's vacant and abandoned land, often in nontraditional ways like creating more green spaces and promoting urban agriculture. The DFC prides itself on its broad community engagement during the outreach phase of the planning process. However, the Strategic Framework has been criticized for essentially being a right-sizing plan: schematizing cutting off services to underpopulated areas of the city in an attempt to "right size" the population-space ratio.[20] But important for our discussion is that the Strategic Framework emphasizes how reliable, comprehensive control over urban property is central to the visions laid out for improving and stabilizing the city.[21]

Blight Removal Task Force

The massive scale of vacant and abandoned property has been a huge hurdle for Detroit: what ought the city do with the more than 80,000 blighted properties within its domain?[22] Demolition is costly, and until the release of the Detroit Blight Removal Task Force Report (hereafter referred to as "Blight Report"), the city was not even sure how many properties in Detroit constituted "blight," needed to be demolished, or which were still standing. Stakeholders from the federal and city governments, local businesses, charities, and nonprofits formed the steering committee of the Detroit Blight Removal Task Force. This task force was spurred by the Obama Administration's 300-million-dollar federal effort to work with the city on issues related to blight, public works, and safety. In the eyes of city authorities and many residents, blighted properties are such a problem in Detroit that the formation of the task force and the resulting Blight Report alone were regarded as a huge step toward improving the conditions of life in Detroit. Among other things, this report defines *blight* and delineates what buildings (including houses) in the city need to be demolished versus preserved. The ability to categorize properties as blighted or not is powerful; it articulates which buildings and houses deserve to remain and which the city feels it is better off without.

Detroit Land Bank Authority

In 2008 the Detroit City Council established the Detroit Land Bank. Mayor Duggan's office revamped it a few years later under the name Detroit Land Bank Authority (DLBA) as part of the Mayor's plans to improve neighborhoods in the city. Land banks are government (or nonprofit) entities designed to help manage property vacancy and abandonment and are understood to be a direct response to the rise in "problem properties" in distressed or declining cities—e.g., vacant, deteriorated, or abandoned properties often with encumbered titles or that are tax delinquent.[23] Land banks have special powers to acquire property titles and are able to clear any liens, clouds, or encumbrances on these titles. The DLBA acquires property by filing nuisance claims against property owners. Owners have a limited time to respond to the claim and to abate the nuisance (e.g., tear down a collapsed front porch). If they do not, the DLBA takes the property to sell via auction, demolish, or hold for future development. Houses around the city are auctioned off through an online system that displays photos, addresses, and an overview of expected repairs. Vacant city-owned lots can be purchased through the DLBA's online system as well. This kind of institution exists to try to streamline the movement of "unused" properties into "productive use," and amasses other properties for large future redevelopment projects.[24]

DETROIT'S NEW PROPERTY REGULATORY SCHEMA

In this section, I analyze the potential impacts for property informality brought about by six new property-related regulations in Detroit that were put into place during the time of my research. These regulations all arise from various efforts to curb decline and promote stabilization and revitalization in Detroit (two of these regulations were adopted statewide). But my aim is to do an important kind of analysis that many scholars have done in various ways before: to consider how the law will shape everyday life in ways not explicitly acknowledged nor fully considered (or perhaps in ways that were *exactly* as designed but not explicitly advertised). The "law on the books" never translates neatly into law in action—the effects are always more varied, unexpected, or even misaligned with the professed intent of the law in the first place.

For example, research by sociologist Kathryn Edin and anthropologist Laura Lein uncovered the disparate impact that the imposition of formal work requirements in the 1996 welfare reforms would have for single mothers in their study.[25] Neither welfare nor low-wage work had previously allowed these mothers to cover their living expenses, so all engaged in informal economic survival strategies. Edin and Lein found that some survival strategies the mothers in their study relied on were more commensurate with formal work than others. Specifically, they argued that network strategies (such as doubling up in apartments or relying on family for childcare) are more conducive to formal work, while side work is not (informal employment such as cutting hair in one's home for example). Moving from welfare to formal work would not allow mothers to continue side work, whereas they could still rely on network survival strategies while formally employed. The authors concluded that the implementation of 1996 welfare policy changes would differentially impact the women in their study depending on the informal economic survival strategies on which they relied. While the new regulations I examine in this chapter are all aimed at stabilizing and revitalizing Detroit, they are situated to differentially impact LAs, RAs, and NAs because of the varied nature of these appropriators' informal practices.

The nature of community input is also consequential for how new policies impact inequality. Creators of both the DFC Strategic Framework and the Blight Report espoused commitments to being locally responsive and conducted outreach and community engagement to achieve this goal. Community meetings were held to get input for the DFC Strategic Framework, residents were trained and hired to collect data for the Blight Report, and "blexting" was unveiled, a platform for residents to send a text to report blight.[26] In part because of these measures, these two documents are touted as being ground-up participatory plans/recommendations. But research shows that residents most likely to participate in community planning processes are those with greater resources—the time to participate, the transportation to meetings, the money to pay for childcare, etc.[27] If appropriators—whose informal practices are often under-the-radar and poorly understood by planning authorities—are participating in community-planning processes, research tells us that more privileged appropriators are going to be more engaged because they are afforded various means that enable them to participate. Certain voices are left out of the planning process and as such, new regulations may not adequately take their ontologically and epistemologically rooted understanding of Detroit's opportunities and obstacles into consideration. Or, to be more cynical (realistic?), perhaps the unequal, unjust outcomes these new regulations are set to have for informal appropriators are exactly part of the design and goal: to remove poor, predominately Black residents' access to the resources of the city and criminalize the practices that enable their survival.

PROMOTING AND EXPANDING:
CO-OPTATIVE FORMALIZATION

Several of the new regulations rolled out during the course of my research co-opt the settler/pioneering practices that LAs engage in. These new regulations promote this kind of lifestyle and expand avenues for legal access to property that accords with a model of investment and future commitment (ownership). Property auctions streamline purchasing cheap properties that need significant renovation; salvaging businesses facilitate easy, legal access to salvaged material; and a new urban agriculture ordinance legalizes farming/gardening practices and expands avenues for purchasing property in the city. In essence, these new regulations enable LAs (and some RAs) to translate illegal appropriation into legal ownership, thereby benefitting from being property owners while still achieving their primary goals and living their urban settler lifestyles. Creating legal avenues for continuing informal practices is what I call co-optative formalization.

"Neighbors Wanted": New Detroit Land Bank
Authority Property Auction

In 2014 Mayor Duggan's new administration took over and revamped the Detroit Land Bank Authority (DLBA). Many of the properties the DLBA holds are in queue for demolition, but others are put up for sale as part of Mayor Duggan's effort to encourage "responsible" homeownership in the city. The DLBA's slogan is "Neighbors Wanted"—referring to the goal of attracting new home-owning residents to Detroit's neighborhoods. The DLBA has an ongoing auction that sells properties weekly, often starting around $1,000.

Previously, inexpensive properties in Detroit were available by auction only through the Wayne County property auction. In the first round, bidding starts at the amount of delinquent taxes owed. Properties that are unsold by the second round start at bids of $500. Anyone holding title to a property that was behind on taxes in the last three years (like holdover squatters who had owned their houses) are prohibited from purchasing properties at the auction,[28] though in practice this isn't often being

observed.[29] The Wayne County Treasurer's website offers little information about these properties, only the address and the dollar amount of
delinquent taxes.

The DLBA's auction website, on the other hand, offers photos and
details about potential improvements needed. The DLBA frequently holds
open houses so interested buyers can tour the properties before bidding
starts.[30] This new property auction makes the process of purchasing
cheap homes to renovate simpler, especially for newer residents from outside the city who haven't yet "hit the pavement" to research and identify an
appropriate tax delinquent property to try to occupy or buy. The DLBA
property auction strictly stipulates that new owners must bring properties
up to code and have them occupied within six months, and thus those able
to participate must possess the various resources necessary to do so, like
time, labor, knowledge, and/or money.

During my time in Detroit, it was surprisingly difficult to find inexpensive houses to purchase in the city because so often they sit in legal limbo
during the tax foreclosure process or because the legal owner cannot be
found. My partner and I searched for a year, trying to find a property we
could afford to buy and try to fix up. We'd weave through neighborhoods
on Detroit's East Side on our way from Hamtramck (where we first lived)
to Belle Isle to let our dogs run around, writing down addresses of houses
that looked vacant but weren't in too rough condition. We couldn't get a
realtor to help us search for a house that was only going to sell for a few
thousand dollars—there's a lot of work involved in that and little commission. Most of these kinds of houses don't enter the real estate market—no
MLS numbers for them or listings on Zillow.

The DLBA's new property auction functions as an avenue for increasing
access to property ownership in Detroit—which is precisely its stated goal
(increasing "responsible" ownership in the city). But more specifically, this
auction is advantageous for people seeking inexpensive properties to renovate. This allows LAs to carry out their homesteading practices legally.
Homesteading does not require that occupation be illegal—LAs often illegally occupy property only until they are able to purchase. LAs have the
stability and distance from necessity to "shop around" for the right
house and want to make long-term commitments to and significant
investments in property. The DLBA's auction bolsters LAs' ability to

pursue homesteading and legally settle the city with an urban pioneering ethos. The DLBA's convenient online advertisement system also enables interested buyers from far away to explore this kind of housing option in the city.

While $500–$1,000 is a scant amount to pay for a house compared to prices nationwide, it can be prohibitive for poor residents like NAs and some RAs, not even taking into consideration the costs for immediate repair, taxes, and long-term upkeep. Remember that, for example, squatter T.J. could not afford a legal divorce—a cost of around $250—and has not been able to afford that for several years. But cost isn't the only obstacle for poor or low-income appropriators being able to take advantage of this new avenue to property ownership in Detroit. Many NAs who were squatting either don't want to own their houses at all or don't want to own them given the deteriorated conditions they are in, considering their own lack of resources to invest in improvements and/or disinterest in the laborious process of renovations. For NAs, squatting is viewed as temporary, not something they want to continue in the future. And/or the risks of squatting are preferable to the risks of being legally housed; the latter comes with obligations to stay abreast of regular monetary payments to avoid eviction.

Holdover squatters were more varied in their views about property ownership. Many former homeowners who squat their properties *do* want to own them (again). But many cannot afford to purchase a property from the DLBA auction nor have the money to bring it up to code. If they lost their home to tax foreclosure, they likely couldn't afford the few thousand dollars per year in taxes, and deferred maintenance (which would increase the costs of required renovations) is common in these situations. Holdover squatters who are former renters often just want to remain in their property as long as they can to avoid paying rent for a duration and save money. I did talk with several who were interested in owning the home they squatted, but none could afford to pay the delinquent taxes on their squatted homes.[31]

Greening Detroit: New Urban Agriculture Ordinance

Greening projects, such as urban farming and the creation of community gardens, have gained popularity in cities. Declining cities have begun to capitalize on this trend as a way to repurpose the vacant land in the city left by decades of depopulation and to help revitalize cities.[32] Such endeavors are increasingly embraced by urban authorities because they can help to clean up and beautify the urban landscape, and they can create economic opportunities and sustenance for impoverished communities.[33]

In Detroit, as authorities and many residents are also embracing urban agriculture, farming and gardening possibilities are being "reintroduced" (and I mean this ironically). Helena, a resident and authority who has worked on issues of agriculture in the city, vehemently derided the idea that farming in Detroit is somehow "new" saying,

> I grew up with it as most African Americans in the city have. Either they came from the South or their parents came from the South, so it's been a part of our culture for a long time. That's why, you know, sometimes it's kind of upsetting when people think that it's a new thing, that some young people are coming in the city now start it, and it really isn't. It's a part of the southern roots of African Americans and other groups.

She explained that in Detroit in the 1700s, there were "ribbon farms"—long lots that stretched down to the river so farmers could access water; and in the 1890s, Mayor Hazen Pingree promoted agriculture in the city as a way to combat poverty.

The Strategic Framework advocates for urban agriculture in Detroit as a way to help put vacant land in the city back into "productive use," to improve the health of local residents, to entice new residents who seek this kind of lifestyle, and to stimulate the economy.[34] These efforts capture the pioneering spirit of folks who are disenchanted by consumer culture and big agri-business; greening opportunities are especially in tune with many LAs' desires and practices.

In the interest of bolstering urban agriculture in the city, Detroit's City Council adopted an urban agriculture zoning ordinance in 2013. Guided by several years of discovery and meetings with local farmers, this ordinance recognizes agriculture as a legitimate land use in the city, sets standards for it, and defines urban agriculture activities (such as farm versus garden, greenhouse versus hoophouse, etc.). Agriculture in Michigan is protected by the 1981 Michigan Right to Farm Act (MRFA), which was designed to protect farmers from nuisance complaints by residents in encroaching suburban developments. But it also restricted municipalities from regulating agriculture. The new ordinance in Detroit thus had to work with rural farmers to create a framework that would work alongside the MRFA and its Generally Accepted Agricultural and Management Practices (GAAMPS). The City of Detroit Planning Commission reached an agreement with the Michigan Agricultural Commission to provide an exemption for the city from these restrictions, enabling them to proceed with the new urban agriculture ordinance.

Along with defining acceptable practices, this ordinance creates regulations where none existed before. The ordinance includes regulations such as restricting mature production of oats, rye, or wheat to avoid rodent problems; delineating site requirements (such as how far back a compost pile must be from the street); and acceptable forms of agriculture (including aquaculture, aquaponics, and hydroponics). This new ordinance regulates the sale of produce and other farm products—e.g., farmer's markets. It also allows pre-existing agricultural operations that do not conform to new requirements to be formalized as a "legal nonconforming use," rather than requiring that the space be altered to meet all the new regulations.[35] This incentivizes legalization (for informal farmers/gardeners to purchase their plots of land) because this nonconforming status excuses them from significant costs to comply (like moving a water catchment system further from the edge of the property).

One significant component of this new urban agriculture ordinance is that it permits purchasing property for the express purpose of agricultural endeavors. Previously, residents in Detroit could not purchase vacant property that was not adjacent to their legally owned residence unless they planned to build on it. Now a resident can, for example, purchase the vacant lots across the street to garden or buy a vacant block in another neighborhood to start a farm because it is a legally regulated use of property in the city. Detroiters can also now legally sell their produce and other "agricultural products" for income.

Some RAs in my study told me about an old rent-a-lot program that allowed community groups and residents to rent lots yearly from the city for a small fee.[36] But they also noted how cumbersome the rental process was because city officials often were not aware of the program or, in one instance, could not find the necessary paperwork.[37] These residents also expressed that renting lots ultimately was not worth it because there was little perceived difference in precarity between renting a lot (because the rental term is yearly) and using it without permission, and more headache involved with the former.[38] In some respects, longtime resident appropriators have become disinterested in certain types of formality because their experiences have demonstrated how cumbersome and unnecessary formality can be.

This new urban agriculture ordinance formalizes and legalizes the practices of LAs who move to the city seeking inexpensive space to garden, grow their own food, farm for a living, and more generally "live off the land" akin to urban pioneers. Lots can be purchased through the city for as little as $200 for a side-lot and for "fair market value" for nonresidence adjacent land.[39] The impact is that some appropriators are able to benefit from an expanded opportunity for property ownership while pursing the practices that are central to the lifestyle they have chosen (like LAs) or that they have come to enjoy over the years (like RAs). On the other hand, NAs in my study didn't undertake agricultural endeavors and weren't interested in doing so, leaving them unable to take advantage of or benefit from this expanded opportunity for property ownership in the city.

Salvaging Detroit

Increasingly, city authorities have made blight removal a priority in their efforts to boost revitalization and improve neighborhood conditions. The 2014 Blight Report advocates that the city pursue deconstruction (over demolition) to remove properties.[40] The report lists "resale opportunities" as the first reason for doing so, followed by several others including environmental sustainability and "a sense of reclaiming Detroit's past for craft and artisanal purposes."[41] Salvage businesses are envisioned as a way to aid recycling, avoid landfills, and save the city money in the process of deconstructing blighted properties. The Blight Report also recommends that the city establish two new construction and demolition centers, which could cater to and be supported by a market for recycled (salvaged) materials.[42]

New businesses and nonprofits around Detroit have popped up that offer salvaged materials neatly organized in for-sale warehouses with steeply discounted prices. New businesses, restaurants, or even remodeled homes often advertise that their tables or wood floors came from some iconic building in the city that is no longer standing. It is a practice that the city and many residents are embracing. "Made in Detroit" is not just a slogan for companies like luxury goods producer Shinola setting up shop in the city. The phrase also implies a reclaiming of the built environment of the city and its history through this cycle of deconstruction, salvaging, and rebuilding. Architectural Salvage Warehouse (est. 2005) and Reclaim Detroit (est. 2011) are two such businesses—popular during the time of my research—that offer salvaged materials for sale in the city. Other businesses rely on salvaged materials for creating new products to sell. Woodward Throwbacks opened in 2013 and sells both salvaged materials as well as new products made from salvaged materials.

Salvage resale businesses enable LAs to meet many of their salvaging goals legally. They can inexpensively access pieces of Detroit's history to use in their home remodels, gardens, and art projects. LAs can be even more deliberate in their selection of materials and purchasing them aligns with their goal of using these materials for a long time. Some salvagers in my study had already begun to use these new options for obtaining building materials. Farmer and salvager Fern explained, "Half of this house is from like the ReStore or Arch Salvage which is over in the west side or from various houses around here that aren't standing anymore." NAs and RAs did salvage at times—mainly for making alterations to their squatted houses or gardens—but for them the added costs of the formal salvage industry may prove prohibitive. NAs and RAs were more likely to scrap rather than salvage, where the goal of deconstructing buildings is to procure income (not usable materials, as salvagers seek).

For some salvagers, the benefits of the activity are twofold: to obtain useful materials and the adventurous element of climbing through abandoned buildings and seeing parts of the city that have been left to ruin. These salvagers can take advantage of salvage businesses for useful materials *and* continue their urban exploration because as of the time of this writing no new laws or regulations were rolled out that target the latter. So while the explorational facet of the informal salvaging practice isn't being formalized, it isn't being further suppressed either. For example, at the time of this writing, resident and (now former) gardener Henry is regu-

larly paid to take outsiders on unsanctioned tours of hidden art throughout the city's abandoned buildings.

The new regulations discussed in this section promote a settler/urban pioneering lifestyle in Detroit. These expanded opportunities for accessing
and owning property in the city serve a dual purpose: they entice new residents and function as creative solutions for repurposing land and property
in the city. Increasing demand for property helps to create a market for real
property in Detroit, turning excess property from a liability into an asset
for the city. LAs, intent on Settling the City, are well positioned to take
advantage of these new property regulations and engage in many of the
practices that these regulations promote (e.g. remodeling properties with
"reclaimed" materials, urban agriculture, rehabbing cheap properties).

Some RAs may also benefit from these expanded opportunities,
depending on their specific orientation toward their practices. Didi, for
example, would likely benefit from being able to purchase the vacant lots
near her where she plants wildflowers. Chuck or other RAs who demolish
blight in their neighborhoods may benefit from a reduction in the burden
of having to tear down houses themselves, but their practices aren't being
formalized into something they can capitalize on like property ownership.
So while LAs (and some RAs) in my study are able to transition their practices from de jure illegal to legal, the same opportunities are not being
created for NAs' (and other RAs') practices. Instead, their practices are
being suppressively formalized and curtailed.

CRIMINALIZING AND ERASING:
SUPPRESSIVE FORMALIZATION

While new avenues for legal property ownership have been created that
promote the settling/pioneering lifestyle, other new regulations aim to
curb certain illegal uses of property and clean up the built environment of
Detroit. Protecting property and curtailing signs of blight and "disorder"
are purported to be necessary in order to cultivate trust in the real estate
market in Detroit and encourage new residents and investors.[43] New
anti-scrapping and squatting laws and the reallocation of federal funds

toward blight demolition are designed to bolster these changes. But criminalizing squatting and scrapping makes these practices riskier. And wide-scale demolition rids the city of the deteriorated properties that appropriators use as a resource for meeting their wants and needs; it *erases* the possibility for these practices to persist. These regulations are situated to negatively impact NAs and RAs moreso than LAs because the latter can formalize their practices to avoid the negative impacts of criminalization. Criminalization and erasure are examples of what I call "suppressive formalization."

New Anti-Scrapping Law

While scrapping that conforms to an ethos of care is largely considered appropriate by Detroiters in my study, there is still a plethora of scrapping that is considered harmful and detrimental to overall neighborhood stability and well-being. Not only can scrapping contribute to a deteriorated built environment and pose hazards for neighbors, but the unchecked proliferation of this practice signals a lack of reliable property law enforcement which may deter would-be investors or new residents.

In an effort to curb illegal metal scrapping in Detroit and the resulting neighborhood deterioration, then State Representative Rashida Tlaib of Michigan's 13th District introduced a new "anti-scrapping" bill. This bill was supported statewide because it also addresses problems like railroad theft in rural areas of Michigan. A local authority who advised on this bill explained that in Detroit the primary motivation behind the law is to curb the harmful effect of scrapping on the built environment: the destruction of buildings that often makes it cost-prohibitive to renovate them.[44] The bill was signed into law in April of 2014, amending a 2008 law (MI HB 4593 and 4595) regulating the sale of metals at scrapyards across the state of Michigan.[45]

This new law aims to reduce the incentives of scrapping and deter scrappers by increasing the potential risks. It makes it harder for "thieves"[46] to sell illegally acquired materials at scrapyards for quick cash and easier for law enforcement to trace stolen material and prosecute scrappers. This new law *only* targets illegally appropriated property that is *sold* at scrapyards, and it makes it harder to obtain immediate cash in exchange for scrapped materials.[47]

Salvaging and scrapping are both informal practices that take materials from buildings, violating the same laws like theft and vandalism. But only scrapping involves taking the materials to the scrapyard to sell for income. Because this law targets informal deconstruction at the point of sale, only those who engage in scrapping to procure income from scrapyards are going to be impacted by this new law, namely NAs or RAs. So while deconstruction-as-salvaging is being formalized via expanded legal access to materials at salvage businesses, deconstruction-as-scrapping is being criminalized, and the NAs and some RAs who participate in scrapping face greater risks trying to procure income this way.

New Anti-Squatting Law

In September of 2014, just a few months after the new scrapping law, a new statewide law was adopted that criminalizes squatting and gives more power of control to property owners. A similar ordinance was initially under consideration by Detroit's City Council, but the state law super-seded the need for a similar local policy.[48] As is the case in most cities, squatters violate property laws when they trespass in Detroit. If the police can verify that an occupant did indeed illegally trespass to enter a prop-erty, they can arrest or cite the occupant. Prior to this new law, without proof that the occupant trespassed (and did not have permission from the owner to be there), the only recourse was for the legal owner to try to evict the occupant through civil court. And, in order for the illegal occupant to be charged with a criminal offense (if the police did not intervene imme-diately), the legal owner had to file trespassing or vandalism charges.[49]

Dealing with squatters has become a public-relations nightmare in Detroit. Barnabas, a local legal expert, explained that for city officials deciding how to respond to squatters "it is not a legal issue, it's a political one." Quentin, a city employee, explained that many people in Detroit call in to complain about "squatters" when they really just do not like their neighbors. He also explained that it makes local government look bad when "the big bad city just throwing these poor people out of their house," a point that was later echoed by two police officers in my study. And recently a squatter sued the city for mistreatment after she and her children were forcefully removed from a property they were occupying. For reasons like these, Barnabas explained, the city has been reluctant to take legal action against squatters by arresting them for trespass or evicting them (even aside from the lack of resources to do so).

However, with the passing of this new law, squatting in Michigan is now a misdemeanor for a first offense and a felony for the second offense.[50] This new law also allows property owners to take more direct action in order to reassert control over their property. They are now allowed to "use force to regain possession of premises occupied by a squatter."[51] This does not authorize assaulting an occupant, but property owners are permitted to physically remove squatters' belongings, for example, and change the locks.

All types of informal occupiers in my study are potentially impacted by this new law should a property owner want them out. Most squatters in my study purposefully occupy tax delinquent properties because of the reduced likelihood of an owner trying to remove them. This new law means they are placed at greater risk if/when new owners purchase the property and want to take control of it. But, LAs in my study are the ones purchasing their properties at auction, so they are less likely to be negatively impacted by this new law. Indeed, this new law smoothes the way for more newcomers to purchase cheap properties at auction and easily take control of and move into them. It helps newcomers, who may want to pursue this homesteading lifestyle by rehabbing a cheap, run-down property, to take legal control of the property they want without being encumbered by the presence of squatters.

Not being able to efficiently remove squatters in Detroit is considered an obstacle to promoting revitalization, as properties facing foreclosure are frequently occupied. In 2015, an estimated 100,000 properties going through foreclosure were occuped.[52] It is cost-prohibitive for new property owners—who may have bought a house for as little as $500 at the county property auction—to have to go through the time and expense of eviction to remove an unwanted squatter. As an example of suppressive formalization, this new regulation has the twinned effect of making NAs/RAs practices harder and riskier, while making it easier for LAs and other newcomers like them to (re)settle the city.

Blight Demolition

Blighted property is a significant problem for declining cities like Detroit. After a city-wide property survey in 2014, 78,506 properties were identified as blighted or having indicators of future blight.[53] In the resulting Blight Report, blight is defined as a property that meets any of a long list of conditions, including a property that: is a fire hazard, has had the utilities disconnected or rendered ineffective, is tax-reverted, is owned or controlled by a land bank, has been vacant for five years and not maintained to code, or is on the demolition list.[54] These blighted properties are popularly conceived as "broken windows,"[55] which signal apathy and lack of social cohesion among residents, contribute to the further deterioration of social relationships and the built environment, and increase crime. Cleaning up signs of disorder (like blight) is considered imperative for improving the physical and social conditions of such neighborhoods and attracting new residents.

Despite scholarly research attesting to the ineffectiveness of demolition as a neighborhood improvement strategy,[56] Mayor Duggan's administration (and other administrations prior) has emphasized the importance of blight removal for improving the conditions of the city. To that end, a massive blight demolition plan was unveiled by the Duggan administration. This demolition plan targets the most stable neighborhoods for blight removal first, aiming to help stabilize these neighborhoods and prevent further decline. This approach is justified by the fact that these neighborhoods have the lowest vacancy rates, so more residents will benefit from proximal blight removal.[57] The potential benefits of blight removal are numerous. Residents face a host of social and environmental ills from structurally unsound, interstitial spaces created by the decaying houses and buildings across the city. Blighted properties are often sites of potential harm to curious passersby or children seeking places to play, and commonly used for illicit activities.[58] As of September 2019, Detroit had demolished 19,870 vacant buildings under this new plan, and 4,560 were in queue.[59]

In 2010, amidst the aftermath of the recession, the US federal government created the Hardest Hit Fund to help struggling homeowners.[60] In fall 2013, 52.3 million dollars were made available to Detroit,[61] which local activists argue should have been allocated to help the thousands of households facing mortgage or tax foreclosure.[62] Instead, however, these funds have been redirected toward blight demolition in the city. In conversation during my participant observation, David Szymanski, who at the time was the Chief Deputy Treasurer of Wayne County, said that the funds had been redirected from foreclosure assistance to demolition because they were not being used. He explained that homeowners were struggling to *prove* their eligibility to receive assistance, as cloudy property titles and property inheritance, lack of formal income or tax records, and other issues common among poor households in declining cities meant that residents could not provide the necessary documentation.

Reallocating funds from foreclosure assistance to blight demolition kicks the can down the road. The lack of market demand for property in Detroit means that when residents lose their houses to foreclosure, most of them end up sitting vacant, become blighted, and have to be demolished. One commonly cited finding is that "in one triangle-shaped area between Grand River, Dexter and Joy, 80 percent of 200 mortgage foreclosures from 2005–13 are blighted or have been seized by the county for unpaid taxes."[63] This change in the allocation of funds negatively impacts marginalized residents by failing to intervene in extensive foreclosures and likely has contributed to the presence of holdover squatters across the city.

Blight removal gets rid of the vacant properties that many of Detroit's poorest residents use for shelter and income. The definitions of blight are so broad that the only vacant properties *not* classified as blight according to the report are privately owned properties that are boarded up, secured, and well maintained. But appropriators rarely target such properties for occupation or demolition because those conditions signal that the legal owner is still watching and caring for the property, and thus occupying such a property would not accord with an ethos of care and would be riskier. Instead, appropriators target tax delinquent or reverted properties, and land bank (government owned) properties because it is unlikely that they will be evicted, even if the city knows that illegal occupants are there.[64] Vacant properties that squatters can take over often lack utilities and are not maintained to code (meeting definitions of blight). By targeting all of the "blighted" properties in the city for demolition, the properties that informal appropriators utilize are being removed as well.[65]

The Blight Report also recommends that the definition of an "occupied" property be redefined to include only "rightful owners or tenants and exclude squatters."[66] This recommendation was not adopted as of this writing, but it illustrates the precarity of squatters' occupation. Currently, a property is defined as "occupied" if it is either legally *or* illegally occupied— i.e., the presence of homeowners, squatters, or renters all constitute a property as occupied. An occupied property cannot be demolished under Ordinance 290-H in Detroit. Redefining an occupied property to exclude illegal occupants would allow properties to be demolished even if squatters are living there. This recommendation was motivated by the goal of quickly cleaning up neighborhoods by speeding up and streamlining the demolition process, which currently is very drawn out and cumbersome, a city official explained, and often delayed by the presence of squatters.[67]

Recently, one of the three major demolition companies in the city estimated that squatters occupy 10 percent of the homes they are slated to demolish.[68] If that estimate held true for all three major Detroit demolition companies (excluding demo companies that only do occasional blight removal in the city), that would mean that sixty of the approximately two hundred houses demolished every week in Detroit are likely occupied.[69] As a suppressive formalization tactic, blight demolition *erases* the possibility for certain survival practices (scrapping and squatting) to persist in the city and may leave NAs with fewer options for meeting needs like income and shelter.[70]

The new regulations discussed in this section can be understood as modes of suppressive formalization in Detroit. The criminalization of scrapping and squatting aims to curb these practices in the city. But the variation in Lifestyle, Routine and Necessity Appropriators' practices means that these new laws will have different impacts "on the ground" for appropriators across these categories. Scrapping is made riskier—but only for appropriators who sell the scrapped materials at scrapyards for income (salvagers practices aren't criminalized by this new regulation). While all informal occupation (squatting) is made riskier by the new law, it is likely to have much more significant harm for NAs and RAs who cannot or don't want to purchase their properties at auction. LAs in my study pursue ownership of their properties (often at auction) and thereby avoid being the occupants of a property that someone else purchases. Blight demolition removes the properties—the urban resource—that informal appropriators (except gardeners/farmers or blotters) use in their practices. But LAs can continue their practices legally through new formal channels for accessing salvaged materials or vacant houses.

FORMALIZATION AND THE REPRODUCTION OF INEQUALITIES IN DETROIT

As Detroit planners and policymakers roll out new plans to promote revitalization, they must deal with the "problem" of property—its abundance, deteriorated condition, and poorly regulated state. New regulations that aim to variously tackle these property problems interact with the informal practices prevalent across the city. The outcome of this interaction is that the informal practices that longtime residents use to get by or keep their heads above water are being threatened. The practices that enable residents to Survive the City are being suppressed via criminalization and erasure. At the same time, many of these new regulations create legal avenues for pursuing an urban pioneering lifestyle. Newcomers intent on Settling the City see their practices increasingly becoming possible legally and their rights to the city solidified via expanded opportunities for various forms of property ownership. Detroit's new property regulatory schema can be understood as exacerbating the precarity of most longtimer appropriators, while establishing and supporting the stability of newcomer appropriators.

Rather than explicitly targeting informality in the city, Detroit's new property regulatory schema is geared toward revitalization. The regulations analyzed here are just six examples that impact informality; more were unveiled before my time in Detroit and others toward the tail end or after (see Conclusion for more examples). Urban authorities/planners in the city don't seem to be using the informality lens to make sense of appropriation in the city nor the impact of new regulations. Ananya Roy notes the inherent tensions between the planning profession and informality: the latter is precisely *unplanned*.[71] The new regulations I analyzed here are positioned to have very different impacts for different residents and the everyday lives of appropriators, and seeing these differences requires engaging with informality. The categories of Suppressive and Cooptative Formalization can be used to assess the potential impacts of these and other property-related regulations the city rolls out.

The disparate impact of these regulations "on the ground" is precisely why authorities in cities of the Global North need to be paying attention to informality—to be looking for it and understanding it. Idealistically, one might hope that *were* authorities in Detroit paying attention to this variation in property informality and among appropriators, the responses may be different. But, more likely, some of this disparate, unequal impact is expected or even encouraged/desired by authorities (and other residents). That these new property regulations differentially impact informal appropriation can be explained in two ways (that are not mutually exclusive).

First, the data collection that informed these strategies (like community meetings and neighbors texting-in information about problem properties on their block) may have excluded the most marginalized Detroiters. Scholarship shows that attempts to democratize local governance by including residents in planning processes fall short of creating inclusive policies because only certain residents are likely to choose to participate. Those most likely to not participate in community meetings and the like are the least well off, most marginalized residents.[72] Many of the new plans, programs, and recommendations have been informed by a great deal of input from Detroit residents. But it is possible these meetings were not well attended by very marginalized residents like NAs, and so their needs and voices may not have been taken into account. Indeed, in my own research, community meetings tended to be attended by *either* LAs or NAs, but there was not much overlap except by RAs. And NAs were most often in attendance at meetings held by service organizations like soup kitchens.

A second way to interpret these findings is that declining cities like Detroit must create the conditions in which gentrification and revitalization are possible. Key to attracting new residents with various forms of capital who can bolster processes of gentrification is developing avenues for affordable or inexpensive property ownership and demonstrating that property rights are protected (by curbing illegal property use). Prior research also shows that removing signs of crime and disorder improve the perception of neighborhoods by outsiders,[73] and that whites are more likely to move to areas with other whites.[74] The survival tactics of Detroit's poorest residents (who are overwhelmingly Black) are negatively impacted by revitalization efforts that aim to curb illegal property appropriation. These revitalization efforts may be making it harder for poor Detroiters—who themselves may be viewed as an obstacle to revitalization—to get by in the city.

One way to think about this variation or these unequal impacts is that different ways of relating to property are being co-opted or suppressed. Settling the City entails ways of relating to property that are very aligned with the ideologies of liberalism: private property is viewed as a bastion of individual freedom and is a relationship that is legitimated via investment, labor, and future commitments. The informal practices of "settlers" easily "fit" with this dominant model, in which individual property rights solidify one's rights to the space of the city (and access to the resources therein) and entail obligations to invest in and care for property. These investments must accord with middle-class tastes (or pioneering tastes in which creativity in form and function are embraced) that require more significant resources (time, labor, and economic) that many NAs or RAs do not have access to nor interest in expending. Property ownership (at least in the domain of homeownership, which is where most existing research has focused) is typically only undertaken with a futural intention—it's only economically worthwhile to buy property (versus rent for example) when one plans to own it for at least several years.

On the other hand, the property relations that tend to characterize Surviving the City are much more temporary, immediate, and entail a kind of "pausing" rather than settling or investing and therefore don't align with the liberal private ownership model. The responsibilities that property ownership entails are burdensome unless one has the capital and other resources to stay abreast of these obligations. Many NAs are more comfortable with the precarity of squatting than renting or owning; the latter requires them to stay on top of regular financial obligations or risk eviction/foreclosure. The dominant property regime in the United States doesn't easily enable formalization of these Surviving the City practices. This is perhaps in part because the ways of relating to property that characterize Surviving the City don't easily translate into a form of ownership that is privileged, prevalent, nor ideologically or institutionally supported.

Here we see that creative, locally responsive planning in Detroit meets its limits in the realm of envisioning alternatives: the buck stops with the application of the liberal private property regime. Because of this, the interface of the formal and informal becomes a mechanism for reproducing race and class inequalities in the urban context.

But what might it look like to respond to Surviving the City via co-optative formalization as well? What if the city of Detroit and other cities like it were to respond to informality in ways that privilege the epistemic and ontological situations of their more marginalized residents? What if these ways of understanding and navigating the city were used to guide planning responses, as they have been in Global South contexts? In declining cities that are often bleeding residents, retaining bodies and minds—even of those often deemed superfluous or undesirable—might be an easy argument to win (or at least easier than in cities like San Francisco where these bodies are overwhelmingly physically/spatially "in the way"). I'll turn to these questions in the next chapter, where I conclude by discussing how policies might more deliberately—and equitably—respond to informality in the context of declining city stabilization and revitalization.

Conclusion

LESSONS FOR INFORMALITY IN THE GLOBAL NORTH

Detroit is changing. I don't agree with popular interpretations of these changes as gentrification, as this is overly simplistic (and obfuscates what I argue elsewhere are reproductive of settler colonial structures of erasure).[1] Nonetheless, a sense of urgency has motivated my timeline for writing this book. Policymakers in cities like Detroit need to take stock of and better understand the informal practices that they may be unknowingly impacting via the enforcement of existing laws or the creation of new ones. I am certainly not suggesting that government ought to completely stay out of these informal practices, as that would mean squatters like DeAngelo are left living without even heat and running water. Or scrappers like Bond would continue to labor intensively under extremely unsafe conditions for meager income. Rather, one of my goals is for city authorities, policymakers, and planners to recognize the varied informal practices that have and continue to shape their cities and citizens' everyday lives, such that plans and policies can be made with an eye toward improving these conditions, rather than ignorantly (or even purposefully) regulating these practices out of existence. Toward this end, I urge scholars and policymakers to think sociologically about informal practices in the United States. This means looking more deeply at the social impact of practices that are illegal or noncompliant. Illegality does not always mean illicit or harmful, but illegality does entail violating social rules. With regard to real property, violating these rules goes against deeply held ideals about the normativity of private property rights and the valorization of private ownership as a social good.

Informality poses ideological and regulatory obstacles for policymakers and urban planners, because informality defies regulations and is "unplanned."[2] Yet there is great need for plans and policies to respond sensitively, productively, and conscientiously to informality. My work and others show that formalizing informality has serious implications for the conditions of life for a wide variety of residents. Allowing legal violations to persist, like noncompliant housing or food vending, undermines the law and can perpetuate conditions that are dangerous for health and safety (like inadequate sewage disposal in houses or lack of refrigeration by food vendors). Tolerating noncompliant work or housing practices can signal that substandard conditions are acceptable for poorer Americans, further perpetuating caste-like divides. But responding with criminalization or heightened enforcement of existing laws like building or health codes can make these modes of getting by riskier, economically burdensome, or entirely unavailable for poor Americans, leaving them worse off in their everyday lives (such as when new colonia regulations essentially ended new developments of this kind, which provide much needed affordable housing[3]).

So how ought government and authorities respond? There is a lot at stake in these policy decisions. I conclude this book by first bringing into conversation the work of policy, legal, and urban planning scholars who have variously addressed the conundrum of formalizing informality in the Global South and some scholarship that has already sought to transfer these lessons to the US context. I focus on existing research on the governance of informal housing because of the centrality of land and space ("property" according to the state) to both housing policies and my study of informal property use in Detroit. I am confident, however, that similar questions and considerations would also be productive in devising strategies to regulate informal economic activities. In putting these examples from various regions in conversation with each other, I do not mean to ignore the specificities of local political, economic, cultural, or legal conditions that scholarship has robustly demonstrated are significant for understanding how informality manifests.[4] Instead, I aim to extrapolate lessons that can be put to work in cities like Detroit where local specificities will, of course, necessarily come into play in actual policy formation.

To these ends, I proffer a series of considerations we ought to address in seeking to respond to informality in socially just ways. I focus on concrete ideas for Detroit and other declining cities grappling with similar urban conditions, but I believe these considerations can translate to other contexts as well. Specifically, I argue that declining cities would do well to implement three "progressive" strategies for addressing informality, including 1) regulatory exceptions, 2) incremental formalization, and 3) expanding notions of property rights.

GOVERNING INFORMALITY

As with all social issues, there are conflicting ideas about how government ought to respond to informality. In the United States, these views tend to diverge along the generalized "left"/"right" political divide.[5] The complexities of governing informality also create tensions for both the left and right. The left tends to be more supportive of social policies that aim to help the poor. Permitting informal practices rather than criminalizing or erasing them can support the survival practices of poor Americans and reduce the punitive risks associated with living in violation of the law. Yet, from the left's perspective, government *ought* to improve the socioeconomic positions of the poor such that they don't *need* to rely on informal economic or housing strategies and endure substandard conditions at work and home. On the other hand, allowing informality to persist may resonate with commitments to limited government on the right, leaving the poor to fend for themselves as increasingly neoliberal governments abdicate social responsibilities. But this laissez-faire approach doesn't crack down on the "criminal" practices of informal actors nor hold them accountable to the rule of law, which are responses valued by the right. From both sides, informality is a failure of government.

Similar tensions exist across different scholarly understandings of the relationship between law and informality. Legal scholar Jane Larson writes that all "informality is an indigenous response to the unproductive use of law."[6] But in what way is law imagined to be unproductive? Hernando de

Soto and other economists in the United States have made the argument that too much regulation gives rise to informality by making the costs of conforming to the law too high and that the solution lies in scaling back regulations so that informal practices no longer violate laws.[7] Other scholars argue the opposite: that informality arises when there is too little law and oversight such that social safety nets deteriorate, and the poor (and, increasingly, the middle class) must rely on self-help survival strategies.[8] These different understandings of the legal and political problems of informality dovetail with different "paradigms"[9] or "epistemologies"[10] of government response to informal housing in cities in the Global South, the most prominent of which are *land titling* and *upgrading*.

In early responses to informal housing settlements around the 1950s,[11] slum clearance, razing, and eviction predominated.[12] In Latin America this led to massive displacement of the poor; whereas in other regions residents were moved into new social housing.[13] Post-democratization in much of Latin America, two response paradigms have dominated formalization policies: land titling and upgrading. It is important to remember these paradigms are not mutually exclusive but broad patterns I am sketching to encourage generalizability and application in varied contexts. (For example, sociologist Xuefei Ren finds various combinations of demolition and removal, or upgrading and integration in her case studies in China, India, and Brazil.[14]) After reviewing these two dominant response paradigms, I will turn to more progressive, outside-the-box regulatory recommendations by informality scholars. In presenting these different regulatory recommendations, I try to concretize them by referencing existing and potential policy responses in cities like Detroit.

Regularization through Titling

Formalization of land rights has typically occurred through titling, wherein residents are given legal title to the land/house they occupy. The purpose of titling is not only to give residents of informal settlements more secure tenure, but also to give them access to wealth via enforceable private property rights over the land/housing they occupy. The aim is for this new wealth (property ownership) to enable participants access to economic markets or credit.[15] But studies show that poverty is not alleviated by this narrow approach to formalization and that in reality these land titles offer residents little ability to gain access to credit or participate in markets, nor improve their employment prospects post-legalization.[16]

Furthermore, titling can lead to gentrification, as residents of informal settlements are not protected from market pressures post-legalization. Studies also find evidence that titling can lead to more informal settlements or land seizures, as other citizens anticipate or come to expect titling in the future.[17] The process of titling can also exacerbate gender inequality as much of the time, legal titles are conferred to male heads of household.[18] Finally, overlapping claims to land/housing can complicate titling processes and exclude many residents of informal settlements.[19] Scholars explain titling as a narrow approach to legalization that largely ignores the broader social context and fails to address the conditions that produced informality in the first place.[20]

Regularization through Upgrading

Upgrading strategies take a more comprehensive approach to regularizing informality, combining legal titling with improvements to the built environment and investments in public services, job creation, and community support structures. This model is predicated on the notion that it is much cheaper to 1) provide services on site than to relocate residents to new housing and 2) promote enablement—help the poor help themselves.[21] These "self-help" neighborhoods are understood to provide public benefit but also act as a mechanism of control over the poor.[22] These broader upgrading programs show more success in improving everyday conditions for residents than just titling.[23] But scholars argue that even upgrading approaches are limited when the *space* of a slum is improved but little is done to invest in or expand residents' capacities and overall well-being.[24] Investments in informally developed spaces cannot alone disrupt enduring obstacles and inequalities.

Titling and Upgrading Strategies in Detroit

In Detroit, some titling programs have been implemented in response to informal occupation practices, but these are limited in scope and are not paired with any sort of comprehensive upgrading efforts.[25] There are past and present programs that offer the opportunity for illegal occupants to gain title to the houses they occupy, but they come with a host of stipulations. Unveiled in 2015, the Occupied Buy-Back program, run out of the Detroit Land Bank Authority, allows eligible occupants of land bank-owned houses to buy them for $1,000. Only former owners, renters, or relatives of former owners; or other squatters who have paid utilities for at least twelve months or have made significant improvements to the property are eligible for this program (thus excluding certain categories of illegal occupants in my study).[26] Eligible buyers must then meet several requirements, like demonstrate financial stability, maintain the exterior of the home, save money for property taxes in an escrow account, and keep the water bill paid. If these requirements are successfully met by the end of a trial period, the deed is conferred to the occupants.[27] While physical upgrades to the property are not offered as part of the program, participants are required to attend quarterly "Home Preservation Workshops" with DLBA partner agencies and receive financial counseling prior to entering the program (as part of determining their eligibility), which could be considered an element of social upgrading.

Starting back in 1983, the city of Detroit established the Nuisance Abatement Program, which enabled the city to take ownership of property that constituted a nuisance for being run-down, blighted, or dangerous, for example.[28] Interested citizens could then gain ownership of a property charged with being a nuisance by fulfilling certain criteria. They had to be accepted after a lengthy approval process, restore the property up to code within a specified time frame, and live in the property. Several nonprofit groups in the city participated by reaching out to communities and neighborhoods to try to assist residents in gaining ownership of properties through this program. The Nuisance Abatement Program was moved from the city prosecutor's office to Wayne County in 2004 and was eventually shut down in April of 2010 due to lack of funding and because it was considered economically untenable. Over the years, thousands of residents applied for this program, but few were accepted, in part, due to a cumbersome approval process. Even fewer were able to fulfill the requirements by renovating up to code and living in the property.[29] For some others, the property owners returned and reclaimed the property even after the applicant had invested thousands of dollars into repairs.

Perhaps because squatters are so spatially dispersed across Detroit, there are no models of localized upgrading programs paired with titling to improve access to utilities, or neighborhood or housing conditions (other than targeted demolition). Instead, with current and past programs, repairing the house up to code and investments to improve utility access (like purchasing hot water heaters or repairing plumbing) are the responsibility of the new owner. For some occupants, the opportunity to own is welcome. If the house is in decent condition and the occupant has regular income to be able to pay future taxes, utilities, and upkeep, such a program may be a good fit. But bringing a property up to code is often a stiff challenge even for many economically stable Detroiters.

The DLBA's "Side Lot" program offers homeowners the opportunity to purchase vacant lots adjacent to their house. Here, history of demonstrable care for a given lot is used by the DLBA to adjudicate competing claims by neighbors—i.e., gardeners and blotters are given priority to purchase over other eligible residents who are not already using and caring for the lot(s).[30] Titling is not a fit for informal practices like demolition, scrapping, or salvaging, as this practice is directed towards appropriating material resources from property (though some of these appropriators may have other interests in property ownership).

Land and home ownership programs are only a useful policy response to informality when occupants are comfortable with and desire the responsibilities and liabilities that go along with legal private ownership. In this study, these programs—examples of co-optative formalization— would likely be a good fit for homesteaders and some holdover squatters, or for the LAs and RAs who blot or farm vacant lots. For occupants/users who envision their tenure as short term or temporary or who lack the resources to take on the financial responsibilities of ownership, gaining legal title is not a good fit for their practices. Even some urban farmers, who have been cultivating land in the city for decades, express hesitation about ownership. Some of these gardens function akin to common space, where neighbors and even passersby are welcome to participate in the space and share food. Thus, for an individual in the neighborhood to own them could burden them with liabilities and responsibilities for spaces that they don't exert (nor want to exert) complete control over. One final consideration is that, especially in a context like Detroit where speculations and glimmers of gentrification are on the horizon, we know that titling doesn't protect residents from displacement or further destabilization if/when market pressures from gentrification arise.

Other broader upgrading strategies may be productive in several dimensions for cities like Detroit. One could imagine a city program that offers supplies to seal squatted homes from the elements or provide kits to construct rain collection devices or 55-gallon drum furnaces to "help the squatters help themselves." And, in cities in the Global North, improving access to utilities may be much simpler than in many contexts in the Global South. Water, sewer, electricity, and gas infrastructure are already in place; occupants just need access to the resource. However, just because utilities can be turned on doesn't change the fact that many people can't regularly afford to pay for them.

Utility provision is another avenue for further investigating informality in the United States. Peter Ward finds many colonia residents living without formal access to basic utilities.[31] And, we mustn't forget that many households in Detroit have been subject to widespread water shut-offs starting in 2014 and the now half-decade long poisoning of Flint, Michigan's water supply (yet another case of residents being horribly neglected, if not institutionally targeted, by their local government). In both instances many residents are procuring access to water informally. Additionally, many other examples of informal economic practices likely abound in Detroit—beyond those that rely on real property like scrapping or salvaging.

TOWARD A PROGRESSIVE REGULARIZATION AGENDA
FOR DETROIT

Urban, policy, and legal scholars have sought to promote more progressive regulatory agendas to avoid deepening inequalities during processes of formalization. There are three key recommendations that arise across informality scholarship and that offer promising lessons for addressing property informality in cities like Detroit: 1) regulatory exceptions, 2) incremental formalization, and 3) expanding notions of property rights.

Regularization through Exceptions

Ananya Roy (and others) have drawn on Giorgio Agamben's state of exception to think through the idea of regulatory exceptions: manifesting as a limited duration of time during which the laws and regulations pertaining to an informal development/practice are suspended.[32] The aim is to prevent the negative impact of enforcing laws or regulations that poor residents cannot afford to conform to, thereby prohibiting constructive practices. For example, the need to prove formal legal right to one's home to get utility connections could be suspended. Or authorities could refrain from enforcing punitive policies in response to nonstandard ways that low-income communities use urban space.[33] Exceptions can also be understood as the government "getting out of the way" to allow a level of flexibility that burdensome formal regulations prohibit.[34]

In the context of cities like Detroit, residents have also questioned why they are required to adhere to certain responsibilities when the city regularly fails its responsibilities. For example, when my partner and I bought our house in Detroit in 2013, an inspector from the city came by and wrote an extensive list of all the building code violations we were responsible for fixing. Soon after, the city stopped sending inspectors out in this manner due to budgetary constraints and no one ever followed up to examine our repairs. If the government can suspend their responsibility to enforce building codes, then they are also able to suspend the responsibility of conforming for residents who cannot afford to. The costly responsibilities of property ownership was sometimes why squatters did not want to legally own their houses: they couldn't afford to repair windows or fix leaky gutters. But building codes (as one regulatory example) are often products of politics as much as safety and are influenced by a range of factors from labor unions to cultural norms.[35] The aesthetics of informal spaces often conflict with normative ideals of order and legitimacy.[36] Codes that regulate safety could be prioritized, while codes that attempt to regulate the appearance or aesthetics of properties could be suspended. This is an example of creating a temporary state of exception.

Another kind of regulatory exception that might be productive for addressing informality in Detroit is to be able to have certain features of one's property formalized as "legal nonconforming." This is typically a way of grandfathering in nonconforming uses or conditions when a new regulation is imposed. But here we can think of ways to not penalize squatters or blotters for altering their properties in ways that don't conform to codes, such that the cost of changing these features isn't a hindrance to ownership. Many squatters rely on inexpensive workarounds such as alternative heating or rain collection devices. This regulatory technique is already employed in Detroit's urban agriculture ordinance: some built structures or arrangements of space that pre-date formalization can be permitted to continue as "legal nonconforming," which incentivizes legalization by failing to penalize agricultural endeavors that don't conform to the new ordinance.

Regularization through Incremental Formalization

To prevent the devaluation of laws and standards—and uphold the legal ideals of equality and equal enforcement—incremental steps toward meeting existing regulations can be taken. Jane Larson calls this the "progressive realization" of legal standards that may be unattainable at the outset.[37] She looks to international human rights law, specifically the International Covenant on Economic, Social, and Cultural Rights for a model.[38] This covenant spells out that rights must be progressively realized to the maximum of available governmental resources.[39] Larson argues that this model respects both legality and equality. The law is applied equally insofar as it requires "maximum available resources" from both government/authorities and residents engaged in informal practices; but it promotes equality by recognizing existing inequalities that impact residents' abilities to comply. Thus this approach doesn't further frustrate goals of social justice by overburdening residents. She explains,

> People who are different can be disadvantaged by treating them the same as others in contexts where they cannot live up to the accepted norm; but they can also be disadvantaged if they are treated as different in a way that reinforces traditional stereotypes or perpetuates their position of exclusion or inferiority.[40]

Larson argues instead for *special treatment* and *substantive equality* not equal treatment and formal equality. These both can be applied to informal housing and informal economic activities like street vending or under-the-table/noncompliant businesses (like daycares or in-home salons/food preparation).

In many Global South contexts, incremental formalization could be said to characterize the progression of informal settlements, as after titling occurs various services (like road infrastructure or utility provision) are slowly introduced over time. In Mexico, for example, "colonias populares" (informal settlements) incrementally formalize over time and, in two to three decades, come to reflect city averages in terms of urban services and housing quality.[41] In Detroit, residents in housing with substandard conditions could be required to renovate to meet building codes slowly over time, in accordance with their available resources. Many other regulatory "exceptions" made initially could be enforced over time as well, including paying full tax or utility bills.

A key point with this approach is that incremental formalization requires both residents *and* government to devote maximum available resources to meeting existing standards.[42] Some property laws aim to curtail informal practices, like anti-squatting laws; while others can be deployed to prevent the conditions that motivate informal property use—like tax reversion that leads to vacant properties, homeless residents, and nonexistent neighbors. The city could focus on devoting "maximum available resources" toward enforcing property-related laws and regulations that are most helpful for community stabilization, such as preventing trash dumping or aiding residents' ability to stay in their homes. Or, the city could devote resources toward low-cost solutions to improve housing conditions for squatters, like providing materials to seal houses from the elements.

Regularization through Expanded Property Rights

Regulatory exceptions and incremental enforcement offer ways of responding to informality that both uphold the cultural ideals of law in the United States and don't exacerbate existing inequalities. But these approaches don't *prevent* informality. The third feature of a progressive formalization agenda—expanding notions of property rights—can be deployed proactively *and* retroactively to address informality. Scholars from various domains have called attention to the harmful impacts of the liberal private property regime for those who lack legal rights to property.[43] The root of this issue, some of these scholars have argued, is not just that some are *excluded* from the domain of property ownership, but that the liberal private property regime makes it possible for this exclusion to exist.[44]

Perhaps most famously, legal scholar Jeremy Waldron argued that life is inherently spatial insofar as all the necessary activities for supporting life must be done *somewhere*.[45] Homeless persons therefore lack the freedom to act when they lack the legal right to the space necessary for carrying these activities out (such as sleeping, bathing, or urinating). Creating urban commons wherein these practices are permitted can help alleviate this burden on homeless citizens.[46] Urban commons are an example of expanding legal rights to space. But thinking even more progressively, not only can we recognize that economic practices also require space but also often resources or permitted uses of real property.[47]

Expanding models of property rights, legal tenure, and claims to property access, use and control could prevent some of the problems created by the exclusion that happens within the liberal property regime. Research finds that experiments with alternative tenure rights in parts of the Global North and South have shown success, such as individual or collective leaseholding over public land, community land trusts, cooperatives, temporary permits or authorized occupations.[48] Others advocate considering "security of tenure" as a continuum of rights and claims that can include the right to remain as well as claims to services and credit.[49] Expanding legitimate tenure claims[50] or rights of access to benefit streams (perhaps more relevant for informal economic practices)[51] can *prevent* informality by creating new ways of legally accessing the space of the city and the resources therein that are a better fit for the diversity of informal practices that persist. Furthermore, the right to control and make decisions over property could be expanded, requiring a kind of ground-up "agenda setting" by informal actors.[52]

The most progressive and possibly most effective way to respond to informality in cities like Detroit in a just and equitable way is through these modes of expanding property rights. For example, alternative tenure rights, akin to what was called an "authorized squat" in London, would promote safety and stability for illegal occupants like squatters.[53] Authorized squats allow occupants to live in a building with a "no rent, no repairs" kind of agreement with the property owner. That is, squatters can live for free, but property owners are released from any responsibility or liability for their occupancy.[54] In a case like Detroit, squatters could be granted authorizations to occupy city-owned properties for a predetermined or ongoing amount of time without penalization. The city could even designate which properties were available for authorized occupation. A June 2016 survey of tax foreclosed properties in Detroit found that 89 percent reported wanting to stay in their home. But, interestingly, only 47 percent reported wanting to buy the property.[55] Expanding property rights could enable these occupants to stay in their homes without necessitating legal ownership.

Relatedly, property occupants in Detroit could be granted the right to access and hookup utilities, regardless of their legal status. Some squatters in my study were capable of paying for utilities and would have done so if they were allowed. Many squatters seemed to think they needed to falsify documents to get DTE (gas/electric) hooked up, but my research assistant's queries to the company in 2019 found that legal occupancy was not something that the company attempted to verify prior to starting service (perhaps they previously did). Conversely, the water company did require and verify legal residency.

Regarding forms of property deconstruction, there is heightened concern for the safety of appropriators. But criminalizing these practices only makes them more dangerous by making practitioners feel they need to be covert or to move quickly, and potentially carelessly. Some sort of expanded right to access resources from real property[56] (i.e., disused building materials) could benefit scrappers and salvagers or perhaps even promote more collaboration among practitioners to share tools, knowledge, and labor.

Property rights also adjudicate decision-making and control capabilities. Many residents in my study—especially RAs—were frustrated by their reliance on an absentee municipality that purported to be responsible for local conditions but did little to positively influence them. Because property informality is uneven and dispersed throughout Detroit, spatially decentralized control and decision-making might make more sense for figuring out how to respond to informal practices.[57] Decision-making rights for vacant/abandoned properties could be localized to the few surrounding blocks. This would allow residents to determine acceptable uses that align with an ethos of care, such as whether a house remains boarded up, squatters are permitted to move in, or the property is allowed to be scrapped and subsequently demolished.

Social justice-oriented scholars have proposed that we ought to "look to the bottom" and listen to those who have experienced the brunt of the social problems we seek to rectify.[58] This ideal can be framed in the context of expanding property rights; as listening to and privileging the epistemic agency of residents involved with informality is necessary for these communities to assert their rights to control and make decisions over property. These residents are akin to Gramsci's "organic intellectuals," who have more vested interest in and practical knowledge of problems and solutions.[59] Ananya Roy calls this the "politics of shit," referencing anthropologist Arjun Appadurai to illustrate her point. He writes, "When a World Bank official has to examine the virtues of a public toilet and discuss the merits of faeces management with the defecators themselves, the poor are no longer abject victims, they become speaking subjects, they become political actors."[60] This is an important proposition that arises in other scholarship concerned with articulating social justice-oriented approaches to regulating informality.[61]

PROPERTY INFORMALITY AMID RISING INEQUALITY IN AMERICA

The spatial turn in sociology has brought a wealth of scholarship that explicitly engages with the role of space and place for understanding social life. Similarly, collaborations between legal scholars and sociologists have helped to affirm the centrality of law for social life and vice versa. But sociologists seem not to be connecting these two disciplinary advancements, as there is a lack of uptake with the socio-legal nature of space and place in our discipline. In the United States (and many other countries shaped by the principles of liberalism), overcoming this gap requires engaging explicitly with real property, as space is carved up and regulated by laws that dictate use, access, and control of these spaces and the benefit-streams they provide. These legal regulations shape the character of these spaces and the social practices/interactions that happen therein.[62]

It might seem, at first glance, that my study affirms the centrality of *space* over *real property* because the law is in many ways insufficient for explaining the practices in this book; practices which persist despite the law. Yet, in the United States where the liberal private property regime is deeply entrenched in ideology and governance, we cannot ignore the law even when it seems absent. The practices in this book violate laws, transgress boundaries, and defy zoning or building codes. But these informal practices are also layered onto and throughout a geographic space that has already been regulated according to these laws, boundaries, and codes. These regulations don't disappear just because they are regularly defied. Formal law is always present.[63] Importantly, while property informality thrives amidst the sociospatial and political conditions of cities like Detroit wherein residents are able to regularly ignore and defy the law, should these conditions change, laws and regulations that already exist need only be enforced.

In using the lens of informality to make sense of a quintessential declining city, I have picked up a thread laid down by sociologists, urbanists, and legal and policy scholars. In Detroit, the ubiquitous yet glossed-over role of property emerges from the shadows to reveal its centrality for understanding everyday life, social and spatial relationships, and inequality in the city. By writing this book, I aim to contribute primarily to three areas of sociological research: informality, urban decline, and property.

Informality is a prominent feature of everyday life for residents in cities like Detroit but hasn't yet been rigorously recognized as such. Here too, the form of the city is literally shaped by property informality, as interventions into the space of the city are carried out in ways that transgress not only laws but authorities' plans and programs. Residents cultivate, clean up, occupy, build on, tear down, and take from the space of the city, altering the conditions of their blocks and neighborhoods. And because relationships with property are always triadic, these informal engagements with the space of the city shape social relationships as well, as informal rights are legitimated in the social arena via obligations of care toward the property and community.

The lives I analyze in this book and the perspectives I have striven to make sense of are not unique to Detroit. The process of urban decline has shaped many cities in the United States (and globally), reminding us that these are not exceptional spaces, but rather a persistent urban form. When I discuss this research with people unfamiliar with cities like Detroit, my interlocuters often balk and shake their heads in amazement. When I speak with people from Youngstown, Ohio, or Buffalo, New York, or certain neighborhoods in Chicago, Philadelphia, or New Orleans, I learn that the conditions and practices in this book are familiar and recognizable in their own communities.

Key discussions among scholars of urban decline have noted the need to better understand the way that the conditions of decline alter social life. And that to strategize ways forward—ways for improving the conditions of life in these cities—we need new models that don't rely on tired growth tropes. Promoting growth may be futile in many declining cities. Striving to achieve forms of stability in a "post-growth" context may be more realistic, productive, and beneficial for residents. If informality is a key dimension of urban life in cities like Detroit, policies ought to reflect this and to consider how informality can be a possibility rather than a problem.

This research reiterates the need for studies of social life to pay attention to the role of property, ubiquitous as it is in our society. The ethos of care that arises in distressed neighborhoods in Detroit to adjudicate the informal right to property challenges some fundamental presumptions about the way property rights organize social relationships and the normativity of private ownership. Different models are possible, and perhaps even more appropriate and socially progressive/productive than private ownership, especially amidst the conditions of post-growth cities, where we cannot expect property to be a source of capital expansion nor for market-competition to incite productive use and care.

Furthermore, this book shows the many fruitful, creative, and inventive possibilities for relating to urban property that persist as informal. Informal property relations expand residents' ability to access property and its resources (materials, income, shelter, food, etc). Some are able to access property temporarily (as in squatters who occupy in a short-term manner), others extractively (as a resource stream), some with a kind of longitudinal trajectory (who want to own property), and finally still others in a manner more consistent with property as a kind of urban commons (such as some blotters and gardeners). These varied property relations enable more residents to engage with the space of the city in ways that fit their diverse needs and wants.

The significance of understanding informal property relations are three-fold. First, informal practices can shape laws and policies: the law some-times *follows* changes in social norms and actions, and as such these informal practices can actually shape formal, legal rules. Second, informal norms are sometimes treated as law and upheld and enforced, even by authorities.[64] And third, there is a kind of interaction effect when formal systems are deployed to govern informal practices. In this book, some residents are threatened when their informal, nonstandard property relations come into contact with formal regulations that map the private ownership model onto practices that don't fit well. When this happens, as I argue is the case in Detroit, some residents are harmed not just by the fact that they endure many hardships due to poverty and oppression but that their tactics and strategies for mediating these hardships are now further threatened as well.

The findings of this book also suggest several things that policymakers and planners ought to consider if they are actually committed to promot-ing positive changes for all residents of declining cities, rather than just newcomers with more capital. Policymakers need to recognize that laws and regulations are impacting informal practices in their city/state/region. Along these lines, they need a better understanding of what these prac-tices are like and what motivates participants. In particular, policymakers need to be informed about the way informality driven by need versus desire differ. Not only do residents from different class backgrounds come up with different solutions to similar urban problems as Ryan Devlin argues,[65] but important variations also exist across class lines *within* the same practices, like squatting. Thus, the enforcement of law has varied—and frequently unintended or unforeseen—impacts in practice.

In seeking to understand how informality shapes residents' lives and the sociospatial environment of a given city/region, authorities would do well to explore these practices detached from the norms implied by law and assess informality and its impacts on their own terms. That is, author-ities ought to ask how these informal practices impact daily life and neigh-borhood conditions, rather than starting from the perspective of whether they violate laws. Informality and its productive dimensions for residents' everyday lives and the form of the city can inform policymaking.

For example, when residents are productively using blighted/abandoned properties in the city—whether by squatting, homesteading, salvaging, or scrapping, for example—authorities ought to think twice before demolishing these properties. Demolition as a revitalization strategy has been criticized,[66] perhaps because, in line with broader upgrading strategies discussed in this chapter, it relies on the notion that changing the environment is enough to change people and their circumstances. As I showed, blight demolition also stands to harm very marginalized appropriators: not everyone has the social capital or resources to get their squatted home off the demolition list. And Detroit needs more residents caring for their homes and their blocks. Scaling out, it is also apparent that widespread tax/mortgage foreclosures and subsequent rampant speculation are not a solution to blight in cities like Detroit but in fact a contributor to and producer of it.[67] That many residents struggle to pay property taxes ought to shape new regulatory responses that keep people in their homes rather than forcing them into increased instability and/or out of the city.

In attempting to devise more socially just and equitable regulatory responses to informality, authorities ought to consider how these practices are a form of planning-by-doing that can be read as ways of negotiating, intervening in, and overcoming obstacles or problems that informal actors face. Legal scholars Eduardo Peñalver and Sonia Katyal, while careful to say that they don't condone people violating property laws (who they call "outlaws"), write that "Given the important position that outlaws have occupied in the evolution of property law, however, we believe that it is essential for the law to retain a certain flexibility in its response to them."[68] Authorities ought to recognize the communicative and redistributive impacts of property informality and be willing to learn from the way informal practices rearticulate just forms of property relations.

More and more scholars are tuning into these informal practices in the United States and other Northern contexts.[69] This could be in part because of convincing arguments by scholars[70] who have been calling for more explicit transnational urban research that draws parallels between, for example, third world slums and inner-city American ghettos[71] or studies of subaltern urban spaces in the United States.[72] Perhaps this recent energy—particularly among urban studies and policy scholars—may also be driven by researchers' attunement to US conditions like growing poverty and inequality, shrinking social support systems, increasingly neoliberal governance, and acutely difficult conditions of work and housing. Informality is, in many ways, a response to the practices of the state—both failures (as in, failure to provide affordable housing) and explicit decisions made to enforce (or not) certain practices or allow regulatory exceptions.

Some of this scholarship on informality in the United States, which tends to explicitly engage in transnational comparison, is not new. Peter Ward's seminal work on colonias in Texas is, at the time of this writing, now two decades old. Ananya Roy's article calling for this kind of transnational engagement was published fifteen years ago. So why the slow uptake among scholars in the Global North, particularly the United States? This is perhaps because the ability for social scientists and other scholars to learn from informality in the Global South is impeded by biases in the United States that view informality as coinciding with the economic, social, and political conditions of developing nations. Jane Larson points to three conditions that scholars tend to look to in explaining Southern informality: "(1) the limited resources of governments in developing countries, (2) legal cultures in which rules are often seen as symbolic or aspirational, and which enforcers routinely bend, and (3) political systems that lack meaningful accountability to the needs of the majority."[73] More and more scholarship demonstrates that similar conditions persist—and/or that different conditions also promote informality—in the Global North as well.

This trend toward scholarly recognition and increased understanding of informality—and explicit use of this framework in research on housing and work/economies—is promising, as it means that more empirical research is being conducted that can challenge the presumed pejorativity of categories like illegal or noncompliant and aid devising more productive and socially responsible policies to address informal practices in places like the United States.

Adopting the lens of informality to make sense of the practices in my study and delving into this burgeoning literature has shaped my own attunement to the prevalence of informality in other spaces and regions. Living and working in Philadelphia after graduate school, I followed a new city ordinance that criminalized squatting (and, housing advocates argue, puts precariously housed renters and owners at further risk as well). This ordinance impacts informally housed residents in the city, even those occupying with permission but without a formal rental agreement. And now living in Eugene, Oregon, my conversations with local planners have quickly shifted to the prevalence of practices like camping and car-living as well as regulatory changes that have attempted to respond sensitively to these informal housing practices in the midst of the COVID-19 pandemic (which, relatedly, is already spurring more out-migration from dense urban centers). Two hours north in Portland, Oregon I am struck by the growing number of small two to three tent camp sites scattered throughout the city which, like many on the West Coast, struggles increasingly with housing affordability. With different sociospatial environments and conditions of real property (i.e., higher demand and higher property values) informal practices like housing procurement take shape in different ways.

Just as increasing economic inequality and growing precarity in the United States and other Northern countries means we may see informality driven by need growing, an increasingly economically strained middle-class may turn to informal practices as well. As millennials inherit fewer economic opportunities, high education and housing costs, and generally see less prosperity than they were raised with, this may lead to more and more disaffected young adults shirking the conventional middle-class dream and relying on informality to carve new paths for themselves. Although I am quite critical of Lifestyle Appropriators in this book, I do not mean to disparage them entirely. I actually have quite a lot in common with many of them in terms of progressive visions; a distaste for mainstream ideals and measures of "success"; and a desire to embrace a way of life that is simpler, more in tune with our environment, and refocused on meaningful experiences rather than material possessions. Indeed, for a generation who is inheriting a sick planet, there are real lessons to be learned from the off-the-grid, creative experiments with alternate models that many appropriators embrace. My critiques are moreso of unreflective or uncritical settler aspirations toward the space and people of Detroit.

But in situating critiques of how settler colonial structures are reproduced, we also need to direct our scrutiny to the power-players orchestrating the resettlement of Detroit: the government and their revitalization strategies, institutions that benefit from land-grabbing, and wealthy investors profiting from organized abandonment. As one example, Quicken Loans —owned by billionaire Dan Gilbert who through his various companies has been buying up cheap highrises in Downtown Detroit over the last decade—was sued by the Justice Department in 2015 for mortgage fraud. The federal government indicted Quicken Loans for violating the False Claims Act for improperly originating and underwriting mortgages insured by the Federal Housing Administration. After countersuing and fighting the charges, Quicken Loans finally settled for 32.5 million dollars in 2019.[74] But the outgrowth and impact has been a massive contribution to mortgage foreclosures in Detroit—which we can recognize as contributing to many of the problems Detroit neighborhoods and residents suffer from. These power-players promote and profit from resettlement in various ways, and it is within these conditions and opportunities that new residents like Lifestyle Appropriators pursue the chance to (re) settle Detroit. Ignorant to the fact that they reproduce settler colonial structures of dominance and erasure, power-players and new residents like LAs seek to roll out visions for the future of Detroit that promote their own comfort and experiences with little regard for the 660,000 residents who are at home in the city. It is these dynamics that I find atrocious and personally frustrating. And if I'm frustrated, imagine how Detroit feels.

These differing orientations toward the city and how they dovetail with informal property use ought to be central in planning the way forward for post-growth cities like Detroit. These may be different from the considerations that are at the center of policymaking in the Global South, but in the North, we can still learn a lot from the decades of experience with formalization strategies in other contexts. And perhaps the most straightforward lesson is to treat informal practices as the strategies of organic intellectuals but with careful attention to the differing knowledge of and experience with the city that appropriators have, as shaped by their positionalities and histories. The informal practices in my study are responses to the lack of accountability and responsibility for the city's property, people, and persistent social problems. Individual owners have abandoned their properties, and local government has failed to maintain property that comes into its possession or enforce laws that demand accountability from absentee owners. Dominant ways of thinking about property control tend to exist in a kind of binary: either an individual is responsible, or the city/state is.

But we can shift how we think about property control from a binary to a continuum: from the individual to the block, community, neighborhood to the city, region, etc. When appropriators and residents root the informal right to property in an ethos of care, they disrupt this dichotomous approach to property control.

It is also important that we pay attention to different scales of accountability and responsibility; the practitioners on the ground and the policymakers from above need to consider their responsibilities to communities and how to be accountable to them. The dominant way of being accountable in the eyes of the state and in considering what responsibilities one owes the state is via the law, asking "Is this legal or illegal?" In cities like Detroit, residents and authorities regularly defy these laws. But this does not always mean failing to be accountable or responsible. Through property informality, residents across the city are accountable to each other, to their families, to their neighbors and communities. They are responsible for homes, land, gardens, and each other's safety and well-being. The lens of informality makes readable a city that transgresses its plans and laws. Adopting this framework is productive for challenging existing assumptions about how to intervene in urban problems and can help us recognize productive ways forward.

Appendix

The data in this book comes from ethnographic and qualitative research conducted while living in Detroit. Participant observation began in September of 2011. I moved to Detroit in December of 2011 and continued active participant observation through January 2016. My true exit from the field did not take place until July 2016 when I moved away from Detroit as I was still gathering information that has been incorporated into this book post-dissertation. I have returned to the field several times post-exit to revisit spaces, follow up with participants, and to explore emerging ideas as Detroit continues to change.

During my time in the field, I conducted sixty-five formal interviews, typically lasting about ninety minutes. These formal interviews were supplemented with participation in meetings held by community groups and nonprofits, and volunteering at soup kitchens, homeless shelters, and community gardens. I rode along with police officers on patrol and visited squatted areas and scrap sites. Generally, I sought out opportunities for participant observation that would bring me into contact with illegal property users, or with residents discussing these issues (such as volunteering with eviction-defense groups). I also collected, analyzed, and frequently coded relevant news articles, discussions on the internet chat site DetroitYes!, and important city documents, reports, and plans. I pored over laws, policies, and ordinances that related in some way or another to illegal property use in Detroit.

I knew from the outset that observation and participation needed to be part of my research design, but what I was studying was different from many classic ethnographies I had read. I wasn't embedded in a group or single place to observe. Rather, participation became important insofar as I came to understand property informality from the perspective of a resident—a homeowner in Detroit. Everyday life in Detroit became research; I didn't leave the field at night when I went home. Completely enmeshed in my dissertation meant that questions about property use, law enforcement, and spatial conditions were always hovering in my mind, popping up at any advantageous moment. I made interview connections everywhere, from conversations overheard at a restaurant to the YMCA to the library with my daughter during story hour.

My interview subjects were chosen according to three different groups. Of the sixty-five interviews, forty-two were *appropriators*—people who are illegally using property by squatting, scrapping buildings, or gardening. Twenty-six were *resident witnesses* who have encountered these activities as part of daily life in Detroit, for example, they lived next door to squatters or were the victims of scrapping. And twenty-three were *institutional actors* who deal with illegal property use in their institutional role, such as city employees (e.g., police officers, firefighters, or urban planners), local lawyers, and representatives from influential nonprofits in the city. Very soon the line between these conceptual categories became blurry. During many interviews that started out as *resident witness* interviews, I discovered the witness was also participating in the illegal use of property. Similarly, often during interviews with *institutional actors*, I turned toward my *resident witness* script because it turned out they lived next door to a squatter. In the text of this book, I focus on interview participants' relationship to appropriation moreso than their status as residents when I introduce who they are. That is, I tend to introduce them as a Routine Appropriator rather than a resident witness even if they were interviewed as both. Figure 6 shows how my use of interview guides overlapped for these categories.

In conducting research, I avoided introducing specific language that might influence participants. I introduced my research by stating that I was interested in the use of vacant property in the city and did not specify interest in illegal practices. During interviews, I refrained from introducing the law or from using potentially loaded terms like "squatting" or "scrapping" until the interview participant had done so first. When possible, I also utilized the language offered to me by participants: some squatters called themselves "homesteaders," some scrappers called their activity "hustling." When I categorized these different practices and present the data through the book, I used labels that were illustrative and common across my interviews.

For two reasons, I initially relied on snowball sampling for interviews. First, I did not intend to study "neighborhood effects" at the outset and therefore focusing on specific neighborhoods was not part of my study design. Relatedly, IRB prohibited recording any geographic data and severely restricted the demo-

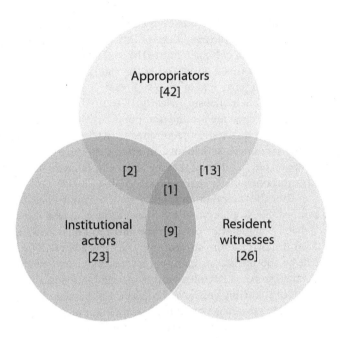

Figure 6. Overlapping use of interview guides.

graphic data I could collect due to concern that residents of very vacant neighbor-hoods could be identified. Second, I expected it would be difficult to find illegal property users who would be willing to speak with me, and snowball sampling can be particularly useful in such scenarios. However, I soon discovered finding participants was easier than expected. Nearly every resident witness I spoke with knew a blotter or squatter (or where to find one). Many squatters knew scrappers (and vice versa). These connections were invaluable. But many of my interview participants were also appropriators I encountered as part of daily life in Detroit. While driving or biking around the city, I frequently traversed different routes to explore as much of the city as I could. Because of this, I often came across poten-tial interview participants. Once I came upon two men taking a fire escape ladder off the Packard Plant in broad daylight. Another time, after coffee with one inter-viewee, he suggested I drive through a nearby neighborhood, naming off several squatters he knew who I might pass by (which I indeed did). Recently burned structures often turned up scrappers, combing through the remains.

Because of this relative ease of finding interview participants, I was able to choose later interview participants to incorporate a broader range of perspectives based on differing backgrounds and identities. As such, my interviews are not representative of any neighborhoods or specific neighborhood conditions in Detroit. When I write about the conditions of Detroit that influence the perception of these practices, I am only speaking to the conditions identified by participants in conversation or that I witnessed in their neighborhoods. I frequently conducted interviews in participants' places of residence or gave them a ride to and from a location of their choosing. Nearly all wanted to talk with me about their neighborhood or show me around and point out the conditions to which I refer in this book. Despite the strict requirements IRB imposed for ensuring the anonymity of my research participants, interviewees were rarely concerned about getting "found out," and I had very few interview requests turned down.

I paid all my interview participants twenty dollars in cash and offered payment before or after the interview, depending on their preference, so that they would feel comfortable stopping the interview at any time. Paying cash was a measured decision I made after considering how to uphold IRB's anonymity requirements—I couldn't ask the university to cut them a check. Nor would gift card/visa cards be appropriate, as many corporate establishments that give out gift cards don't have stores in Detroit's distressed neighborhoods, and many businesses in Detroit at that time only accepted cash. I remember distinctly how I cringed when another researcher, planning to start a new project in the city after only visiting a few times, asked me if she thought she should offer her focus group participants Starbucks gift cards. There was only one Starbucks in the city that I knew of at that time, located in Midtown, miles from where her interview participants lived. The ethically problematic part of offering cash payments was that I found out some of the people I interviewed used the money to purchase drugs.

I recorded interviews using the "Voice Notes" app on my iPhone and was permitted by IRB to only require verbal consent given the importance of allowing participants to maintain anonymity. These interviews were transcribed by a professional transcription service, selected in part because the owner and most of the staff were Black. The owner assured me that many of the staff would be familiar enough with African American Vernacular English (which many of my interview participants used) to transcribe accurately. I coded these transcriptions using Dedoose and had three research assistants code for inter-rater reliability. I coded in iterations soon after each interview was complete; first looking for patterns which I further explored in subsequent interviews and which I refined in subsequent rounds of coding. Due to phone malfunctions, I lost two interview recordings. In one, the participant—a white male Lifestyle Appropriator in his thirties—was largely so incoherent that I chalked it up to a lesson for me to check my recording. Rhiannon's interview recording was also lost, but I was able to reconstruct missing details from notes and follow up conversations with her. I took notes during and reflections after every interview. For participation observation, I took notes (and sometimes recorded) depending on the context and the feasibility of doing so. For example, I could not take notes while pulling weeds at the garden where I worked one summer, but I took notes during community meetings.

All quoted material are direct quotes from transcripts. The interviews were transcribed verbatim, so I sometimes removed "uhs" and "ums" or repetitive words that distracted from the meaning of a quote. Ellipses represent a minor omission of quoted material to bring important words together in a manageable and presentable way; always without altering the meaning of what was said. Some parts of interviews are written but not audio recorded; these are also represented with quotation marks. Bracketed words or phrases within quotes represent words I added to improve the clarity of the quote, such as replacing "it" with [squatting] so as to more clearly communicate the meaning of the quote. Parentheses within quotes are additional information that is germane for understanding the quote.

Maintaining anonymity was of primary importance, both in order to stay in compliance with IRB requirements but also to uphold this promise to my research participants (even though most often they were not at all concerned about having their identity known). Anyone who has lived in Detroit knows what a small town it can be . . . As a city that has a similar population to Portland, Oregon, it never ceased to amaze me how everyone seems to know everyone, or everyone seems linked by one or two degrees of separation. This perception could also have been shaped by the Midwestern friendliness that I encountered in the majority of my interactions with people—even strangers—in Detroit. But this sense that "everyone knows everyone" also meant that in writing this book I had to be cautious to remove identifying details. University of Michigan's IRB was concerned, for example, that if I collected too much demographic data and revealed the neighborhoods where participants lived, that residents in very vacant neighborhoods could be identified. I was concerned that, much like a small town, many folks in Detroit could identify others by their stories. And the identity of the people in my study seems to be particularly fascinating to others. When I give talks, for example, reporters and audience members commonly try to guess the identity of people in my research if they know anyone in Detroit or even if they have just read news articles on similar topics. For people in Southeast Michigan, perhaps this desire to pin down someone's identity is in part because they too have encountered scrappers in the city, or they wonder if the single Black mother squatting that I reference is the same one they read about in a news article on Detroit.

To handle this, I sometimes altered minor details when writing this book, such as how many children someone had or if they were married. If I changed someone's race, I switched it with another person's in the same category to keep the demographic composition of these categories the same. I don't disclose any specific neighborhood information (just general areas of the city), and didn't officially record this either, though I myself know where these practices all took place. Identities are tricky in a study like this. It can be ethically problematic to reveal hidden practices because we cannot control what happens to our data after we publish it. At the same time, if authorities in cities like Detroit take heed to what the data in this book reveals, the hidden practices could become models for renegotiating property access and control in more constructive and socially just ways.

Notes

PREFACE

1. Williams 2018.
2. Aguilar and MacDonald 2015.
3. See Schlichtman and Patch 2014.
4. Interview with Jayne, September 10, 2014.
5. Interview with Doug, June 19, 2013.
6. Explored in chapters 8 and 9; see Herbert and Brown *in progress*.
7. Anderson 1990.
8. Hyra 2017, 19.
9. Massey and Denton 1993.
10. Hyra 2017, 90.
11. Borrowing one of David Harding's terms (2010).
12. Hyra 2017, 91.

INTRODUCTION

1. Lefebvre 1996.
2. As Debbie Becher (2014) finds similarly in Philadelphia.
3. Wegmann 2015.
4. Fairbanks 2009; Becher 2014.

5. Ward 1999.

6. Bernt 2017; see Haase et al. 2014, 1525 for heuristic model.

7. Peñalver and Katyal 2010.

8. See David Garland (2005) on the informal legality of public torture lynchings in twentieth-century America.

9. Castells and Portes 1989.

CHAPTER 1. URBAN DECLINE AND INFORMALITY

1. Hollander et al. 2009.

2. Woetzel et al. 2016.

3. Steinmetz 2009.

4. Sugrue 1996, 14.

5. Bernt 2015.

6. US Census 2010.

7. In Figure 3 the middle class is defined as "those living in households with a household income between 80 percent and 200 percent of the national median income," and the upper middle class is defined as "those living in households with incomes between 200 percent and 300 percent of the national median household income" (Detroit Future City 2019, 22).

8. See Beauregard 1994, for example.

9. Haase et al. 2014, 1520.

10. Bernt 2015.

11. Herscher 2012.

12. Peñalver and Katyal 2010.

13. Hackworth 2014.

14. Glaeser and Gyourko 2005; Galster 2017.

15. Bernt 2015.

16. Pallagst 2008.

17. Wiechmann and Bontje 2015.

18. Hackworth 2014.

19. See Hackworth 2015 for discussion.

20. Hackworth and Nowakowski 2015; Elliott 2018.

21. US Census 2010.

22. US Census 2010.

23. The term "shrinkage" is more popular outside of the United States, perhaps because "the social consequences—exclusion, poverty and homelessness—are happening to a much more dramatic extent in the US than in European cities" (Wiechmann and Pallagst 2012, 273).

24. Molotch 1976; Hackworth 2014.

25. Beauregard 2003; Pallagst 2008, 14.

26. Bontje 2004.

27. Perlman 1976.

28. de Soto 1989.

29. Auyero 2000.

30. Bayat 1997.

31. Holston 2009.

32. Roy 2002.

33. Roy 2011, 227.

34. Chatterjee 2004, 40.

35. Bayat 2000, 533.

36. AlSayyad 2004.

37. Bayat 2007.

38. Peñalver and Katyal 2010.

39. Castells and Portes 1989, 12.

40. Feige 1990, 990.

41. Castells and Portes 1989.

42. Roy 2005; Robinson 2006; Connell 2007.

43. Smart 1986; Pruijt 2003; Uitermark 2004; Martínez 2014; Starecheski 2016; Vasudevan 2017.

44. Kearns 1979; Pruijt 2013.

45. Venkatesh 2006.

46. Duneier et al. 1999.

47. Gowan 2009.

48. Edin and Lein 1997a.

49. Gowan 1997; Edin and Shaefer 2015.

50. Mukhija and Loukaitou-Sideris 2014, 4; see chapter 8 this book.

51. Durst and Wegmann 2017, 113.

52. See Ewick and Silbey 1992, for example.

53. Castells and Portes 1989.

54. Mukhija and Loukaitou-Sideris 2014.

55. See Ward 1999; Larson 2002; Durst 2015; Sullivan and Olmedo 2015.

56. See Ward 1999 for comprehensive discussion.

57. Mukhija 2014; Wegmann 2015.

58. Wegmann 2015.

59. Durst and Wegmann 2017.

60. Harris 2018.

61. Harris 2018, 9.

62. Harris 2018, 12.

63. Roy 2005.

64. Roy 2011, 233.

65. Roy 2011, 231.

66. Roy 2011, 233.

67. Lefebvre 1991.

68. Carruthers and Ariovich 2004.

69. Durst and Wegmann 2017, 1.

70. See Elliott 2018 for discussion.

71. Roy 2005.

72. See Ren 2017, for recent example.

73. Fairbanks 2009.

CHAPTER 2. REGULATIONS AND ENFORCEMENT

1. Mukhija 2014; Wegmann 2015.

2. Kamel 2014.

3. Ward 1999.

4. Massey and Denton 1993.

5. Wilson 1987; Krivo et al. 1998.

6. Holston and Caldeira 2008, 18.

7. This count does not include vacant houses or other buildings that are properly boarded up, secured, surveilled, and regularly maintained, because they do not constitute blight. See Detroit Blight Removal 2014, 3.

8. This does not include privately owned vacant land. See City of Detroit 2013, 88; Detroit Strategic Framework 2012, 11.

9. Sugrue 1996; Steinmetz 2009.

10. Hackworth 2014.

11. US Census 2010.

12. Hackworth 2014, 3.

13. Akers 2013; Hackworth 2014; Mallach 2014.

14. See Sternlieb and Burchell 1973; Salins 1980; White 1986, 313; Hackworth 2014, 3 for discussion.

15. For clear description of some of these conditions see Millington 2013 or Steinmetz 2008.

16. Harris 2018.

17. Steinmetz 2008.

18. Bomey and Gallagher 2013, 6.

19. Hackworth 2014, 23.

20. US Census 2010.

21. Detroit Future City 2017, 60.

22. Cwiek 2015.

23. Akers and Seymour 2018.

24. Way 2010; Durst and Wegmann 2017.

25. US Census 2010.

26. In the second round of the Wayne County Treasurer's property auction, bidding starts at 500 dollars.

27. Lincoln Institute 2012.

28. Atuahene and Hodge 2018.

29. Leopold et al. 2015.

30. Detroit Future City 2017, 63.

31. Leopold et al. 2015.

32. Tighe and Ganning 2016.

33. Atuahene and Hodge 2018.

34. Mallach 2014.

35. Hackworth 2007.

36. Farley 2015.

37. Free Press Staff 2014; while property taxes are commonly handled by counties, in 2004 the City of Detroit began real and personal property tax collection (City of Detroit 2019b).

38. City of Detroit 2013, 9.

39. The Proposal for Creditors states that, "the City urgently needs to upgrade or replace the following IT systems, among others: payroll; financial; budget development; property information and assessment; income tax; and DPD [Detroit Police Department] operating system" (City of Detroit 2013, 19).

40. City of Detroit 2013, 70.

41. City of Detroit 2013, 81.

42. Chirico et al. 2016.

43. For detailed discussion of tax foreclosure in Detroit see Dewar et al. 2015.

44. Loveland 2016.

45. Hackworth 2014, 3.

46. Ikonomova 2017a.

47. Loveland N.D.

48. Interview with Clarence, July 15, 2013.

49. Kinder 2016.

50. Talen 2015; Douglas 2018.

51. City of Detroit 2013, 82.

52. Interview with Quentin, October 22, 2013.

53. See Hackworth 2014, 23–24.

54. City of Detroit 2013, 14.

55. For comparison, Pittsburgh clears 34.0 percent, Milwaukee 23.3 percent, St. Louis 23.5 percent, and Cleveland 11.4 percent (City of Detroit 2013, 9).

56. City of Detroit 2013, 9.

57. City of Detroit 2013, 13.

58. City of Detroit 2013, 13.

59. Interviews with Isaac and Cedric, August 2, 2013.

60. Interviews with Isaac and Cedric, August 2, 2013; interview with Frank, July 2, 2013.

61. Interview with Sondra, March 20, 2014.

62. The original application of this law typically pertained to situations in rural areas where, for example, neighbor A accidentally built a fence two feet onto neighbor B's property. Fifteen years later, neighbor B tries to tell neighbor A to get off her property. Neighbor A can claim adverse possession since she has been using the property for so long and so explicitly that neighbor B could have claimed ownership over the land the fence was built on long prior.

63. *Rozmarek v Plamondon* 1984.

64. Interview with Nathan, March 11, 2014.

65. Becher 2014.

66. As Bartram 2019 also finds in Chicago.

67. Fairbanks 2009.

68. Becher 2014; Bartram 2019.

69. Mallach 2014.

70. Cities where squatters are mentioned in major news sources post-recession include Flint and Detroit, MI; North Lauderdale, FL; Las Vegas, NV; Buffalo, NY; Richmond and Oakland, CA; and Chicago, IL.

CHAPTER 3. FROM ILLICIT TO INFORMAL

1. Castells and Portes 1989.

2. Castells and Portes 1989.

3. Herbert 2018a.

4. Singer 2000.

5. Shlay 2006.

6. Hardin 1968.

7. Demsetz 1967.

8. Taub et al. 1984; Galster 1987; Dietz and Haurin 2003.

9. Sampson 1991; Rohe and Stewart 1996; Rossi and Weber 1996; DiPasquale and Glaeser 1999; Harkness and Newman 2002; McCabe 2013.

10. Goetz and Sidney 1994; Rollwagen 2015.

11. Castells and Portes 1989.

12. Kearns 1979; Pruijt 2013.

13. Gowan 1997; Edin and Shaefer 2015.

14. Wilson and Kelling 1982.

15. Mele 2000; Peñalver and Katyal 2010.

16. While this chapter illustrates the informal social legitimacy of appropriation, appropriators have personal justificatory narratives that vary in important ways, which are examined in detail in chapter 8.

17. Table 2 provides an overview of the practices that fall under the categories of Occupation and Deconstruction.

18. Kearns 1979; Pruijt 2013.

19. See Kinder 2016 for a similar discussion of a "tipping point" for vacant properties.

20. I did not interview resident witnesses who lived in Highland Park or Hamtramck (both municipalities nearly completely surrounded by Detroit). However, I included the Hamtramck context to discuss this institutional actor's perspective because in that moment of the interview he was discussing his own neighborhood, not where he worked in Detroit. His perspective, set against the backdrop of Hamtramck's conditions, is illuminating.

21. Interview with Boris, October 24, 2013.

22. Interview with Lamar, November 4, 2013.

23. For further discussion of such practices in Detroit, see Kinder 2016.

24. See, for example, Anderson 1990; Huo and Tyler 2000; Lundman and Kaufman 2003.

25. Lefebvre 1996.

26. Blackstone 1765; Peñalver and Katyal 2010.

CHAPTER 4. BEYOND POLITICS OR POVERTY

1. Lefebvre 1996.

2. Snow and Anderson 1993, 37.

3. Devlin 2017.

4. Finn 2014.

5. See Hou 2010 and Douglas 2018, for more examples.

6. Mukhija and Loukaitou-Sideris 2014.

7. Talen 2015.

8. For a critical standpoint, see Douglas 2018.

9. Bermann and Marinaro 2014; Devlin 2018.

10. Bayat 2000; Bayat 2007; Chatterjee 2004.

11. Kearns 1979; Uitermark 2004; Aguilera and Smart 2017.

12. Weinstein 2008.

13. Roy 2011.

14. Fischer 2014, 2.

15. Devlin 2017; 2018.

16. Devlin 2017, 3.

17. See Herbert 2018b for close examination of squatting among Necessity Appropriators.

18. Millar 2018.

19. Thompson 1963, 12.

20. Heidelberg Project: https://www.heidelberg.org/ and Blight Busters: https://detroitblightbusters.org/.

21. Bernt 2015.

CHAPTER 5. NECESSITY APPROPRIATORS

1. Tax foreclosure of rent-to-own houses is an all too prevalent predatory practice in Detroit. See Akers and Seymour 2018, for more discussion.

2. See McKinney-Vento 2009.

3. Goux and Maurin 2003; Pilkauskas et al 2014.

4. The local tax law was amended in 1999, shortening the foreclosure timeline for delinquent properties down from six to seven years to three years (Dewar et al. 2015).

5. I interviewed Joe on a separate occasion because he injected heroin the first time I met them and was too high to participate in the conversation much.

6. Glacier Rig N.D.

CHAPTER 6. LIFESTYLE APPROPRIATORS

1. Participants in my study used various terminology for their practices. What Kevin is referring to here is the practice I have labeled "salvaging."

2. Many appropriators mentioned having looked up properties online. During my time in Detroit, there were two common ways this was done. Tax and ownership information are available on the city's website for a small fee. And, after a citywide survey documenting the condition of all property parcels, this data was made available through Loveland Technologies on a website called Motor City Mapping along with ownership information and tax status. Now much of this information is available for cities across the country on a website called Land Grid (also a product of Loveland Technologies).

3. Tax delinquent status is not a reliable measure of the level of care for an occupied property, as many households in Detroit struggle to keep up with high tax bills.

4. Allen recalled going to BSEED which oversees construction, property maintenance, environmental compliance, and zoning codes (https://detroitmi.gov /departments/buildings-safety-engineering-and-environmental-department), but as of 2019 the city's website notes that the Detroit Building Authority is in charge of demolitions (https://detroitmi.gov/departments/detroit-building-authority).

5. Re-stores are businesses that sell building materials/supplies that are reused, like old doors, lights, or windows.

CHAPTER 7. ROUTINE APPROPRIATORS

1. Becher 2014.
2. Because I did not have this typology to organize my research when I was conducting interviews, I did not seek out interviews with holdover squatters who fit the categories of Routine versus Necessity Appropriators.
3. See Mallach 2014 for a breakdown of how this is profitable in Detroit.
4. Loveland Technologies 2016.
5. Akers and Seymour 2018.
6. Of 405 respondents for this question; Loveland Technologies 2016.
7. City records show that Didi does own the lots she mentions in her interview, but the timeline of purchasing them may be off. Prior to 2014 residents in Detroit could not buy property that was not adjacent to their legally owned property unless they planned to build on it—so likely Didi couldn't have purchased the lot immediately next to her house last. But, on the other hand, perhaps there are ways that Detroit residents got around this obstacle before the new 2014 ordinance made it possible to do so.
8. Similar to those analyzed by Kinder 2016.
9. Tyree Guyton's story is well known in Detroit and can be interpreted as an example of Routine Appropriation that transitioned into a Lifestyle practice. See Herron et al. 2007 and https://www.heidelberg.org/.

CHAPTER 8. SURVIVING THE CITY OR SETTLING THE CITY?

1. Ager 2015.
2. Nickum 2014.
3. Bruni 2015.
4. Gustafson 2011.
5. See Finn 2014 for discussion.
6. Devlin 2018.
7. Devlin 2017, 13.
8. Cover 1983; Peñalver and Katyal 2010.
9. Peñalver and Katyal 2010, 25.
10. Cover 1983, 5.
11. Ewick and Silbey 2003, 1345.
12. Cover 1983; Ricoeur 1984–88; Ewick and Silbey 2003.
13. Taylor 2002.
14. Zukin 1987.
15. Spain 1993.
16. Stratton 1977; Brown-Saracino 2009.

17. First-wave gentrifiers is a term used to describe outsiders who move into a neighborhood prior to any typical signs of gentrification but who, in retrospect, are acknowledged to have been the initial "wave" of gentrifiers (and are often subsequently economically displaced as gentrification accelerates). First-wave gentrifiers are often artists, bohemians, or middle-class intellectuals who have rejected mainstream suburban ideals and sought out buildings or homes to renovate in inexpensive, racially diverse, urban neighborhoods. See Lloyd 2006.

18. Smith 1996.

19. Veracini 2011.

20. Veracini 2013.

21. Glenn 2015.

22. Safransky 2014.

23. Hyra 2017.

24. Douglas 2018.

25. Kinder 2016.

26. Riggs 2015, 566–569.

27. Peñalver and Katyal 2010, 56.

28. Becher 2014.

29. Becher 2014.

30. Becher 2014.

31. Wilson 1987.

32. Hackworth 2019.

33. Wilson 1987; Krivo et al. 1998, 68–69.

34. Wilson 1987.

35. Stack 1975; Edin and Lein 1997b; Small 2004; Sampson 2012.

36. Peñalver and Katyal 2010.

37. Detroit's Coleman A. Young Municipal Building used to be called the City-County building, so Detroiters often reference city-county for a general nod toward local government.

38. The federal government allocated Hardest Hit Funds to Michigan post-recession which many residents argue were misused. This is what Bond is referring to.

39. Lisa is also referring to the perceived mismanagement of the Hardest Hit Funds.

40. Interview with Grant, June 29, 2013.

41. See, for example, Appadurai 2004 or Desmond 2016 for cultural/economic ways of thinking about how this manifests.

42. The exception here being the few RAs who had come to enjoy their practices over time, like blotter Didi or gardener Jerome.

43. Piliavin et al. 1996; Wong, Culhane, and Kuhn 1997.

44. Ownership for scrappers would not make sense, whereas for many salvagers what they take *becomes part* of something they own and further benefit from

(such as their home, or a piece of art they can circulate or sell). Holdover squatters had differing perspectives about pursuing ownership. For former homeowners, many tried to buy their properties back at auction, but a new law forbade bidding at the auction if you were behind on your taxes in the past three years (see chapter 9). Many, but not all, farmers/gardeners and blotters were open to or interested in ownership.

45. Starecheski 2016.
46. Massey and Denton 1993.
47. Becher 2014.
48. Brown-Saracino 2009.
49. Devlin 2017.

CHAPTER 9. REGULATING INFORMALITY, REPRODUCING INEQUALITY

1. Akers 2013.
2. Detroit Future City 2012; McGraw 2015.
3. Pallagst 2008; Hollander et al. 2009; Bernt 2015; see Akers 2013 and Hackworth 2014 on Detroit specifically.
4. Safransky 2014.
5. Ward 1999; Larson 2002.
6. Ward 1999; Mukhija and Loukaitou-Sideris 2014.
7. As I will discuss more toward the end of this chapter, the impact of these new regulations for Routine Appropriators depends to a certain extent on whether or not RAs have come to embrace their practices and want to continue them for the future.
8. Oliver and Shapiro 1995; Shlay 2006.
9. See Conclusion for more in-depth discussion of the lessons of formalizing informality.
10. Williams 1991.
11. Bartram 2019.
12. Delgado 1997; Larson 2002.
13. See Holston 2009, for example.
14. Wegmann 2015.
15. Ward 1999.
16. Ward 1999.
17. Roy 2005.
18. Feloni and Lee 2018.
19. Gallagher 2017.
20. Hackworth 2015.
21. Detroit Future City 2012; McGraw 2015.

22. Detroit Blight Removal 2014, 100.

23. Center for Community Progress, N.D.

24. Center for Community Progress, N.D.

25. Edin and Lein 1997a.

26. Clark 2014.

27. Valverde 2012; Rios 2014.

28. Michigan Public Act 501 2014.

29. Detroit Journalism Cooperative 2018.

30. Detroit Land Bank Authority 2019.

31. Some of the holdover squatters I spoke with were renters who had been hoping to keep their homes from being foreclosed by paying the back taxes in exchange for their landlord giving them the title to the property. None I spoke with were able to pay the delinquent back taxes to achieve this. In a city with rampant overassessments and high tax rates, accumulating thousands of dollars in delinquent taxes over the course of three years (the timeline to tax foreclosure) is not difficult.

32. Safransky 2014.

33. Detroit Future City 2012.

34. Detroit Future City 2012.

35. Busdicker 2013.

36. There are several ways to do this, see Busdicker 2013.

37. I also could not find out much information about the old rent-a-lot program from city officials. A new similar program is underway by Mayor Duggan's office, but the time frame residents in my study referred to was prior to Duggan taking office. I could not find information on the city's website, and while city employees and local authorities had heard of the program, they also could not provide documentation of it.

38. Interview with Jerome, October 26, 2013; interview with Didi, May 3, 2014.

39. Busdicker 2013, 3.

40. Deconstruction is "the exercise of human hands physically taking apart a structure" whereas demolition refers to the more common approach of using machinery to demolish a built structure. Deconstruction allows useful materials to be saved in the process. See discussion in Detroit Blight Removal 2014, pages 148–155.

41. Detroit Blight Removal 2014, 148.

42. Detroit Blight Removal 2014, 156.

43. Detroit Future City 2012.

44. Interview with Alondra, October 24, 2013.

45. Heise 2014.

46. Associated Press 2014.

47. This law: 1) restricts payment methods for certain commonly stolen items (like copper wiring), requiring, for example, that payment be mailed to a verified address rather than allowing an immediate cash payment (section 445.426); 2) creates a record of transactions to enable law enforcement to better prosecute scrappers (section 445.427); 3) makes the sale or purchase of certain property items prohibited, such as "public fixtures" like manhole covers, copper from transformers on light poles, and materials clearly marked as belonging to someone other than the seller (section 445.430); and 4) makes certain transactions a felony punishable with fines and/or jail time (section 445.433) (Muxlow et al. 2008).

48. AlHajal 2014.

49. Heisc 2014.

50. Misdemeanor offense carries a maximum $5,000 fine, maximum 180 days jail time. Felony offense carries a maximum $10,000 fine, maximum two years jail time (Heise 2014).

51. Heise 2014.

52. Harpaz 2015.

53. Detroit Blight Removal 2014, 14.

54. Detroit Blight Removal 2014, 13.

55. Wilson and Kelling 1982; Sampson and Raudenbush 2004.

56. Hackworth 2016.

57. Detroit Blight Removal 2014.

58. Interview with Frank, July 2, 2013.

59. City of Detroit 2019a.

60. US Department of the Treasury 2018.

61. Detroit Blight Removal 2014, 240–241.

62. Ikonomova 2017b.

63. MacDonald and Kurth 2015.

64. Prior to the law's implementation, a city official explained that the city could not afford to evict all the squatters in city-owned property (Interview with Quentin, October 22, 2013). But with the new squatting law, the city has other tools it can deploy to remove illegal occupants.

65. It is questionable how long it will actually take to demolish all of the blighted properties in the city. During the time of this research, the city reportedly demolished about two hundred per week (Gallagher 2014).

66. Detroit Blight Removal 2014, 111.

67. Interview with Ginnifer, September 13, 2013.

68. Williams 2015.

69. See Gallagher 2014.

70. I say "may leave" here because it is unclear how much demand there is among informal appropriators for blighted property in comparison to the supply and how much demolition will decrease this supply and how quickly. Local housing rights

activists expressed concern over the impact of demolition for the survival of poor families in the city but also similarly speculated that demolition may not be keeping pace with the rise of blight and thus there may still be a steady "supply" of blighted property for appropriation.

71. Roy 2005.

72. Valverde 2012.

73. Sampson and Raudenbush 1999; Sampson and Raudenbush 2004; Hwang and Sampson 2014.

74. Quillian and Pager 2001; Charles 2003.

CONCLUSION

1. See Herbert and Brown, In Progress.

2. Roy 2005.

3. Ward 1999.

4. AlSayyad 1993; Ren 2017.

5. See Ward 1999, 69, for example.

6. Larson 2002, 158.

7. de Soto 1989.

8. Such as Castells and Portes 1989 and Sassen 2006.

9. Fernandes 2011.

10. Roy 2005.

11. And again in the 1990s, Roy 2005.

12. Roy 2005; Fernandes 2011.

13. Smart 2003.

14. Ren 2017.

15. de Soto 2000.

16. Gilbert 2002; Kagawa and Turkstra 2002.

17. Fernandes 2011; Murphy 2014.

18. Roy 2002.

19. Roy 2005; Fernandes 2011.

20. Gilbert 2002; Kagawa and Turkstra 2002; Fernandes 2011.

21. Roy 2005.

22. Duhau 2014.

23. Fernandes 2011.

24. Perlman 2004; Roy 2005.

25. Some of these titling programs in Detroit are also examples of co-optative formalization but are more explicitly responses to informality in the city than some of the regulations discussed in chapter 9.

26. The program is open to the individuals who meet some or all of the criteria listed below: The last owner of record before public ownership; People rent-

ing the property at time of foreclosure; Has a family member that was the last owner of record before public ownership; Have paid utilities in the property for at least twelve months; Can demonstrate that they have made significant improvements to the property (Lewand-Monroe 2016, 10). As another example of co-optative formalization, this program is likely to only be available to more economically stable holdover squatters (who have the requisite history with the house) or homesteaders who have made substantial improvements to the property.

27. Lewand-Monroe 2016, 10.

28. The Nuisance Abatement Program (NAP) can also be understood as a revitalization (or perhaps more appropriately *stabilization* at that time in the city's history) program which had ramifications for squatters in the city. Housing rights advocates in the city explained that organizations like ACORN had tried to use the NAP to help squatters gain legal titles to homes, but many squatters lost money and were evicted from houses because they didn't have prior approval to take over the property. Interview with Nathan, March 11, 2014. Finding record and information of this program was difficult, so much of this information comes from an interview with a former employee who was closely involved in the Nuisance Abatement Program.

29. Kimani 2004.

30. Interview with Dean, October 14, 2013.

31. Ward 1999.

32. Ward 1999; Roy 2005; Agamben 2005.

33. Rios 2014.

34. Browne et al. 2014.

35. Valverde 2012.

36. Rios 2014.

37. Larson 2002.

38. United Nations 1966.

39. Larson 2002, 178.

40. Larson 2002, 162.

41. Duhua 2014.

42. Larson 2002.

43. Waldron 1991; Roy 2003; Blomley 2009; Ehrenfeucht and Loukaitou-Sideris 2014; Herbert 2018a.

44. Blomley 2009.

45. Waldron 1991.

46. Ehrenfeucht and Loukaitou-Sideris 2014.

47. Kettles 2014.

48. Kearns 1979; Royston and Ambert 2002; Fernandes 2011; Angotti 2017.

49. McAuslan 2002; Sims 2002; Roy 2005, 154.

50. Payne 2001.

51. This idea has found traction in rural and environmental research, see Ribot and Peluso 2003; Larson et al. 2010.

52. Roy 2005.

53. Or, perhaps, *used to be* as increasing criminalization of squatting in countries in Europe has halted some of these more progressive approaches to responding to squatters (see Vasudevan 2017).

54. Kearns 1979.

55. These questions had different response rates, so it's unclear how much overlap there is, Loveland Technologies 2016.

56. See Ribot and Peluso 2003; Larson et al. 2010.

57. Loukaitou-Sideris and Mukhija 2014.

58. Matsuda 1987; Roy 2005.

59. Matsuda 1987.

60. Appadurai 2001 referenced in Roy 2005, 37.

61. Ward 1999; Larson 2002.

62. See Becher 2014; Sullivan 2018; Bartram 2019, for examples.

63. Ewick and Silbey 1998.

64. Garland 2005.

65. Devlin 2017.

66. Hackworth 2016; Ackers 2017.

67. Others have noted this—Hackworth 2018; Ackers and Seymour 2018.

68. Peñalver and Katyal 2010, 125.

69. See Devlin 2018 in NYC; Iveson et al. 2018 in Sydney, Australia; Nelson et al. 2019 in New Orleans; Harris and Patterson 2017 in Hamilton, Ontario; Fairbanks 2009 or Becher 2014 in Philadelphia.

70. See Roy 2005, 2011; Robinson 2006; Auyero 2011; and Schindler 2014.

71. Roy 2005; Auyero 2011.

72. Schindler 2014.

73. Larson 2002, 154-155.

74. Department of Justice 2015; Eisen 2019.

Bibliography

PUBLISHED SOURCES

Agamben, Giorgio. 2005. *State of Exception*. Trans. by Kevin Attell. Chicago: University of Chicago Press.

Ager, Susan. 2015. "Detroit is Cool Again." *National Geographic*, May 2015. http://www.nationalgeographic.com/taking-back-detroit/see-detroit.html.

Aguilar, Louis and Christine MacDonald. 2015. "Detroit's white population up after decades of decline." *Detroit Free Press*, September 17, 2015. https://www.detroitnews.com/story/news/local/detroit-city/2015/09/17/detroit-white-population-rises-census-shows/72371118/. Accessed May 25, 2019.

Aguilera, Thomas and Alan Smart. 2017. "Squatting, North, South and Turnabout: A Dialogue Comparing Illegal Housing Research." In *Public Goods versus Economic Interests: Global Perspectives on the History of Squatting*. Ed. Freia Anders and Alexander Sedlmaier. New York: Routledge.

Akers, Joshua. 2013. "Making Markets: Think Tank Legislation and Private Property in Detroit." *Urban Geography* 34(8): 1070–95.

Akers, Joshua. 2017. "A new urban medicine show: on the limits of blight remediation." In *Why Detroit Matters: Decline, Renewal, and Hope in a Divided City*, edited by Brian Doucet, 95–116. Chicago, IL: Policy Press.

Akers, Joshua, and Eric Seymour. 2018. "Geoforum Instrumental Exploitation: Predatory Property Relations at City's End." *Geoforum* 91: 127–40.

AlHajal, Khalil. 2014. "Detroit looks to alert property owners, trespassers to new anti-squatting laws." *Mlive*, October 13, 2014. http://www.mlive.com /news/detroit/index.ssf/2014/10/detroit_looks_to_alert_propert.html. Accessed June 2, 2016.

AlSayyad, Nezar. 1993. "Informal Housing in a Comparative Perspective: On Squatting, Culture, and Development in a Latin American and a Middle Eastern Context." *Review of Urban and Regional Development Studies* 5: 3–18.

AlSayyad, Nezar. 2004. "Urban Informality as a 'New' Way of Life." In *Urban Informality: Transnational Perspectives from the Middle East, Latin America, and South Asia*, edited by Ananya Roy and Nezar AlSayyad. Lanham, MD: Lexington Books.

Anderson, Elijah. 1990. *Streetwise: Race, Class, and Change in an Urban Community*. Chicago: University of Chicago Press.

Angotti, Tom. 2017. "Uruguay's Housing Cooperatives: Alternatives to the Private Market." In *Urban Latin America: Inequalities and Neoliberal Reforms*, edited by Tom Angotti. Lanham, MD: Rowman & Littlefield.

Appadurai, Arjun. 2001. "Deep Democracy: Urban Governmentality and the Horizon of Politics." *Environment and Urbanization*, 13(2): 23–43.

Appadurai, Arjun. 2004. "The Capacity to Aspire: Culture and the Terms of Recognition," in *Culture and Public Action*, edited by Vijayendra Rao and Michael Walton. Stanford: Stanford University Press.

Associated Press and Crain's Staff. 2014. "Michigan Senate OKs Scrap Metal Bill; Snyder Expected to Sign." *Crain's Detroit*, March 20, 2014. https:// www.crainsdetroit.com/article/20140320/NEWS01/140329993/michigan -senate-oks-scrap-metal-bill-snyder-expected-to-sign.

Atuahene, Bernadette, and Timothy R. Hodge. 2018. "Stategraft." *Chicago-Kent College of Law*, 1–41.

Auyero, Javier. 2000. *Poor People's Politics: Peronist Survival Networks and the Legacy of Evita*. Durham: Duke University Press.

Auyero, Javier. 2011. "Researching the Urban Margins: What Can the United States Learn from Latin America and Vice Versa?" *City & Community* 10(4): 431–36.

Bartram, Robin. 2019. "Going Easy and Going After: Building Inspections and the Selective Allocation of Code Violations." *City & Community* 18(2): 594–617.

Bayat, Asef. 1997. *Street Politics: Poor People's Movements in Iran*. New York: Columbia University Press.

Bayat, Asef. 2000. "From 'Dangerous Classes' to 'Quiet Rebels': the Politics of the Urban Subaltern in the Global South." *International Sociology* 15(3): 533–57.

Bayat, Asef. 2007. "Radical Religion and the Habitus of the Dispossessed: Does Islamic Militancy Have an Urban Ecology?" *International Journal of Urban and Regional Research* 31(3): 579–90.

Beauregard, Robert A. 1994. *Voices of Decline: The Postwar Fate of U.S. Cities.* Hoboken, NJ: Wiley-Blackwell.

Beauregard, Robert A. 2003. "Aberrant Cities: Urban Population Loss in the United States, 1820–1930." *Urban Geography* 24(8): 672–90.

Becher, Debbie. 2014. *Private Property and Public Power: Eminent Domain in Philadelphia.* New York: Oxford University Press.

Bermann, Karen, and Isabella Clough Marinaro. 2014. "'We Work It out': Roma Settlements in Rome and the Limits of Do-It-Yourself." *Journal of Urbanism* 7(4): 399–413.

Bernt, Matthias. 2015. "The Limits of Shrinkage: Conceptual Pitfalls and Alternatives in the Discussion of Urban Population Loss." *International Journal of Urban and Regional Research* 40(2): 441–50.

Blackstone, Sir William. 1765. *Commentaries on the Laws of England.* Oxford: Clarendon Press.

Blomley, Nicholas. 2009. "Homelessness, Rights, and the Delusions of Property." *Urban Geography* 30(6): 577–90.

Bomey, Nathan, and John Gallagher. 2013. "How Detroit Went Broke: The Answers May Surprise You—and Don't Blame Coleman Young." *Detroit Free Press*, September 15, 2013. http://archive.freep.com/interactive/article/20130915/NEWS01/130801004/Detroit-Bankruptcy-history-1950-debt-pension-revenue#. Accessed March 6, 2017.

Bontje, Marco. 2004. "Facing the Challenge of Shrinking Cities in East Germany: The Case of Leipzig." *GeoJournal* 61: 13–21.

Browne, Ginny, Will Dominie, and Kate Mayerson. 2014. "Mediating Informality in the Food Cart Industry." In *The Informal American City: From Taco Trucks to Day Labor*, edited by Vinit Mukhija and Anastasia Loukaitou-Sideris. Cambridge: The MIT Press.

Brown-Saracino, Japonica. 2009. *A Neighborhood That Never Changes: Gentrification, Social Preservation, and the Search for Authenticity.* Chicago: University of Chicago Press.

Bruni, Frank. 2015. "The Spirit and Promise of Detroit." *New York Times Opinion Pages*, September 9, 2015. http://www.nytimes.com/2015/09/09/opinion/frank-bruni-the-spirit-and-promise-of-detroit.html. Accessed June 2, 2016.

Busdicker, Libby. 2013. "A Summary of the Urban Agricultural Amendments to Detroit's Zoning Ordinance." Michigan State University College of Law, East Lansing, Michigan. www.law.msu.edu/clinics/food/busdickerfact.pdf. Accessed December 20, 2016.

Carruthers, Bruce G., and Laura Ariovich. 2004. "The Sociology of Property Rights." *Annual Review of Sociology* 30(1): 23–46.

Castells, Manuel and Alejandro Portes. 1989. "World Underneath: The Origins, Dynamics and Effects of the Informal Economy." In *The Informal Economy: Studies in Advanced and Less Developed Countries*, edited by Manuel Castells, Alejandro Portes, and Laura A. Benton. Baltimore: Johns Hopkins University Press.

Center for Community Progress. N.D. "Frequently Asked Questions on Land Banking." https://www.communityprogress.net/land-bank-faq-pages-449.php. Accessed December 13, 2019.

Charles, Camille Zubrinsky. 2003. "The Dynamics of Racial Residential Segregation." *Annual Review of Sociology* 29(1): 167–207.

Chatterjee, Partha. 2004. *The Politics of the Governed: Reflections on Popular Politics in Most of the World*. New York: Columbia University Press.

Chirico, Michael, Robert P. Inman, Charles Loeffler, John MacDonald, and Holger Sieg. 2016. "An Experimental Evaluation of Notification Strategies to Increase Property Tax Compliance: Free-Riding in the City of Brotherly Love." *Tax Policy and the Economy* 30(1): 129–61.

City of Detroit. 2013. "Proposal for Creditors." City of Detroit Emergency Manager's Office. June 14, 2013.

City of Detroit. 2019a. "Detroit Demolition Program." *Detroit Building Authority*. https://detroitmi.gov/departments/detroit-building-authority/detroit-demolition-program.

City of Detroit. 2019b. "Property Taxes FAQ." *Office of the Assessor*. https://detroitmi.gov/departments/office-chief-financial-officer/ocfo-divisions/office-assessor#Property-Tax-Assistance.

Clark, Anna. 2014. "Will 'Blexting' Help With Detroit Blight?" *Next City*, July 28. https://nextcity.org/daily/entry/detroit-blight-blexting-houses-motor-city-mapping. Accessed December 2, 2019.

Connell, Raewyn. 2007. *Southern Theory: Social Science and the Global Dynamics of Knowledge*. Cambridge, UK: Polity Press.

Cover, Robert M. 1983. "The Supreme Court, 1982 Term—Forward: Nomos and Narrative." *Harvard Law Review* 97(1): 4–68.

Cwiek, Sarah. 2015. "Second Round of Wayne Co. Property Auction Starts this Week." *Michigan Radio*, National Public Broadcasting. October 4, 2015. https://michiganradio.org/post/second-round-wayne-co-property-auction-starts-week. Accessed December 2, 2016.

Delgado, Richard. 1997. "Rodrigo's Twelfth Chronicle: The Problem of the Shanty." *Georgetown Law Journal* 85(3): 667–90.

Demsetz, Harold. 1967. "Toward a Theory of Property Rights." *The American Economic Review* 57(2): 347–59.

Department of Justice. 2015. "United States Files Lawsuit Alleging that Quicken Loans Improperly Originated and Underwrote Federal Housing Administration-Insured Mortgage Loans." *Office of Public Affairs: Justice News*. April 23, 2015. https://www.justice.gov/opa/pr/united-states-files-lawsuit-alleging-quicken-loans-improperly-originated-and-underwrote. Accessed July 20, 2020.

Desmond, Matthew. 2016. *Evicted: Poverty and Profit in the American City*. New York: Crown Publishing.

de Soto, Hernando. 1989. *The Other Path: The Economic Answer to Terrorism*. New York: Basic Books.

de Soto, Hernando. 2000. *The Mystery of Capital: Why Capitalism Triumphs in the West and Fails Everywhere Else*. New York: Basic Books.

Detroit Blight Removal Task Force. 2014. "Every Neighborhood Has A Future . . . And It Doesn't Include Blight." Detroit, Michigan. 2nd printing, June 2014.

Detroit Journalism Cooperative. 2018. "Owe taxes? That's OK. Wayne County Will Still Sell You Foreclosed Homes." *Detroit Journalism Cooperative*. https://www.detroitjournalism.org/2017/10/18/owe-taxes-thats-ok-wayne-county-will-still-sell-foreclosed-homes/. Accessed May 16, 2019.

Detroit Land Bank Authority. 2019. "Rules for Purchasing Properties." *Detroit Land Bank Authority Website*. https://buildingdetroit.org/rules/. Accessed May 17, 2019.

Detroit Future City. 2012. *Detroit Strategic Framework Plan*. Detroit: Inland Press.

Detroit Future City. 2017. *139 Square Miles*. Detroit: Inland Press.

Detroit Future City. 2019. *Growing Detroit's African-American Middle Class: The Opportunity for a Prosperous Detroit*. Detroit.

Devlin, Ryan Thomas. 2017. "Asking 'Third World Questions' of First World Informality: Using Southern Theory to Parse Needs from Desires in an Analysis of Informal Urbanism of the Global North." *Planning Theory* 17(4): 568–87.

Devlin, Ryan Thomas. 2018. "A Focus on Needs: Toward a More Nuanced Understanding of Inequality and Urban Informality in the Global North." *Journal of Cultural Geography* 36(2): 121–43.

Dewar, Margaret, Eric Seymour, and Oana Druţă. 2015. "Disinvesting in the City: The Role of Tax Foreclosure in Detroit." *Urban Affairs Review* 51(5): 587–615.

Dietz, Robert D. and Donald R. Haurin. 2003. "The Social and Private Micro-Level Consequences of Homeownership." *Journal of Urban Economics* 54(3): 401–50.

DiPasquale, Denise and Glaeser, Edward L. 1999. "Incentives and Social Capital: Are Homeowners Better Citizens?" *Journal of Urban Economics* 45(2): 354–84.

Douglas, Gordon C. C. 2018. *The Help-Yourself City: Legitimacy and Inequality in DIY Urbanism*. New York: Oxford University Press.

Duhau, Emilio. 2014. "The Informal City: And Enduring Slum or a Progressive Habitat?" In *Cities from Scratch: Poverty and Informality in Urban Latin America*, edited by Brodwyn Fischer, Bryan McCann and Javier Auyero. Durham, NC: Duke University Press.

Duneier, Mitchell, Ovie Carter, and Hakim Hasan. 1999. *Sidewalk*. New York: Farrar, Straus and Giroux.

Durst, Noah J. 2015. "Second-Generation Policy Priorities for Colonias and Informal Settlements in Texas." *Housing Policy Debate* 25(2): 395–417.

Durst, Noah J., and Jake Wegmann. 2017. "Informal Housing in the United States." *International Journal of Urban and Regional Research* 41(2): 282–97.

Edin, Kathryn, and Laura Lein. 1997a. "Work, Welfare, and Single Mothers' Economic Survival Strategies." *American Sociological Review* 62(2): 253–66.

Edin, Kathryn, and Laura Lein. 1997b. *Making Ends Meet: How Single Mothers Survive Welfare and Low-Wage Work*. New York: Russell Sage Foundation.

Edin, Kathryn, and Luke Shaefer. 2015. *$2.00 a Day: Living on Almost Nothing in America*. New York: Houghton Mifflin Harcourt Publishing.

Ehrenfeucht, Renia and Anastasia Loukaitou-Sideris. 2014. "The Irreconcilable Tension between Dwelling in Public and the Regulatory State." In *The Informal American City: Beyond Day Labor and Taco Trucks*, edited by Vinit Mukhija and Anastasia Loukaitou-Sideris. Cambridge: The MIT Press.

Eisen, Ben. 2019. "Quicken Loans Settles Financial-Crisis-Era Suit with Justice Department." *The Wall Street Journal*, June 14, 2019. https://www.wsj.com/articles/quicken-loans-settles-financial-crisis-era-suit-with-justice-department-11560540509. Accessed July 20, 2020.

Elliott, Meagan M. 2018. "Imagined Boundaries: Discordant Narratives of Place and Displacement in Contemporary Detroit." Dissertation. University of Michigan, Ann Arbor.

Ewick, Patricia, and Susan S. Silbey. 1992. "Conformity, Contestation, and Resistance: An Account of Legal Consciousness." *New England Law Review* 26: 731–49.

Ewick, Patricia, and Susan S. Silbey. 1998. *The Common Place of Law: Stories from Everyday Life*. Chicago: University of Chicago Press.

Ewick, Patricia, and Susan S. Silbey. 2003. "Narrating Social Structure: Stories of Resistance to Legal Authority." *American Journal of Sociology* 108(6): 1328–72.

Fairbanks II, Robert P. 2009. *How It Works: Recovering Citizens in Post-Welfare Philadelphia*. Chicago: University of Chicago Press.

Farley, Reynolds. 2015. "The Bankruptcy of Detroit: What Role Did Race Play?" *City & Community* 14(2): 118–37.

Feige, Edgar L. 1990. "Defining and Estimating the Underground and Informal Economies: the New Institutional Economics Approach." *World Development* 18(7): 989–1002.

Feloni, Richard and Samantha Lee. 2018. "Billionaire Dan Gilbert Has Invested $5.6 billion in Nearly 100 Properties in Detroit—see the Full map of Exactly What He Owns. Business *Insider*, August 30. https://www.businessinsider.com/dan-gilbert-detroit-properties-bedrock-map-2018-8. Accessed May 25, 2019.

Fernandes, Edésio. 2011. "Regularization of Informal Settlements in Latin America." *Lincoln Institute of Land Policy*. Policy Focus Report Series/Code PF023.

Finn, Donovan. 2014. "DIY Urbanism: Implications for Cities." *Journal of Urbanism: International Research on Placemaking and Urban Sustainability* 7(4): 381–98.

Fischer, Brodwyn. 2014. "Introduction." In *Cities from Scratch: Poverty and Informality in Urban Latin America*, edited by Brodwyn Fischer, Bryan McCann, and Javier Auyero. Durham: Duke University Press.

Free Press Staff. 2014. "What Detroit's Bankruptcy Plan Could Mean for City Services," *Detroit Free Press*, February 22. https://web.archive.org/web/20151012055336/http://www.freep.com/article/20140221/NEWS01/302220027/city-services-and-plan-of-adjustment. Accessed April 16, 2018.

Gallagher, John. 2008. "Detroit: Land of Opportunity: Acres of Barren Blocks Offer Chance to Reinvent City." *Detroit Free Press*, December 15.

Gallagher, John. 2014. "Detroit Blight Removal Campaign Ramps Up, Long Way to Go." *Detroit Free Press*, December 14, 2014. http://www.freep.com/story/money/business/michigan/2014/12/14/detroit-blight-duggan/20360959/. Accessed June 3, 2016

Gallagher, John. 2017. "See What's in Detroit Future City's Strategic Plan." *Detroit Free Press*, November 9, 2017. https://www.freep.com/story/money/business/john-gallagher/2017/11/09/detroit-future-city-plan/848131001/. Accessed May 25, 2019.

Galster, George. 1987. *Homeowners and Neighborhood Reinvestment*. Durham: Duke University Press.

Galster, George. 2017. "Why Shrinking Cities are Not Mirror Images of Growing Cities: A Research Agenda of Six Testable Propositions." *Urban Affairs Review* 55(1): 355–72.

Garland, David. 2005. "Penal Excess and Surplus Meaning: Public Torture Lynchings in Twentieth-Century America." *Law and Society Review* 39(4): 793–833.

Gilbert, Alan. 2002. "On the Mystery of Capital and the Myths of Hernando De Soto: What Difference Does Legal Title Make?" *International Development Planning Review* 24(1): 1–19.

Glacier Rig. N.D. "Historical Copper Prices and Prices Chart." InvestmentMine. http://www.infomine.com/investment/metal-prices/copper/all/. Accessed July 11, 2020.

Glaeser, Edward L., and Joseph Gyourko. 2005. "Urban Decline and Durable Housing." *Journal of Political Economy* 113(2): 345–75.

Glenn, Evelyn Nakano. 2015. "Settler Colonialism as Structure." *Sociology of Race and Ethnicity* 1(1): 52–72.

Goetz, Edward G., and Mara Sidney. 1994. "Revenge of the Property Owners: Community Development and the Politics of Property." *Journal of Urban Affairs* 16(4): 319–34

Goux, Dominique and Maurin, Eric. 2003. "The Effect of Overcrowded Housing on Children's Performance at School." *Journal of Public Economics* 89(5–6): 797–819.

Gowan, Teresa. 1997. "American Untouchables: Homeless Scavengers in San Francisco's Underground Economy." *International Journal of Sociology and Social Policy* 17(3–4): 159–90.

Gustafson, Kaaryn S. 2011. *Cheating Welfare: Public Assistance and the Criminalization of Poverty.* New York: New York University Press.

Haase, Annegret, Dieter Rink, Katrin Grossmann, Matthias Bernt, and Vlad Mykhnenko. 2014. "Conceptualizing Urban Shrinkage." *Environment and Planning A: Economy and Space* 46(7): 1519–34.

Hackworth, Jason. 2007. *The Neoliberal City: Governance, Ideology, and Development in American Urbanism.* Ithaca: Cornell University Press.

Hackworth, Jason. 2014. "The Limits to Market-Based Strategies for Addressing Land Abandonment in Shrinking American Cities." *Progress in Planning* 90: 1–37.

Hackworth, Jason. 2015. "Rightsizing as Spatial Austerity in the American Rust Belt." *Environment and Planning A: Economy and Space* 47(4): 766–82.

Hackworth, Jason. 2016. "Demolition as Urban Policy in the American Rust Belt." *Environment and Planning A: Economy and Space* 48(11): 2201–22.

Hackworth, Jason. 2018. "Race and the Production of Extreme Land Abandonment in the American Rust Belt." *International Journal of Urban and Regional Research* 42(1): 51–73.

Hackworth, Jason. 2019. *Manufacturing Decline: How Racism and the Conservative Movement Crush the American Rust Belt.* New York: Columbia University Press.

Hackworth, Jason and Kelsey Nowakowski. 2015. "Using Market-Based Policies to Address Market Collapse in the American Rust Belt: The Case of Land Abandonment in Toledo, Ohio." *Urban Geography* 36(4): 528–49.

Hardin, Garrett. 1968. "The Tragedy of the Commons." *Science* 62(3859): 1243–8.

Harding, David J. 2010. *Living the Drama: Community, Conflict, and Culture among Inner-City Boys.* Chicago: University of Chicago Press.

Harkness, Joseph, and Sandra J. Newman. 2002. "Homeownership for the Poor in Distressed Neighborhoods: Does this Make Sense?" *Housing Policy Debate* 13(3): 597–630.

Harpaz, Beth J. 2015. "Buyer Beware of Detroit's $500 Foreclosed Properties," *The Detroit News.* March 16. https://www.detroitnews.com/story/news/local /detroit-city/2015/03/16/detroit-foreclosed-properties-auction/24829395/. Accessed May 25, 2019.

Harris, Richard and Ashleigh Patterson. 2017. "Landlords, Tenants and the Legal Status of Secondary Suites in Hamilton, Ontario." *The Canadian Geographer* 61(4): 540–49.

Harris, Richard. 2018. "Modes of Informal Urban Development: A Global Phenomenon." *Journal of Planning Literature* 33(3): 267–86.

Heise, Kurt. 2014. Public Acts 223–225. Michigan Compiled Laws.

Herbert, Claire W. 2018a. "Like a Good Neighbor, Squatters Are There: Property and Neighborhood Stability in the Context of Urban Decline." *City & Community* 17: 236–58.

Herbert, Claire W. 2018b. "Squatting for Survival: Precarious Housing in a Declining U.S. City." *Housing Policy Debate* 28(5): 797–813.

Herbert, Claire W. and Michael Brown. *In progress.* "Race, Property, and Erasure: Rethinking Gentrification's 'Displacement' through a Settler Colonial Lens."

Herron, Jerry, Aku Kadogo, Daniel S. Hoops, Hilda Vest, Jenenne Whitfield, John Beardsley, Marilyn L. Wheaton, Marion E. Jackson, Michael H. Hodges, and Neal Shine. 2007. *Connecting the Dots: Tyree Guyton's Heidelberg Project.* Detroit: Painted Turtle.

Herscher, Andrew. 2012. *The Unreal Estate Guide to Detroit.* Ann Arbor: University of Michigan Press.

Hollander, Justin B., Karina M. Pallagst, Terry Schwarz, and Frank J. Popper. 2009. "Planning Shrinking Cities." *Progress in Planning* 72(4): 223–32.

Holston, James and Teresa Caldeira. 2008. "Urban Peripheries and the Invention of Citizenship." *Harvard Design Magazine* 28, 19–23.

Holston, James. 2009. *Insurgent Citizenship: Disjunctions of Democracy and Modernity in Brazil.* Princeton: Princeton University Press.

Hou, Jeffrey. 2010. *Insurgent Public Space: Guerilla Urbanism and the Remaking of Contemporary Cities.* New York: Routledge.

Huo, Yuen J. and Tom R. Tyler. 2000. *How Different Ethnic Groups React to Legal Authority.* San Francisco: Public Policy Institute of California.

Hwang, Jackelyn and Robert J. Sampson. 2014. "Divergent Pathways of Gentrification: Racial Inequality and the Social Order of Renewal in Chicago Neighborhoods." *American Sociological Review* 79(4): 726–51.

Hyra, Derek S. 2017. *Race, Class, and Politics in the Cappuccino City.* Chicago: University of Chicago Press.

Ikonomova, Violet. 2017a. "Here is a Horrifying Map that Shows Every Detroit Tax Foreclosure since 2002." *Detroit Metro Times*, July 7. https://www .metrotimes.com/news-hits/archives/2017/07/07/here-is-a-horrifying-map-that-shows-every-detroit-tax-foreclosure-since-2002. Accessed April 7, 2018.

Ikonomova, Violet. 2017b. "Anti-foreclosure Activists Make Last-Ditch Effort to Spare Thousands of Detroiters from Eviction." *Detroit Metro Times,* October 4. https://www.metrotimes.com/news-hits/archives/2017/10/03/anti-foreclosure-activists-make-last-ditch-effort-to-spare-thousands-of-detroiters-from-eviction. Accessed May 25, 2019.

Iveson, Kurt, Craig Lyons, Stephanie Clark, and Sara Weir. 2019. "The Informal Australian City." *Australian Geographer* 50(1): 11–27.

Kagawa, Ayako and Jan Turkstra. 2002. "The Process of Urban Land Tenure Formalization in Peru." In *Land, Rights, and Innovation: Improving Tenure Security for the Urban Poor,* edited by Geoffrey Payne. London: ITDG Publishing.

Kamel, Nabil. 2014. "Learning from the Margin: Placemaking Tactics." In *The Informal American City: From Taco Trucks to Day Labor,* edited by Vinit Mukhija and Anastasia Loukaitou-Sideris. Cambridge: The MIT Press.

Kearns, Kevin C. 1979. "Intraurban Squatting in London." *Annals of the Association of American Geographers* 69(4): 589–98.

Kettles, Gregg. 2014. "Crystals, Mud, and Space: Street Vending Informality." In *The Informal American City: From Taco Trucks to Day Labor,* edited by Vinit Mukhija and Anastasia Loukaitou-Sideris. Cambridge: The MIT Press.

Kimani, Khary. 2004. "Nobody Home." *Detroit Metro Times*, January 7, 2004. https://www.metrotimes.com/detroit/nobody-home/Content?oid=2177811 Accessed July 15, 2020.

Kinder, Kimberley. 2016. *DIY Detroit: Making Do in a City Without Services.* Minneapolis: University of Minnesota Press.

Krivo, Lauren J., Ruth D. Peterson, Helen Rizzo, and John R. Reynolds. 1998. "Race, Segregation, and the Concentration of Disadvantage: 1980–1990." *Social Problems* 45(1): 61–80.

Larson, Anne M., Deborah Barry, Ganga Ram Dahal, and Carol J. Pierce Colfer. 2010. *Forests for People: Community Rights and Forest Tenure Reform.* New York: Taylor & Francis.

Larson, Jane E. 2002. "Informality, Illegality, and Inequality." *Yale Law and Policy Review* 20(1): 137–82.

Lefebvre, Henri. 1991. *The Production of Space*. Translated by Donald Nichol-son-Smith. Oxford: Blackwell Publishers Ltd.

Lefebvre, Henri. 1996. *Writings on Cities*. Translated and edited by Eleonore Kofman and Elizabeth Lebas. Cambridge, MA: Blackwell.

Leopold, Josh, Liza Getsinger, Pamela Blumenthal, Katya Abazajian, and Reed Jordan. 2015. "The Housing Affordability Gap for Extremely Low-Income Renters in 2014." Research Report, Urban Institute. https://www.urban.org/research/publication/housing-affordability-gap-extremely-low-income-renters-2014/view/full_report. Accessed May 25, 2019.

Lewand-Monroe, Carrie. 2016. "Detroit Land Bank Authority Quarterly Report." City of Detroit.

Lincoln Institute of Land Policy and Minnesota Taxpayers Association. 2012. "50-State Property Tax Comparison Study." April 2012. http://www.lincolninst.edu.

Lloyd, Richard. 2006. *Neo-Bohemia: Art and Commerce in the Post-Industrial City*. New York: Routledge.

Loukaitou-Sideris, Anastasia and Vinit Mukhija. 2014. "Conclusion: Deepening the Understanding of Informal Urbanism." In *The Informal American City: From Taco Trucks to Day Labor*, edited by Vinit Mukhija and Anastasia Loukaitou-Sideris. Cambridge: The MIT Press.

Loveland Technologies. N.D. "Detroit Parcel Map Top Owners." https://makeloveland.com/us/mi/wayne/detroit#b=neighborhoods. Accessed December 2, 2016.

Loveland Technologies. 2016. "Foreclosure Survey Results: A Report by Loveland Technologies for Wayne County Treasurer, Eric Sabree." http://www.taxforeclosuresurvey.com/. Accessed April 16, 2018.

Lundman, Richard. J. and Robert L. Kaufman. 2003. "Driving while Black: Effects of Race, Ethnicity, and Gender on Citizen Self-reports of Traffic Stops and Police Actions." *Criminology* 41(1): 195–220.

MacDonald, Christine and Joel Kurth. 2015. "Foreclosures Fuel Detroit Blight, Cost City $500 Million." *The Detroit News*. June 3. https://www.detroitnews.com/story/news/special-reports/2015/06/03/detroit-foreclosures-risky-mortgages-cost-taxpayers/27236605/. Accessed May 25, 2019.

Mallach, Alan. 2014. "Lessons From Las Vegas: Housing Markets, Neighborhoods, and Distressed Single-Family Property Investors." *Housing Policy Debate* 24(4): 769–801.

Martínez, Miguel A. 2014. "How Do Squatters Deal with the State? Legalization and Anomalous Institutionalization in Madrid." *International Journal of Urban and Regional Research* 38(2): 646–74.

Massey, Douglas S. and Nancy A. Denton. 1993. *American Apartheid: Segregation and the Making of the Underclass*. Cambridge: Harvard University Press.

Matsuda, Mari J. 1987. "Looking to the Bottom: Critical Legal Studies and Reparations." *Harvard Civil Rights-Civil Liberties Law Review* 22: 323–99.

McAuslan, Patrick. 2002. "Tenure and the Law: The Legality of Illegality and the Illegality of Legality." In *Land, Rights, and Innovation: Improving Tenure Security for the Urban Poor*, edited by Geoffrey Payne. London: ITDG Publishing.

McCabe, Brian J. 2013. "Are Homeowners Better Citizens? Homeownership and Community Participation in the United States." *Social Forces* 91(3): 929–54.

McGraw, Bill. 2015. "Redesigning Detroit: Mayor Mike Duggan's Blueprint Unveiled." *The Center for Michigan | Bridge Magazine on MLive.* August 18. http://www.mlive.com/news/detroit/index.ssf/2015/08/redesigning_detroit_the_mayors.htm. Accessed June 2, 2016.

McKinney-Vento Homeless Assistance Act. 2009. Pub. L. 100–77, July 22, 1987, 101 Stat. 482, 42 U.S.C. § 11301 et seq.

Mele, Christopher. 2000. *Selling the Lower East Side: Culture, Real Estate, and Resistance in New York City.* Minneapolis: University of Minnesota Press.

Michigan Public Act 501. 2014. "An act to provide for the assessment of rights and interests . . . " Amends sec. 78m of 1893 PA 206 (MCL 211.78m) http://legislature.mi.gov/doc.aspx?2013-SB-0295. Accessed December 13, 2019.

Millar, Kathleen. 2018. *Reclaiming the Discarded: Life and Labor on Rio's Garbage Dump.* Durham: Duke University Press.

Millington, Nate. 2013. "Post-Industrial Imaginaries: Nature, Representation and Ruin in Detroit, Michigan." *International Journal of Urban and Regional Research* 37(1): 279–96.

Molotch, Harvey L. 1976. "The City as a Growth Machine: Toward a Political Economy of Place." *American Journal of Sociology* 82(2): 309–32.

Mukhija, Vinit. 2014. "Outlaw In-Laws: Informal Second Units and the Stealth Reinvention of Single-Family Housing." In *The Informal American City: From Taco Trucks to Day Labor*, edited by Vinit Mukhija and Anastasia Loukaitou-Sideris. Cambridge: MIT Press.

Mukhija, Vinit and Anastasia Loukaitou-Sideris. 2014. "Introduction." In *The Informal American City: From Taco Trucks to Day Labor*, edited by Vinit Mukhija and Anastasia Loukaitou-Sideris. Cambridge: MIT Press.

Murphy, Edward. 2014. "In and Out of the Margins: Urban Land Seizures and Homeownership in Santiago, Chile." In *Cities from Scratch: Poverty and Informality in Urban Latin America*, edited by Brodwyn Fischer, Bryan McCann and Javier Auyero. Durham: Duke University Press.

Muxlow, Tlaib, Pagel, Victory, Lauwers, Zemke, Faris, Brown, Callton, Price, Zorn, MacGregor, Hobbs, Switalski, Talabi, Kandrevas and Roberts. 2008. *Scrap Metal Regulatory Act. Michigan Compiled Laws.*

Nelson, Marla, Renia Ehrenfeucht, Traci Birch, Anna Brand, Tara Lambeth, and Jessica Williams. 2019. "Getting By and Getting Out: How Louisiana Bayou Residents are Adapting to Environmental and Economic Change." *Presentation.* Panel on Informal Housing in the U.S. Urban Affairs Association Conference, Los Angeles, CA. April 24–27.

Nickum, Ryan. 2014. "Detroit is Better than Any Other U.S. City and Here's Proof." *Huffington Post.* February 27. http://www.huffingtonpost.com /ryan-nickum/detroit-is-better_b_4862037.html. Accessed June 2, 2016.

Oliver, Melvin L. and Thomas M. Shapiro. 1995. *Black Wealth/White Wealth: A New Perspective on Racial Inequality.* New York: Routledge.

Pallagst, Karina. 2008. "Shrinking Cities—Planning Challenges from an International Perspective." Special Issue on Cities Growing Smaller, *Urban Infill* 1: 6–16.

Payne, Geoffrey. 2001. "Urban Land Tenure Policy Options: Titles or Rights?" *Habitat International* 25(3): 415–29.

Peñalver, Eduardo M. and Sonia Katyal. 2010. *Property Outlaws: How Squatters, Pirates, and Protesters Improve the Law of Ownership.* New Haven: Yale University Press.

Perlman, Janice. 1976. *Myth of Marginality: Urban Poverty and Politics in Rio de Janeiro.* Oakland: University of California Press.

Perlman, Janice. 2004. "Marginality—From Myth to Reality in the Favelas of Rio de Janeiro, 1969–2002." In *Urban Informality: Transnational Perspectives from the Middle East, Latin America, and South Asia,* edited by Ananya Roy and Nezar AlSayyad. Lanham, MD: Lexington Books.

Piliavin, Irving, Bradley R. Entner Wright, Robert D. Mare, and Alex H. Westerfelt. 1996. "Exits from and Returns to Homelessness." *The Social Service Review* 70(1): 33–57.

Pilkauskas, Natasha V., Irwin Garfinkel, and Sara S. McLanahan. 2014. "The Prevalence and Economic Value of Doubling Up." *Demography* 51(5): 1667–76.

Pruijt, Hans. 2003. "Is the Institutionalization of Urban Movements Inevitable? A Comparison of the Opportunities for Sustained Squatting in New York City and Amsterdam." *International Journal of Urban and Regional Research* 27(1): 133–57.

Pruijt, Hans. 2013. "The Logic of Urban Squatting." *International Journal of Urban and Regional Research* 37(1): 19–45.

Quillian, Lincoln and Devah Pager. 2001. "Black Neighbors, Higher Crime? The Role of Racial Stereotypes in Evaluations of Neighborhood Crime." *American Journal of Sociology* 107(3): 717–67.

Ren, Xuefei. 2017. "Governing the Informal: Housing Policies Over Informal Settlements in China, India, and Brazil." *Housing Policy Debate* 28(1): 1–15.

Ribot, Jesse C. and Nancy Lee Peluso. 2003. "A Theory of Access." *Rural Sociology* 68(2): 153–81.

Ricoeur, Paul. 1984–88. *Time and Narrative*, 3 vols. Chicago: University of Chicago Press.

Riggs, Thomas (ed.) 2015. "Homestead Act of 1862." *Gale Encyclopedia of U.S. Economic History*, Volume 2, 2nd Edition. Cengage.

Rios, Michael. 2014. "Learning from Informal Practices: Implications for Urban Design." In *The Informal American City: From Taco Trucks to Day Labor*, edited by Vinit Mukhija and Anastasia Loukaitou-Sideris. Cambridge: The MIT Press.

Robinson, Jennifer. 2006. *Ordinary Cities: Between Modernity and Development*. London: Routledge.

Rohe, William M. and Leslie S. Stewart. 1996. "Home ownership and Neighborhood Stability." *Housing Policy Debate* 7(1): 37–81.

Rollwagen, Heather. 2015. "Constructing Renters as a Threat to Neighbourhood Safety." *Housing Studies* 30(1): 1–21.

Rossi, Peter H. and Eleanor Weber. 1996. "The Social Benefits of Homeownership: Empirical Evidence from National Surveys." *Housing Policy Debate* 7(1): 1–35.

Roy, Ananya. 2002. *City Requiem, Calcutta: Gender and the Politics of Poverty*. Minneapolis: University of Minnesota Press.

Roy, Ananya. 2003. "Paradigms of Propertied Citizenship: Transnational Techniques of Analysis." *Urban Affairs Review* 38(4): 463–91.

Roy, Ananya. 2005. "Urban Informality: Toward an Epistemology of Planning." *Journal of the American Planning Association* 71(2): 147–58.

Roy, Ananya. 2011. "Slumdog Cities: Rethinking Subaltern Urbanism." *International Journal of Urban and Regional Research* 35(2): 223–38.

Royston, Lauren and Cecile Ambert. 2002. "Going Against the Grain: Alternatives to Individual Ownership in South Africa." In *Land, Rights, and Innovation: Improving Tenure Security for the Urban Poor*, edited by Geoffrey Payne. London: ITDG Publishing.

Rozmarek v Plamondon. 1984. 419 Mich 287, 295; 351 NW2d 558.

Safransky, Sara. 2014. "Greening the Urban Frontier: Race, Property, and Resettlement in Detroit." *Geoforum* 56: 237–48.

Salins, Peter D. 1980. *The Ecology of Housing Destruction: Economic Effects of Public Intervention in the Housing Market*. New York: New York University Press.

Sampson, Robert J. 1991. "Linking the Micro- and Macrolevel Dimensions of Community Social Organization." *Social Forces* 70(1): 43–64.

Sampson, Robert J. 2012. *Great American City: Chicago and the Enduring Neighborhood Effect*. Chicago: University of Chicago Press.

Sampson, Robert J. and Stephen W. Raudenbush. 1999. "Systematic Social Observation of Public Spaces: A New Look at Disorder in Urban Neighborhoods." *American Journal of Sociology* 105(3): 603–51.

Sampson, Robert J. and Stephen W. Raudenbush. 2004. "Seeing Disorder: Neighborhood Stigma and the Social Construction of 'Broken Windows'." *Social Psychology Quarterly* 67(4): 319–42.

Sassen, Saskia. 2006. "The Informal Economy: Between New Developments and Old Regulations." *The Yale Law Journal* 103(8): 2289–304.

Schatz, Bryan. 2018. "California's Housing Crisis Is so Bad, Families Are Squatting Abandoned Homes Just to Survive." *Mother Jones*, March/April. https://www.motherjones.com/crime-justice/2018/04/retake-the-house/. Accessed May 25, 2019.

Schindler, Seth. 2014. "Understanding Urban Processes in Flint, Michigan: Approaching 'Subaltern Urbanism' Inductively." *International Journal of Urban and Regional Research* 38(3): 791–804.

Schlichtman, John Joe and Jason Patch. 2014. "Gentrifier? Who, Me? Interrogating the Gentrifier in the Mirror." *International Journal of Urban and Regional Research* 38(4): 1491–508.

Shlay, Anne. 2006. "Low-Income Homeownership: American Dream or Delusion?" *Urban Studies* 43(3): 511–31.

Sims, David. 2002. "What is Secure Tenure in Urban Egypt?" In *Land, Rights, and Innovation: Improving Tenure Security for the Urban Poor*, edited by Geoffrey Payne. London: ITDG Publishing.

Singer, Joseph W. 2000. *Entitlement: The Paradoxes of Property*. New Haven: Yale University Press.

Small, Mario Luis. 2004. *Villa Victoria: The Transformation of Social Capital in a Boston Barrio*. Chicago: University of Chicago Press.

Smart, Alan. 1986. "Invisible Real Estate: Investigations into the Squatter Property Market." *International Journal of Urban and Regional Research* 10(1): 29–45.

Smart, Alan. 2003. "Sharp Edges, Fuzzy Categories and Transborder Networks: Managing and Housing New Arrivals in Hong Kong." *Ethnic and Racial Studies*, 26(2): 218–33.

Smith, Neil. 1996. *The New Urban Frontier: Gentrification and the Revanchist City*. New York: Routledge.

Snow, David A. and Leon Anderson. 1993. *Down on Their Luck: A Study of Homeless Street People*. Oakland: University of California Press.

Spain, Daphne. 1993. "Been-Heres versus Come-Heres: Negotiating Conflicting Community Identities." *Journal of the American Planning Association* 59(2): 156–71.

Stack, Carol B. 1975. *All Our Kin: Strategies for Survival in a Black Community*. New York: Basic Books.

Starecheski, Amy. 2016. *Ours to Lose: When Squatters Became Homeowners in New York City*. Chicago: University of Chicago Press.

Steinmetz, George. 2008. "Harrowed Landscapes: White Ruingazers in Namibia and Detroit and the Cultivation of Memory." *Visual Studies* 23(3): 211–37.

Steinmetz, George. 2009. "Detroit: A Tale of Two Crises." *Environment and Planning D: Society and Space* 27(5): 761–70.

Sternlieb, George and Burchell, Robert W. 1973. *Residential Abandonment: The Tenement Landlord Revisited*. New Brunswick, NJ: Center for Urban Policy Research.

Stratton, Jim. 1977. *Pioneering in the Urban Wilderness*. New York: Urizen.

Sugrue, Thomas. 1996. *The Origins of the Urban Crisis: Race and Inequality in Post-War Detroit*. Princeton: Princeton University Press.

Sullivan, Esther and Carlos Olmedo. 2015. "Informality on the Urban Periphery: Housing Conditions and Self-Help Strategies in Texas Informal Subdivisions." *Urban Studies* 52(6): 1037–53.

Sullivan, Esther. 2018. *Manufactured Insecurity: Mobile Home Parks and Americans' Tenuous Right to Place*. Oakland: University of California Press.

Talen, Emily. 2015. "Do-It-Yourself Urbanism: A History." *Journal of Planning History* 14(2): 135–48.

Taub, Richard D., Garth Taylor, and Jan Dunham. 1984. *Paths of Neighborhood Change: Race and Crime in Urban America*. Chicago: University of Chicago Press.

Taylor, Monique M. 2002. *Harlem: Between Heaven and Hell*. Minneapolis: University of Minnesota Press.

Thompson, E. P. 1963. *The Making of the English Working Class*. New York: Random House.

Tighe, J. Rosie and Joanna P. Ganning. 2016. "Do Shrinking Cities Allow Redevelopment Without Displacement? An Analysis of Affordability Based on Housing and Transportation Costs for Redeveloping, Declining, and Stable Neighborhoods." *Housing Policy Debate* 26 (4–5): 785–800.

Uitermark, Justus. 2004. "Framing Urban Injustices: the Case of the Amsterdam Squatter Movement." *Space and Polity*, 8(2): 227–44

United Nations. 1966. "International Covenant on Economic, Social and Cultural Rights," December 19. 993 U.N.T.S. 3, 5. 210.

United States Census. 2010. Detroit, Quickfacts. https://www.census.gov/quickfacts/fact/table/US/PST120217.

United States Department of the Treasury. 2018. "Hardest Hit Fund Program Purpose and Overview." https://www.treasury.gov/initiatives/financial-stability/TARP-Programs/housing/hhf/Pages/default.aspx. Accessed May 25, 2019.

Valverde, Mariana. 2012. *Everyday Law on the Street: City Governance in an Age of Diversity*. Chicago: University of Chigaco Press.

Vasudevan, Alexander. 2017. *The Autonomous City: A History of Urban Squatting*. New York: Verso.

Venkatesh, Sudir A. 2006. *Off the Books: The Underground Economy of the Urban Poor*. Cambridge: Harvard University Press.

Veracini, Lorenzo. 2011. "Introducing Settler Colonial Studies." *Settler Colonial Studies* 1(1): 1–12.

Veracini, Lorenzo. 2013. "'Settler Colonialism': Career of a Concept." *The Journal of Imperial and Commonwealth History* 41(2): 313–33.

Waldron, Jeremy. 1991. "Homelessness and the Issue of Freedom." *UCLA Law Review* 39: 295–324.

Ward, Peter. 1999. *Colonias and Public Policy in Texas and Mexico: Urbanization by Stealth*. Austin: University of Texas Press.

Way, Heather. 2010. "Informal Homeownership in the United States and the Law." *Saint Louis University Public Law Review* 29(1): 113–92.

Wegmann, Jake. 2015. "Research Notes: The Hidden Cityscapes of Informal Housing in Suburban Los Angeles and the Paradox of Horizontal Density." *Buildings & Landscapes: Journal of the Vernacular Architecture Forum* 22(2): 89–110.

Weinstein, Liza. 2008. "Mumbai's Development Mafias: Globalization, Organized Crime and Land Development." *International Journal of Urban and Regional Research* 32(1): 22–39.

White, Michelle J. 1986. "Property Taxes and Urban Housing Abandonment." *Journal of Urban Economics* 20(3): 312–30.

Wiechmann, Thorsten, and Karina M. Pallagst. 2012. "Urban Shrinkage in Germany and the USA: A Comparison of Transformation Patterns and Local Strategies." *International Journal of Urban and Regional Research* 36(2): 261–80.

Wiechmann, Thorsten and Marco Bontje. 2015. "Responding to Tough Times: Policy and Planning Strategies in Shrinking Cities." *European Planning Studies* 23(1): 1–11.

Williams, Corey. 2015. "Squatters Slow Detroit's Plan to Bulldoze Vacant Homes." *Detroit Free Press*, January 29. http://www.freep.com/story/news/local/michigan/detroit/2015/01/29/detroit-squatters-blight/22516137/. Accessed May 25, 2019.

Williams, Frederick. 2018. "Don't Think They Know." In *Composing Other Ways: Structuralism, Realism, and the Technics of Control and Resistance*, by Michael Philip Brown. Dissertation. Michigan State University.

Williams, Joan C. 1991. "Dissolving the Sameness/Difference Debate: A Post-Modern Path Beyond Essentialism in Feminist and Critical Race Theory." *Duke Law Journal* 2:296–323.

Wilson, James Q., and George L. Kelling. 1982. "Broken Windows: The Police and Neighborhood Safety." *The Atlantic*, March.

Wilson, William Julius. 1987. *The Truly Disadvantaged: The Inner City, the Underclass, and Public Policy*. Chicago: University of Chicago Press.

Woetzel, Jonathan, Jaana Remes, Kevin Coles, and Mekala Krishnan. 2016. "Urban World: Meeting the Demographic Challenge in Cities." *McKinsey Global Institute Report*. https://www.mckinsey.com/featured-insights/urbanization/urban-world-meeting-the-demographic-challenge-in-cities. Accessed November 29, 2019.

Wong, Yin-Ling Irene, Dennis P. Culhane, and Randall Kuhn. 1997. "Predictors of Exit and Reentry among Family Shelter Users in New York City." *The Social Service Review* 71(3): 441–62.

Zukin, Sharon. 1987. "Gentrification: Culture and Capital in the Urban Core." *Annual Review of Sociology* 13(1): 129–47.

INTERVIEWS

Allen, September 30, 2013
Alondra, October 24, 2013
Annette, August 2, 2013
Ashley, November 1, 2013
Barnabas, October 4, 2013
Bobby, February 11, 2014
Bond, February 5, 2014
Boris, October 24, 2013
Carlos, March 14, 2014
Cedric, August 2, 2013
Chuck, November 8, 2013
Clarence, July 15, 2013
Craig, July 27, 2013
Dean, October 14, 2013
DeAngelo, September 27, 2013
Delilah, June 24, 2014
Didi, March 5, 2014
Doug, June 19, 2013
Eloise, December 12, 2014
Fern, February 25, 2014
Francine, June 16, 2013
Frank, July 2, 2013
Gavin, February 18, 2014

Ginnifer, September 13, 2013
Grant, June 29, 2013
Harold, January 17, 2014
Helena, November 6, 2013
Henry, June 29, 2013
Isaac, August 2, 2013
Jackie, July 4, 2013
Jayne, September 10, 2014
Jerome, October 26, 2013
Jillian, June 24, 2013
Jim, March 13, 2014
Joe, July 7, 2013
John, July 31, 2013
Kevin, February 25, 2014
Knox, June 20, 2013
Lamar, November 4, 2013
Latasha, August 2, 2013
Leroy, October 28, 2013
Leslie, January 31, 2014
Lisa, March 13, 2014
Marsey, March 8, 2014
Max, September 6, 2014
Maxine, February 13, 2014
Nathan, March 11, 2014
Nina, June 13, 2013
Oliver, February 25, 2014
Paul, January 14, 2014
Quentin, October 22, 2013
Rhiannon, December 12, 2014
Rita, February 25, 2014
Rob, July 31, 2013
Robert, July 24, 2013
Samantha, June 24, 2014
Sarah, September 23, 2013
Scott, November 8, 2013
Ted, November 8, 2013
Theo, September 18, 2013
T.J., January 31, 2014
Toby, October 1, 2013
Violet, January 14, 2014
Walter, September 22, 2013

Wes, November 14, 2013
William, July 8, 2013

CONVERSATIONS DURING FIELDWORK

Harriet, February 10, 2015
Sondra, March 20, 2014
Terrence, February 20, 2014

Index

Founded in 1893,
UNIVERSITY OF CALIFORNIA PRESS
publishes bold, progressive books and journals
on topics in the arts, humanities, social sciences,
and natural sciences—with a focus on social
justice issues—that inspire thought and action
among readers worldwide.

The UC PRESS FOUNDATION
raises funds to uphold the press's vital role
as an independent, nonprofit publisher, and
receives philanthropic support from a wide
range of individuals and institutions—and from
committed readers like you. To learn more, visit
ucpress.edu/supportus.